Awareness
of Language:
An Introduction

4·50

Awareness of Language: An Introduction

Eric Hawkins

Professor Emeritus, University of York

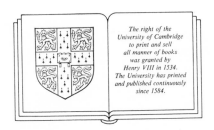

The right of the
University of Cambridge
to print and sell
all manner of books
was granted by
Henry VIII in 1534.
The University has printed
and published continuously
since 1584.

CAMBRIDGE UNIVERSITY PRESS 1984

Cambridge

London   New York   New Rochelle

Melbourne   Sydney

Published by the Press Syndicate of the University of Cambridge
The Pitt Building, Trumpington Street, Cambridge CB2 1RP
32 East 57th Street, New York, NY 10022, USA
296 Beaconsfield Parade, Middle Park, Melbourne 3206, Australia

First published 1984

Printed in Great Britain at
the University Press, Cambridge

Library of Congress catalogue card number: 83-25234

British Library cataloguing in publication data
Hawkins, Eric
  Awareness of language.
  1. Languages, Modern—Study and teaching
  I. Title
  418'.007'1   PB35
ISBN 0 521 28853 3

CE

Contents

Foreword

This book has two aims. The first is to interest parents and teachers as well as administrators and advisers in a new development in language education that is rapidly gaining ground. It has become known as 'awareness of language'.

Besides offering a rationale for this new approach and suggesting how it might bridge the gap between mother tongue and foreign language teaching, Part 1 examines alternative strategies for promoting 'language across the curriculum' and gives examples of recent initiatives by schools and examining boards.

Part 2 fulfils the book's second aim, which is to offer practical guidance to teachers working with the Cambridge University Press series for schools entitled 'Awareness of Language'. This series consists of short topic books designed to promote class discussion of the everyday miracle of human language. Helping to get rid of prejudice about other people's language, often rooted simply in fear of what is strange, is an important objective of the series. The topic books challenge pupils to ask such questions as:

> What makes human language so special?
> Can we communicate without words?
> How do we use language?
> How are languages learned by the baby and in school?
> Is written language just written speech?
> Is learning to read in English harder than in other languages?
> How many languages are spoken in our country today?
> What similarities are there between languages?
> Where did our language come from, how has it changed and how is it changing?

When these questions are discussed in class and at home (through projects involving parents) it is hoped that the presence in schools of pupils from the ethnic minorities will become a positive advantage *because of* the variety of their language backgrounds. The exchange of different language experiences can promote confidence, tolerance of difference, and understanding; multi-lingualism may thus come to be seen as the enrichment it surely is, rather than as one more problem for the hard-pressed teacher.

ACKNOWLEDGEMENTS

This book would not have been written without the encouragement and wise advice of Rosemary Davidson of Cambridge University Press.

I also owe a great debt to Penny Carter, Bronwen Rees and others at Cambridge University Press, and to Brita Green of the Language Department, University of York, who read an earlier draft with meticulous care and whose scholarly comments and generous help enabled me to avoid many errors.

I alone am responsible for the many shortcomings that remain.

E.W.H.
Hull
April 1983

Thanks are due to the following for permission to reproduce material in their copyright:
The Royal National Institute for the Blind, 224 Great Portland Street, London.

for
E.M.B.H.

The background

AN ELEMENT MISSING FROM THE SCHOOL CURRICULUM

The decision taken in 1972 to set up a national inquiry, to be conducted by the Bullock Committee, into the teaching of literacy in schools was a response to growing anxiety in Parliament and the press. If the report of the inquiry (*A Language for Life*, 1975) did little to reassure public opinion, the subsequent failure of most schools and teacher training institutions to respond to Bullock has led many commentators to see mother tongue teaching as a 'disaster area'.

It is to those aware of this mounting anxiety that this book is addressed. It is hoped that it may be especially helpful to those who are responsible for pupils growing up in our tense inner cities, whose classes contain pupils from a diversity of language backgrounds or children who speak a 'non-standard' dialect at home.

The main cause of anxiety in 1972 was the shocking evidence that, after a century of universal education, schools were proving unable to help children to profit from the teaching offered unless they came into school equipped from home with the tools for verbal learning which the school process requires. Those who came to school without the essential verbal skills were seen to fail at the first hurdle – learning to read – and to fall further behind with every year that they stayed at school. The effect of schooling was to *widen the gap* between the children whose homes gave them the verbal learning tools and those who did not get the tools at home (Bullock, p. 22).

To this anxiety there has more recently been added another. It is becoming clear that there is something missing from the language education offered to *all* children. Nowhere does our present curriculum offer children help in learning to understand language itself, the unique characteristic of the 'articulate mammal'. One consequence of this is that young parents are given no preparation or guidance to help them to face their responsibility as their baby's chief language informant and model in the early formative months and years.

More serious still is the linguistic parochialism and prejudice which is endemic in our community to a degree rarely found in other societies. Like other, insidious forms of prejudice it is the product of insecurity and fear of the unknown.

LANGUAGE IN EDUCATION

There has been no lack of discussion of the role of language in the curriculum, especially since the Bullock Report was published, but much of the discussion has been side-tracked by muddled thinking on two issues.

Firstly, an acrimonious and largely peripheral debate about 'verbal deprivation' has centred on *spoken* language, ignoring the fact that it is failure to get confident command of the *written* form of English that causes shipwreck for a large part of the school population.

The second muddle has concerned the curriculum itself. When we speak of the 'school curriculum', which model do we have in mind? Most discussion of the 'curriculum' takes for granted a horizontal (or synchronic) model. This is the curriculum as the headteacher sees it when drawing up the year's timetable. It is the model that is assumed in phrases such as 'language *across* the curriculum'. This way of viewing the curriculum encourages the view that the head of the school should have autonomy in drawing it up. Indeed this claim of curricular autonomy for each individual school is often put forward as a precious defence against centralised planning.

There is, however, another model of the curriculum. This is the 'child's eye' model: the succession of experiences met by the child growing up through the system and moving from one school to another. Slogans such as 'language across the curriculum' have helped to distract attention from the haphazard nature of the child's language experience. If we try to see the curriculum as the child meets it (the 'vertical' or diachronic curriculum), it is at once clear that for each school to claim autonomy, without consultation and in the absence of detailed guidelines worked out regionally and nationally, is unfair to all pupils and most unfair to the very pupils who most need the school's help.

This is not to suggest that the horizontal curriculum must not be coherently planned at each stage. Bullock argued this case cogently. If schools have failed to respond to Bullock, it is partly because no clear mechanism was spelled out in the report for bringing teachers together across their disciplines; most notably there were no suggestions for bringing together the English and the foreign language teachers. It is one of the chief advantages of the 'awareness of language' approach, with which this book is concerned, that the new courses being developed in a growing number of schools encourage teachers, across the *language* curriculum as well as across other curricular boundaries, to come together in boards of studies to plan and teach the new language syllabus.

There is another practical advantage in putting a specific space for discussion of language itself into the horizontal curriculum. When the children in a class come from different language backgrounds, or dialect backgrounds, it is helpful to have a regular opportunity for them to tell one another about their language experiences. In this discussion all start level. All can feel that they have something to contribute. Experiences that they share, such as the acquisition of language by the baby, can, if properly handled, unite children.

While the introduction of 'awareness of language' into the curriculum seeks to integrate language experience across the curriculum, it is equally essential in the vertical programme. It ensures that at the outset of the secondary course all pupils, whatever their previous experience, have a chance to sharpen the tools for verbal learning on which the secondary course depends.

Not the least daunting aspect of this challenge is the adventure into a foreign language. At present some two-thirds of the children who begin French at 11 or older are ill-prepared and lack the essential learning tools. Their homes cannot or will not offer the necessary encouragement, with the consequence that foreign language study beyond the age of 13 is becoming a minority subject, with sixth form classes dwindling and languages other than French disappearing from school timetables in the state sector.

We see 'awareness of language', therefore, as an attempt to give coherence, both horizontally and vertically, in the child's programme, at a critical moment: the difficult transition from the primary to the secondary school. It is such a programme that is spelled out in the six topic books of the Cambridge University Press series.

'Awareness of language' in the curriculum is no panacea to cure all ills. It must take its place as part only of a progressive programme for providing the tools for verbal learning and giving back, to the pupils who have been cheated of it, the precious 'adult time' (individual dialogue with an adult) on which Bullock rightly insisted as every child's birthright. Within such a programme our aim is to offer an approach to language teaching that will bring teachers together across disciplines and school frontiers to plan and teach it, while helping all pupils, but especially the slower learners, to make sense of what is too often a fragmented and haphazard linguistic apprenticeship.

A DEFINITION OF 'AWARENESS OF LANGUAGE'

Because the concept of 'awareness of language' is a new one the term may mean different things to different readers. A more detailed definition of the objectives may be useful at the outset. The concept for which we are arguing can be summarised in the following way.

The new element in the curriculum is intended for the age range 10/11 to 13/14 in comprehensive or middle schools, or the top end of primary schools. It seeks to bridge the difficult transition from primary to secondary school language work, and especially to the start of foreign language studies and the explosion of concepts and language introduced by the specialist secondary school subjects.

It also bridges the 'space between' the different aspects of language education (English/foreign language/ethnic minority mother tongues/ English as second language/Latin) which at present are pursued in isolation, with no meeting place for the different teachers, no common vocabulary for discussing language.

The chief aim of the new element will be to challenge pupils to ask questions about language, which so many take for granted. A subsidiary aim will be to prepare the way for a language element in the 'child-care' courses for fourth and fifth years, exploring the role of the young parent in the baby's language development. Further, by offering a forum where language diversity can be discussed, the new curriculum element will seek to challenge linguistic prejudice and parochialism. The best weapon against prejudice is open discussion and greater awareness.

Since insight into pattern in language has been shown to be a key element in aptitude for foreign language acquisition, and in the 'processing' of verbal messages in the mother tongue, our new curriculum topic will seek to give pupils confidence in grasping the patterns in language. A contrastive study, at an appropriate level, of such patterns with those met in other languages (foreign languages studied in class as well as the ethnic minority tongues of classmates) will be part of this growing insight into the way language works to convey meaning.

Learning to *listen*, which means first getting clear expectations as to what it is one is to listen *for*, will form another major element in the programme. This is especially important for pupils embarking on a foreign language who must 'superimpose' new listening habits on mother tongue habits of which they are not aware. 'The education of the ear ... is a prerequisite for efficient foreign language study' (MacCarthy, 1978, p. 14).

Since it is clear that pupils will get very little from our present school curriculum, with its emphasis on verbal skills, unless they can read with confidence and come to relish using the written language as a tool for learning, our programme will try to offer a fresh approach to the match between the spoken and the written forms of language. It will attempt to demystify some aspects of the system of spelling that has come down to us, comparing it with other spelling systems that may be met, in French or Spanish, for example, or in the ethnic minority mother tongues. At the same time the origins of our curious, left to right, alphabetic writing can be explored and it can be compared with other widely used writing forms, many of which are based on quite different principles: right to left, syllabic, logographic etc.

There will obviously be a degree of information-giving in answering the questions that pupils will ask when their curiosity is aroused about topics they may not have thought about before: questions about language origins, language change, dialects, borrowings etc. At the same time the new approach that we are advocating will call for a classroom method relying chiefly on pupils' activities, in which it is hoped they will practise the difficult but rewarding skills of working in pairs. These activities will include projects encouraging them to gather their own data from the world outside school, as often as possible involving their parents as informants and partners in the investigation.

A RATIONALE

Frequently, when the new concept of 'awareness of language' in the curriculum has been discussed, the question has been raised: Are you not simply wanting to introduce into school a watered-down version of the study commonly known in universities as 'linguistics'?

Our answer can be quite clear. Of course there is common ground in the programme outlined above and some parts of a university course in 'linguistics/language' and no apology need be offered for this. This is not the only area of the curriculum where it can be shown that children who will not go to university will benefit from exploration, at an appropriate level, of some of the themes studied at university. The teacher of 'nature study' does not need to apologise for the subject simply because his or her own degree was called 'biology', 'botany' or 'zoology'. There is, however, more to the programme that we are advocating than 'watered-down linguistics', as a moment's sympathetic consideration of the above outline will make clear.

We are seeking to light fires of curiosity about the central human characteristic of language which will blaze throughout our pupils' lives. While combating linguistic complacency, we are seeking to arm our pupils against fear of the unknown which breeds prejudice and antagonism. Above all we want to make our pupils' contacts with language, both their own and that of their neighbours, richer, more interesting, simply more fun.

THE SHAPE OF THE BOOK

In Part 1 we set out the rationale for 'awareness of language' in the curriculum and examine some approaches that have been suggested. Some possible misunderstandings are also examined. We also give an account of recent initiatives by enterprising teachers in developing courses within the general framework of 'awareness of language', and of new papers in GCE examinations that are relevant.

In Part 2 we offer background notes for teachers considering the introduction of the topic books for pupils published in the series 'Awareness of Language'. Each of the six sections in Part 2 has a short selected further reading list for those teachers who wish to pursue the topics in more detail.

The Appendices include a programme of listening games for the classroom for teachers who wish to prepare their pupils for tackling foreign language studies with the best possible verbal learning tools. This 'learning to listen' programme is also designed to help pupils who lack confidence in reading and those whose mother tongue is not English and who may need specific help in comprehension of spoken English. It lays stress on listening for *meaning*, as well as on more formal listening games. Particular attention is given to games involving comparison of messages received via the ears with messages via the eyes. This 'cross-modal' activity is constantly called on during the school day. It underlies successful learning of the foreign language. It also spells success or failure in many other school subjects in the secondary school, where the pupil meets a succession of teachers' voices and changes of vocabulary, as each lesson bell summons the class to a new discipline.

Part 1

1 Anxieties about language education

HARSH REALITIES OF MOTHER TONGUE LEARNING

One of the effects of the spread of non-selective schooling in the 1960s was to reveal to observers outside the school system, and perhaps to some within it, the nature of the crisis in mother tongue learning.

Previously the '11 plus' selection process had identified, and placed in grammar schools, the 25% or so of pupils from encouraging homes whose verbal skills, thanks largely to their environment, were precocious. They alone received an 'academic' education, including foreign language study, difficult reading, specialised vocabularies etc. The remaining three-quarters of each age group were confined to the secondary modern school, which offered a syllabus making more modest demands on verbal skills.

With the ending of selection at 11, pupils began to be taught in 'mixed ability' groups which were, in fact, largely a misnomer for groups of mixed social background. The extent to which the verbal skills formerly called for in the two kinds of secondary course had differed could no longer be disguised. It took somewhat longer for educationists to realise how greatly such verbal skills were the product of early family opportunity. Loose talk of 'mixed ability' persisted despite the growing evidence of research such as the work reported in the Plowden Report (1967). This showed that the factor of 'parental encouragement' is such a determining influence on verbal performance in the primary school that the concept of a child's 'ability', divorced from parental influence, loses most of its meaning.

Anxiety about mother tongue learning had, in fact, begun to be expressed before the drift towards the comprehensive school began. Already in the 1950s there were cries of alarm. Some of these were linked with concern about the universities' lowering of their entrance requirements for students not specialising in languages. The Report of the Central Advisory Council for Education in 1959 (The Crowther Report) had this to say:

We are all agreed that 'mastery of language' is one of the most important elements of a general education and one where there is little ground for complacency about the effectiveness of present teaching methods... The abolition of compulsory Latin ... provides an opportunity, which ought to be seized, for rethinking the whole basis of the teaching of linguistics in the schools.   (Crowther, *15 to 18*, p. 211)

The Crowther Committee was concerned with the (approximately) 10% of pupils who at that time stayed on at school beyond 15. The Latin requirement for entrance to university had been dropped, except at Oxbridge, before Crowther reported and in 1967 most universities dropped even the requirement of a minimal reading knowledge in a foreign language. A minority of the Crowther Committee pressed for the Latin requirement to be retained:

until such time as thought and experiment have clearly shown that there are other ways of 'doing what Latin does'.

As to exactly what Latin does do, the debate has recently been carried a stage further by research at the London Institute of Education by David Corson (1981). His studies in comprehensive schools have shown what he calls a 'lexical barrier' separating pupils who possess the Latinate vocabulary and those who do not. The latter regularly bypass 'hard' words and are at a disadvantage when faced with the secondary school curriculum and when seeking employment. Corson reported striking improvement in command of English by inner-city children who were taught Latin. This is not the place to follow the argument but we shall return to this hypothesis when we discuss theories of 'verbal deficit' (p. 79).

The universities did not listen to Crowther on the Latin requirement. Instead some of them mounted an isolated rearguard action. In 1962 the five northern universities introduced their 'test in the use of English', which was compulsory for all candidates for entry. Unfortunately the science faculties at two of the universities at once found that the test was diverting applicants away from their doors towards other universities which did not make such inconvenient demands on sixth formers' ability to express themselves in writing. After only two years' trial, therefore, the test was dropped.

The call for 'rethinking' of language courses was, however, echoed by the Secondary Schools Examinations Council. In its last report to the minister, in 1964, before being merged into the new Schools Council for Curriculum and Examinations, the SSEC recommended that the GCE English paper at 'A' level (i.e. at the age of 18) should include an optional paper in 'language' as an alternative to the traditional 'English literature' paper. This new paper should cover: 'a study of the structure of the language; the different types of English, dialects and slang; the relation of language to individual thought and behaviour and also its social implications'.

In fact 18 years were to pass before the GCE Boards began to produce papers which answered this challenge. English teachers and examiners showed no unseemly haste in answering the call for rethinking!

If there was growing unease about mastery of English by the ablest 10% of pupils who aspired to university, what of the 90% who would never approach 'A' level?

The anxiety about the pupils who left school at the statutory age was not so much that they could not pass a test in the *use* of English as that many of them could not *read* – how many it is hard to say. The fact that there are estimated to be 2 million illiterates in the adult population of the UK after 100 years of compulsory education is one measure of the problem. K. Gardner estimated (1968) from his studies of school leavers that 1 in 4 was 'functionally illiterate'. They might decipher headlines in a newspaper but could not fully take in the story underneath, or not confidently enough to remain interested.

Concern grew steadily in the decade following Crowther. In 1972 the National Foundation for Educational Research published a survey which, in the words of the Bullock Report, 'generated a good deal of concern about the reading standards of today' (p. 16).

The flurry this caused was trivial, however, compared with the bombshell of the report of the National Child Development Study in the same year (Davie et al., 1972). This revealed the extent to which illiteracy or semi-literacy was still common among children from particular home backgrounds, despite all the efforts made by teachers. Nearly half of all children of unskilled manual workers (Class V) were 'poor readers' at age 7. This compared with only 1 in 12 poor readers from homes in the administrative class (Class I). (It should also be remembered that Class V is ten times more numerous than Class I.)

The finding that half of the enormous group of Class V children were poor readers after two years in the infant school was not, in fact, the most disturbing part of the picture. More saddening for the conscientious teacher and administrator was the evidence that the effect of schooling is to widen the gap between the 'haves' and the 'have-nots' in reading skills: 'Several studies have shown that the position worsens as the children grow older, there being a progressive decline in the performance of the lower socio-economic groups between the ages of 7 and 11' (Bullock, p. 22). What was becoming clear was that unless children brought into school from their homes the language skills that they would need to succeed at school, teachers were unable to help them.

This finding has recently had striking confirmation from the surveys of literacy in London schools carried out by the Inner London Education Authority. Table 1, taken from the ILEA Survey of 1980, shows the reading scores of an especially disadvantaged group: the children of parents of West Indian origin. One of the disadvantages known to contribute to reading failure is the deprivation of 'adult time': the opportunity for uninterrupted dialogue with an adult who can give the child individual attention at the critical age when the child is learning to match his expanding conceptual universe to the linguistic symbols of the mother tongue. Deprivation of this individual dialogue means that the child's conceptual map is both imprecise and patchy. It is unreliable as a platform on which school learning can build.

The West Indian child is especially at risk of deprivation of 'adult time'. The Rampton Report (1981) showed that nearly 70% of West Indian married women go out to work, compared with the national average of just over 40%. The number of West Indian men on night shifts is twice the national average for whites. The number of one-parent families is much higher among West Indians and in consequence more West Indian children spend their waking hours in the critical years for language acquisition in the care of child-minders, sharing the single adult 'minder' with some ten or twenty other children. Research by Sandra Scarr (1983) has shown that 32% of West Indian homes are inadequately supplied with play materials compared with 6% of white homes. Predictably the ILEA survey showed that the reading scores of West Indian children are very low at age 8 compared with more fortunate groups and that the ten point gap at age 8 widens with every year that they remain at school.

It is self-evident that lack of fluency in reading must inhibit performance not only in English but in all subjects calling for book learning, and that the learning handicap of hesitant reading must grow progressively more crippling as the pupil meets the language demands of secondary education. How disastrously the West Indian pupil is handicapped, however, was not realised until the Rampton Committee reported in 1981.

Table 1 *Mean reading scores at age 8, 10, and 15 (National average score = 100)*

Age in years	UK Non-Immigrant	West Indian
8	98.1	88.1
10	98.3	87.4
15	97.8	85.9
Number of children tested: 12,539		1,465

(The survey was based on a cohort of children born between September 1959 and September 1960.)

At the request of the committee, the DES Statistics Branch included a question on pupils' ethnic origins in its school leavers survey for 1978/79, which was conducted in six LEAs, and covered approximately half of the school leavers from ethnic minorities in the country. This was the first time that school leavers had been identified in such a way that the performance of the different groups could be compared.

The results in English Language were striking. Only 9% of the West Indian pupils scored 'higher grades' (i.e. grades A to C in GCE or grade 1 in CSE) compared with 21% of Asian pupils (for many of whom English must have been a second language) and 29% of other school leavers in the same LEAs. That weakness in English may affect learning in other subjects is suggested by the scores in mathematics where the discrepancy between the three groups (West Indian, Asian and Indigenous) was equally marked. Only 5% of the West Indians scored higher grades in maths compared with 20% of Asians and 19% of other school leavers. Most striking of all was the picture revealed of the levels of achievement across all subjects. *Only 3% of the West Indians obtained higher grades in five subjects compared with 18% of Asians and 16% of other leavers.* This meant that out of every 100 West Indian pupils, 97 left school without the performance in five subjects that is usually taken to be necessary for a good sixth form attack on 'A' levels. For 97 out of 100, therefore, the door to further education, and thus to specialist careers and decision-making posts, was closed.

The importance of 'adult time' in all this is underlined by the evidence from those West Indian pupils who *do* succeed in the school system. The research findings are summarised in the survey conducted by Monica Taylor for the Rampton Committee (Taylor, 1981). She quotes Holberton (1977) who suggests that the West Indian *achiever*: 'finds home a place where he can follow interests and hobbies; has grown ups who are prepared to spend time with him . . . has parents who do not mind an argument about some things . . . does not spend a great deal of time with his peers'.

Work with West Indian achievers shows the importance of a stable model of mature adult roles, and of uninterrupted dialogue with an adult, of talking 'with' rather than authoritarian being talked 'at'. It is in stable family ties that children from Asian families often enjoy a marked advantage which is reflected in their school performance. This, as Rampton showed, often surpasses the performance of those of their white contemporaries who share the family characteristics of the underachieving West Indian pupils, but who have no colour prejudice to contend with.

Prejudice against minorities is, of course, ever present, and even the best-intentioned efforts to combat it can be a cause of resentment if considered as patronising. Ethnic prejudice has, in the past, however, sometimes acted as a stimulus to effort. The Jews, over hundreds of years, in nearly every country in Europe, at different times, faced hardship and cruelty and the most insulting discrimination without ever losing their determination to maintain high standards in literacy. The strength of the Jewish family tradition, the key to language transmission, seems to explain the triumph of high levels of literacy over persecution. A similar family tradition may help to explain the comparatively high attainment of Asian pupils in contrast to the achievement of children whose family structure offers less chance of 'adult time' in the critical formative years.

Repeated studies in the UK and elsewhere have shown the close correlation between home background and reading scores. Detailed examination of the performance of indigenous Class V and of many West Indian pupils and comparison of their scores with those of Asian children in British schools points to 'adult time' as a key factor, reinforcing material factors such as poverty, bad housing and the injustices and prejudices of the host community. The accumulating evidence pointing to lack of 'adult time' as an important predictor of school failure seems to underline the need for the kind of 'preparation for parenthood' courses in school for which we are arguing, containing a carefully designed language element.

Another aspect, however, of the West Indian child's learning difficulties also appears to reinforce our argument for rethinking 'language' in the curriculum. It is suggested by some sensitive observers that even when the West Indian child does enjoy the precious adult dialogue and learns to match his language accurately with his conceptual universe, nevertheless the particular variety of English learned at home is so different from the school variety as to cause problems which teachers are either unable or unwilling to help the child to overcome. This problem has been sensitively discussed by, for example, Edwards (1979) and Trudgill (1974). We shall return to this on p. 61.

Whatever other solutions are proposed to help the West Indian child, it seems clear that an essential basis must be a much greater awareness, among teachers as well as parents, of how children's use of language and the school's attitude to language interact to affect learning. It is just such awareness and greater sensitivity that we hope may develop from the introduction into the curriculum of a discussion of language itself.

DEEPER ANXIETIES: LINGUISTIC PAROCHIALISM

In the BBC documentary film *Anglo-Saxon Attitudes* (September 1982) a white Leicestershire schoolgirl is quoted as saying of her Indian classmates: 'You can't even go into the girls' toilets without hearing those Indian girls jabbering away in their stupid Punjabi language.' The word 'stupid' is revealing; it shows not only the speaker's rejection of what is strange but her expectation that her hearers would fully share her attitude.

We may have here a cause for deeper concern about the language education offered in schools. There is at present no place in the curriculum for discussing with pupils the phenomenon of language itself, as the distinguishing characteristic of the 'articulate mammal', or the relationship of English to other languages spoken in the UK and abroad. It is no accident that British society is marked by a high degree of linguistic parochialism.

Linguistic tolerance does not come naturally; it has to be learned and to be worked at. The first reaction to language that cannot be understood (as to other forms of social behaviour that are different) is suspicion, frustration, even anger. It is hard to believe that people who can behave so mysteriously (linguistically) can be at all like us. The ancient Egyptians, unable to decipher the hieroglyphics used by the scribes, called writing the 'speech of the Gods'. It was too strange to be human. The Norse sagas told that it was the god Odin who invented runic writing.

To be able to step outside our mother tongue and see it in some kind of perspective is a difficult lesson. The school curriculum at present offers little help, except in the foreign language lesson. Jerome Bruner, discussing the difficulty of helping children to achieve greater 'awareness' of language, quotes Vygotsky:

The word, to the child, is an integral part of the object it denotes. Such a conception seems to be characteristic of primitive linguistic consciousness. We all know the old story about the rustic who said he was not surprised that the savants with all their instruments could figure out the size of the stars and their courses – what baffled him was how they found out their names.

(Bruner, 1975, p. 73)

The American linguist Yuen Ren Chao makes a similar point:

Monolingual persons take language so much for granted that they often forget its arbitrary nature and cannot distinguish words from things. Thus primitive peoples often believe that putting a curse on somebody's name could actually harm his person. Persons unused to foreign languages tend to find something perverse in the way foreigners talk. Even Oliver Goldsmith could not get over the perversity of the French, who would call cabbage 'shoe', instead of calling cabbage 'cabbage'. The story is told of an English woman who always wondered why the French call water 'de l'eau', the Italians 'dell'acqua' and the Germans call it 'das Wasser'. 'Only we English people' she said, 'call it properly "water". We not only call it water, but it *is* water.'

(Yuen Ren Chao, 1968, p. 2)

This linguistic parochialism goes very deep in our society. One reflection of it is the isolationism of mother tongue teachers in our schools and teacher training establishments. As we shall see when we examine the main strategy proposed by the Bullock Report, it is a parochialism that fatally flawed even that imaginative inquiry.

In fact English teachers and foreign language teachers have a great deal in common. Both kinds of language teacher offer subjects that serve as 'vehicles' for learning other things. Any shortcomings in their pupils' mastery of the vehicle become apparent for all to see as soon as they have to use it. How often do pupils have to perform publicly in the other areas of the curriculum, such as history or physics? The shared tribulations of the English and the foreign language teacher suggest that they ought to make common cause in planning their different but complementary contributions to their pupils' language experience.

There may be, in a large urban school, as many as five kinds of language teaching going on in adjacent classrooms:

  (i) teaching of English (as mother tongue)
 (ii) teaching of foreign languages (such as French)
(iii) teaching of English as second language (for ethnic minorities)
(iv) teaching of ethnic minority mother tongues (Urdu, Arabic, Chinese etc.)
 (v) teaching of Latin (occasionally classical Greek)

The five kinds of language teacher have been educated in different traditions. In the course of their training, when they have received any training, they have had no opportunity to observe their tutors co-operating with tutors in other subjects and nobody has suggested to them that such co-operation is necessary or possible. They never enter one another's classrooms, seldom discuss together the content of their schemes of work. Most serious of all is their failure to work out a common vocabulary in which to discuss language with the pupils who commute in bewilderment between their classrooms, hearing the parts of speech and the tenses referred to confusingly by a rich variety of names.

If we add to this confusion the very different approaches to language *use* met in the classrooms of the other subject specialists, such as the scientists' demands concerning laboratory notes or the historians' requirements concerning essays, we have a picture of a truly haphazard and fragmented language experience, which HMI (in the working paper *Curriculum 16 to 19*, 1977) found quite unacceptable:

Anyone, by following a group of pupils through a day in a secondary school, can prove that their language experiences are largely a matter of chance . . . The pupil's own use of language may be subject to spasmodic correction . . . [but] many pupils [who have a view of language as a mine field] do not understand the characteristics of language in the context of learning . . . fail to develop confidence and incentive to participate that are vital . . . We cannot be satisfied with the preparation we give to young people for the language needs of their lives.

WHOSE RESPONSIBILITY TO PLAN A COHERENT LANGUAGE CURRICULUM?

If we were concerned only with the fragmentation of the horizontal curriculum to which HMI called attention, the responsibility might seem to lie squarely with the head of the school and with his heads of departments, especially since the autonomy of each head in curriculum planning is vigorously defended. If heads of individual schools (backed by their governing bodies) are to claim autonomy one might expect them at least to show that they can produce a more coherent curriculum than that described above by the HMI working paper.

In fact the incoherence of the curriculum viewed horizontally or synchronically is compounded by an even greater incoherence when looked at vertically or diachronically as the child meets it, growing up through the system. This 'vertical' dimension seems to have gone largely unnoticed in curriculum discussion. The haphazard nature of the successive experience of language offered to the child is the price that is paid for the fetish of the autonomy of each individual head of school.

In fact the 'autonomy' exercised by the average secondary head in planning the curriculum is largely a myth. Heads of secondary schools have no qualifications in curriculum planning. Most of them, on appointment, have had experience of teaching only their own specialist subject. After success in an interview they are presumed suddenly to be invested with understanding of the place in the curriculum of subjects of which they have little recent knowledge and which they have never taught. Those who opposed the setting up of the Schools Council in 1964, and who now oppose national guidelines from HMI, apparently take the view that giving autonomy in curriculum decisions to heads so ill-equipped to take them is a precious safeguard against central direction.

Though the head may make the timetable, curricula are, in practice, shaped in an unplanned, fortuitous way by agencies designed for quite other purposes. The GCE Boards have in the past been the chief influences, yet the Boards are staffed by people chosen for their expertise in *testing*. They have no standing at all, or ought to have none, in determining curricula. The universities, also, exercise a powerful influence, which extends well beyond the small fraction of the school population who aspire to attend university, or the even smaller fraction who eventually qualify for entry. Employers, too, have their say.

Surrounded by these powerful agencies, school heads have as little real scope for manoeuvre as they have qualifications to take decisions. They may get what advice they can from their senior colleagues, who may or may not be acquainted with the best contemporary practice in their subject in this country or abroad. What they almost never do, as national inquiries such as Plowden (1967) and Cockroft (1981) have shown, is to consult with the primary or middle schools from which they recruit their pupils, in order to plan a coherent vertical curriculum.

One requirement of such a vertical curriculum would be that children should be given the tools for verbal learning that are needed at each stage. This would mean restoring 'adult time' to those cheated of it by society. It would mean a progressive course of learning to listen ('thinking with the ears') on which the teacher of foreign languages could later build. It would mean trying to match expectations aroused at one stage of schooling to the experiences provided at the next while avoiding wasteful repetition. None of this would be possible without the planning that crosses school frontiers.

This is not to suggest that schools should lose their right to take initiatives, to choose their own textbooks, to make their own schemes of work, and to promote new courses. The way forward out of traditional ruts and complacent routine can often best be found by individual initiative. An excellent example is offered by the very 'awareness of language' courses which we are advocating. The pioneering, school-based experiments at schools such as, for example, Hessle High School, Banbury School, Henry Box School, North Westminster School and many others have shown what can be done (see our accounts of these initiatives, pp. 42 to 48).

All these experiments fall properly within the responsibility of the secondary school and give more, not less, coherence to the vertical curriculum as the child meets it, arriving from the junior school. However, language courses will be even more successful if suitably prepared for at earlier stages. Initiatives which involve both feeder and receiving schools will come best from LEAs. But here, too, claims to have complete autonomy must be treated with caution.

THE LEA AND CURRICULUM PLANNING

A factor which affects claims by LEAs to be autonomous in curriculum planning is the increasing number of pupils who change from one LEA to another in the course of their schooling. Records of such movements between LEAs are no longer kept. When the Plowden Committee (1967) tried to discover the extent of pupil mobility across LEA frontiers, the DES was unable to provide figures. The Plowden National Survey, however, showed that nearly 1 in 4 of all pupils in primary schools had changed their LEA at least once by the age of 11. Further, Ministry of Labour figures suggested that the incidence of such mobility had increased by 20% in the previous decade.

What is the figure now, nearly two decades on from Plowden? If we add the numbers who move during their secondary years, which Plowden did not count, we get the astonishing figure of between one-third and one-half of all pupils finishing schooling in a different LEA from the one in which they started. Where does that leave claims that LEAs should have the final voice in planning a coherent vertical curriculum?

In fact the apparent conflict between the need for guidelines and the value of local initiatives can be resolved. The way forward is to agree far clearer definitions than we have recently had of the responsibilities that belong to the different levels of decision making in the system. Five such levels can be identified, each with its proper freedoms and restraints:

1 The classroom teacher alone can, and should, determine the shape each lesson should take within the guidelines of the department of which he is a member.

2 The head of department rightly plans the syllabus, in discussion with colleagues, and chooses books. If curriculum initiatives are possible that do not involve breaking the vertical coherence of the learning that the child meets, it is at department level that they will probably be most effectively promoted. Some initiatives, such as the 'inter-faculty' co-operation that Bullock asked for, and that our 'awareness of language' programme demands, will be taken by departments forming joint boards of studies. Also it is on heads of department that the greatest responsibility for the continuous training of the department members rests, and, in some schools, too little is demanded of them in the way of leadership and keeping abreast of their subject.

3 The head of school, in consultation with heads of departments, will plan timetables, ensuring proper horizontal coherence in the programmes offered to pupils, but also in consultation with heads of feeder schools, ensuring that the vertical curriculum makes sense. It is here that the present system abjectly fails.

4 LEAs, through their advisers and inspectors, have a duty to promote induction courses for young teachers and continuous, career-long, in-service training for all teachers, especially heads of departments. On LEAs falls the duty of ensuring maximum vertical coherence in the curriculum of each subject across school boundaries.

5 The DES and the Schools Council (if it is allowed to live), advised by HMI, ought to give clear overall national guidelines. In the early days of the Board for Education, and until its demise in the Education Act of 1944, such guidelines were drawn sharply. The Board instructed LEAs unashamedly about the general lines of courses for which it was prepared to grant aid from national funds. In the post-war years there has been an erosion of DES authority and an assumption of decision making about the curriculum at LEA level for which very many LEAs have shown themselves ill-equipped. A flagrant example of betrayal of trust has been the decision of so many LEAs to change the nature of foreign language teaching in their schools by withdrawing, for financial reasons, all native-speaking assistants from their classrooms. This disastrous step caused the Parliamentary Select Committee for Education, Science and Arts to recommend, in its Second Report to the House of Commons, that since it is 'absolutely vital that pupils should have access to native speakers of the foreign languages concerned . . . the DES should take on responsibility for the Foreign Language Assistants programme . . . which . . . should be funded centrally' (*The Secondary School Curriculum and Examinations*, 1981, p. 31).

At all the above five levels of decision making there is room for initiatives but it is essential that national guidelines should be agreed to give coherence to the whole. The greatest weakness, hitherto, has been lack of leadership from the centre. It is the slowest learners who have suffered most from the vertical incoherence of school programmes. Happily recent developments at the centre give promise of clearer leadership.

It is not only between school and school that there must be vertical coherence in the curriculum. The secondary school also has a duty to prepare its school leavers for the linguistic challenges they will face in society and in further education. Not least of these is the challenge of being a good parent. The Bullock Report devoted considerable space to the linguistic aspects of 'preparation for parenthood'. The response so far has been negligible, with one shining exception.

This exception (which we describe in a later section, pp. 46 to 48) is the course of Language in Child Care developed at Banbury School by Paul Baker of the Banbury Teachers' Centre and Peter Downes, head of modern languages at Banbury School. The course was further developed at the Henry Box School, Witney, where Downes became headmaster and later at Hinchingbrooke School, Cambridgeshire, when he moved there.

So far we have touched on two main causes for concern about language education: the failure of schools to help pupils who do not bring from home the necessary verbal tools for learning and the obvious deficiencies in both the horizontal and the vertical curricula.

Some observers might say that the failure to teach reading skills to disadvantaged groups, such as West Indian children, was the single most disastrous aspect of language education. Others might single out the failure to educate school leavers in linguistic tolerance, or to challenge the prevalent parochialism in our society concerning both foreign language skills and the variety of languages spoken as mother tongues by our citizens. By any reckoning the rethinking of language education that Crowther called for in 1959 was, by 1972, when the Bullock inquiry was set up, long overdue.

But where was the rethinking to start? Whose responsibility was it that language education was acknowledged as being a disaster area and that the very children who could get nowhere without the school's help were the ones who were not given the tools with which to learn?

In our next chapter we look at some of the answers to these questions offered by the Bullock inquiry and examine why, despite its great merits, that imaginative report failed to show the way forward.

2 The Bullock Report - a great opportunity lost

CLARITY ABOUT ENDS; CONFUSION ABOUT MEANS

Margaret Thatcher's decision, in 1972, to set up a national inquiry into the 'teaching of reading and other uses of English' was the clearest recognition of the mounting anxiety expressed in Parliament and the press about the state of English teaching. Such national inquests are rare. They are never held more than once in a generation. When such an inquiry fails to effect reform improvement may be put back for decades.

The failure of teachers and administrators to implement the Bullock proposals is the more tragic because the committee adopted a bolder approach to its problem than perhaps the Secretary of State intended. Scorning a narrow limitation of its brief to 'reading', the committee determined to investigate the whole field of 'language in education', accepting that this might range from 'the influence of the home on early language development' to 'teaching of English in the secondary school' (Bullock, 1975, p. xxxi). Something of the spirit in which the committee interpreted its task may be seen from these radical proposals:

Teachers
'We believe it is essential that all teachers in training, irrespective of the age range they intend to teach, should complete satisfactorily a substantial course in language and the teaching of reading.' (p. 336)

Parents
Parents should be helped to understand the process of language development in their children and play their part in it! Moreover 'long before they become parents' older pupils should be made aware of the adult's role in young children's linguistic and cognitive development. (pp. 54 to 55)

Children

'There should be more adults involved in the school to afford a one-one or one-two relationship with the children as often as possible', and for this purpose the teacher should have the support of trained 'aides' who have taken a course on language development in the early years (pp. 65 to 66).

The report, a formidable volume of 650 pages, is full of insights and is still required reading for all teachers, whatever their specialism. It has become best known for the slogan, not invented by the committee, but given wide currency by the in-service work that followed the report: 'language across the curriculum'.

This admirable concept, that responsibility for pupils' language education ought to be accepted by all teachers, regardless of their special subject, forms an important strand in the programme of 'awareness of language' with which we are concerned in this book. Indeed many advocates of 'awareness of language' as an element in the curriculum see it as the best way of making a reality of the Bullock proposals.

The phrase 'language across the curriculum', however, had the disadvantage that it seemed to focus attention only on the 'horizontal' model of the curriculum. Nevertheless Bullock's insistence on the responsibility of the whole teaching staff for language development was welcome, and would have been more so if only the committee had thought through its proposal more thoroughly and asked more searching questions about its implications.

Unfortunately the committee seems to have been inhibited in the thinking through of its proposals by the insistence of a majority of its members that deliberate strategies designed to give pupils the tools for verbal learning must be avoided. Their view was that language skills must be acquired 'naturally', through the normal classroom activities and especially through 'expressive' use of language. Deliberate attempts to teach language skills were, to most members of the committee, anathema.

It is true that a contrary view surfaces here and there in the report, and not only in the Note of Reservation appended by one of the committee's experienced headmaster members. In fact, as we shall see, the report's final judgement on strategies such as 'learning to listen' is full of contradictions. Nevertheless the opposition to deliberate strategies underlies much of the discussion and seems to have contributed to a kind of paralysis of the will to implement the challenging proposals made. We can see this if we examine three of the Bullock proposals which are entirely in line with the programme of 'awareness of language' for which we are arguing. They are:

(i) responsibility of all teachers for language across the curriculum
(ii) the inclusion of language education in the initial training of all teachers
(iii) the restoration of 'adult time' to children cheated of it by home circumstances.

'LANGUAGE ACROSS THE CURRICULUM'

'Language across the curriculum' is the title of Chapter 12 of the Bullock Report which, with the two previous chapters (on oral and written language respectively), constitutes Part Four, 'Language in the Middle and Secondary Years'. Chapter 12 sets out what is meant by 'language across the curriculum':

The primary school teacher [as class teacher] already has it in his power to establish a language policy across the curriculum . . . he is likely to conceive of his task in terms of integrated rather than subject oriented work. In the secondary school, however, subject teachers tend to regard the role of language as outside their concern. (p. 189)

To summarise the sense of this passage, this leads subject teachers specifically to:

(i) overlook the ways in which language is closely linked with the mental processes that their subject tends to foster
(ii) neglect pupil (expressive) talk as a means of learning
(iii) insist on transactional writing at the expense of expressive writing which is a valuable way for the pupil to 'find his way into a subject'
(iv) take too narrow a view of reading
(v) fail to teach techniques of note-taking and other ways of 'learning to learn'
(vi) fail to see how their own language affects children's learning and to undervalue the art of getting children to talk to them.

To remedy these shortcomings *all* subject teachers need to accept responsibility for an agreed policy for language 'across the curriculum'. It follows that all teachers must be trained for the language aspect of their role.

This concept, as the chapter makes clear, was not an original one. The London Association for the Teaching of English had organised a series of conferences culminating in the publication in 1969 of a discussion document *A Language Policy Across the Curriculum* prepared by H. Rosen (reproduced in Barnes et al., 1969, p. 160). In 1971 the National Association for the Teaching of English had invited teachers of all subjects to its annual conference and devoted the programme to the subject of language across the curriculum. Subsequently HMI organised a series of short courses on the subject and the Schools Council and the London Institute of Education cooperated with a number of LEAs in a project called *Writing Across the Curriculum.*

The Bullock Committee, reviewing the history of these developments, ruefully accepts that despite widespread interest and official encouragement:

> there are still comparatively few schools which have introduced it as a policy... It cannot be pretended that such a policy is easy to establish.
>
> (p. 192)

Events since Bullock reported have proved that this is still true.

The Bullock programme remains a paper programme only. Though it made an important contribution to thinking about the role of language in the curriculum the report is flawed in its failure to grapple with the problems of implementation. The two despairing paragraphs reviewing possible ways of implementing 'language across the curriculum' betray the failure of nerve of the committee:

> We have considered ways in which it [i.e. the policy of 'language across the curriculum'] might take effect, but to endorse any of them would be to produce a prescription that would not suit the circumstances of every school... English departments are hard-pressed ... to ask them to add this important task to their existing commitments would be asking a great deal...

A committee of departments then?

> but it could be countered that it takes an individual head to give real leadership...
>
> (p. 193)

And so the 'strong recommendation' peters out in contradiction and confusion from which schools could not deduce what exactly it was that any individual teacher was being recommended to do.

Compounding this failure of decision was the failure to allot any role in 'language for life' to the study of foreign languages. Throughout its 650 pages the report avoids making any reference to the place of foreign language study in the curriculum, and in all the commentaries that poured out after Bullock, as well as in the inservice programmes that it inspired, this curious linguistic parochialism was perpetuated. 'Across the curriculum', therefore, in the Bullock context clearly did not mean 'across the *language* curriculum' and foreign language teachers seemed to have no role in it.

LANGUAGE TRAINING FOR ALL TEACHERS

The area in which Bullock made perhaps its most radical and imaginative proposals followed logically from the committee's main premise. If all teachers, with the exception we have noted, were to play their part in 'language across the curriculum', they must have adequate training. The Bullock conclusion was quite specific. In *all* initial three- or four-year training courses there must be a compulsory 'module' on language in education. 'We consider that the basic course should occupy at least 100 hours, and preferably 150' (p. 338).

To indicate what the basic module should contain, two examples were suggested. These are reprinted for reference in Appendix B. The two examples propose different approaches. One, more child-centred, takes as its starting point the student's own language and the language of children in school. The other, more theoretical, begins with a review of the process of language change and an introduction to current developments in linguistics.

For students following a one-year postgraduate course of training the committee considered that education in 'language' was equally necessary, though they might have to have a modified course. A minimum programme for such students is described. To summarise it briefly, it would include:

(i) the nature of language; as a system of rules; social effects; dialects
(ii) the functions of language, including language and personal growth
(iii) language and thought
(iv) language and learning ('the central problem for the teacher') including the teacher's language and 'language across the curriculum'
(v) the acquisition of language
(vi) the development of language, including differences between speech and writing
(vii) reading – its acquisition and role in learning

The whole of this discussion in Bullock, with its detailed proposals for 'language in education' programmes for teachers, is one of the most valuable parts of the report. The response of teacher trainers has been, with a few exceptions, to dismiss the proposals as too demanding. Less radical recommendations might have been more readily acceptable, especially since the post-Bullock years were years of financial stringency. The collapse of the Institute of Education structure based on the universities and of the area training organisations in the late 1970s left a vacuum in the planning of teacher education which has not been filled.

Again no mechanism was proposed for implementing a radical

proposal. As a result, after a decade, there is little sign of response from teacher trainers responsible for B.Ed. or PGCE courses.

THE CHILD'S NEED FOR 'ADULT TIME'

The third area where Bullock saw what was needed but failed to think through the hard detail of the steps to be taken was the child's need for individual dialogue with an adult. We have referred to this earlier (p. 14) as the factor of 'adult time'.

Bullock goes back to the Plowden Committee's study of this and quotes the research commissioned by Plowden on the effect of 'parental encouragement' on school achievement: 'the most powerful variable was found to be the School Handicap Score (SHS) a weighted sum of Father's Occupation, Father's Education, Mother's Education, Number of Books in the Home and (minus) the Number of Siblings'. Bullock also quoted a series of research studies in many countries showing how: 'a child's family background gives a clear prediction of his achievement in reading at age 10 and age 14' (p. 23).

We must return to this evidence, and to the recent research at the Thomas Coram Institute in London and at the University of Manchester, which gives fresh confirmation of the importance of 'adult time' for children when facing their first great intellectual hurdle, the breakthrough to literacy. The response of the Bullock Committee to the evidence was radical and imaginative. It made a series of proposals which have gone almost unnoticed in all the torrent of commentary to which its report gave rise and which have evoked little response from LEAs.

The first of the Bullock insights was that if parents are to play their demanding role successfully they will need preparation: 'It has to be recognised that many adolescent pupils are simply not ready to cast themselves in the role of future parents and for them the study of language in parenthood . . . through films, demonstrations and practical experience, would lead to an awareness of the adult's role in the young child's linguistic and cognitive development' (p. 55).

The report goes on to develop the proposal with examples of work being done in schools and samples of material that can be used. However the work should not end when teenagers leave school. Bullock seized on the role that the clinics should play: 'we believe that it may well be in the ante-natal clinics, which are attended by a high percentage of expectant mothers, that the case for language needs can be made with the greatest effect. Language is thus placed in the general context of child care' and, quoting a health visitor: 'when you give your child a bath, bathe him in language' (p. 58).

The education of parents is thus for Bullock a large part of the long-term solution. In the short term, however, 'adult time' must somehow be given back to the children who have been cheated of it. The Bullock Committee recognised the implications of this for schools: 'We believe that there should be more adults involved in the school, to afford a one–one, or a one–two, relationship with the children as often as possible' (p. 67).

In this connection Bullock strongly endorsed the Plowden Committee's recommendation (Plowden, 1967, p. 330) for the employment of properly trained 'teachers' aides', a proposal that has so far been given no chance of implementation because of the outright opposition of the teachers' unions. Bullock not only endorsed the Plowden case but added the further recommendation that all such aides working with young children should have a course of training in language development.

This part of the Bullock Committee's argument for giving back to children the 'adult time' that they need was cogent and forward-looking. Unfortunately the implications of the proposals were not worked out. If all children who need Bullock's one-to-one dialogue with an adult are to get it, the obvious question raised is: Where are the adults to come from?

It is unrealistic to ask for one fully trained teacher for every pupil. Teachers' aides, however, could be trained to do this work and there are a number of possible sources of recruitment: mothers whose own families are in school or have grown up and who have, as it were, served their own apprenticeship as parents; pensioners; unemployed adults (of whom there are likely to be well over 3 million for the foreseeable future); and the best source of all – the university and college students who are currently given the priceless privilege of three or four years' freedom to study on well-equipped campuses at public expense.

Students are privileged to be freed from all other responsibilities, to live in an ideal environment, and to be allowed to devote their time solely to a chosen course of study. They are given this opportunity because they have had the good fortune (favourable health, family encouragement, adequate intellectual endowment, especially verbal endowment etc.) required to succeed in our school system. It is entirely fair that in a democracy, where everybody cannot enjoy the same opportunities, those who do have this unique privilege should accept that it carries obligations. The graduate acquires, during three or four years of self-directed pursuit of a chosen discipline, an intellectual and spiritual capital that will enrich the whole of adult life. This transcends any argument about the purely material value of a degree on the market. The opportunity to give back something, simply by sharing time, interest and individual dialogue with a young, less fortunate learner, could quickly come to be seen as a normal feature of the university privilege, if our society cared enough to make the point to young people.

That many students can give back this precious 'adult time' to younger learners has been shown in a pioneering book by Sinclair Goodlad, *Learning by Teaching* (1979). Goodlad, a senior lecturer at the Imperial College of Science and Technology, London, describes, among a variety of schemes, his own course at Imperial College, in which science and engineering students acted as tutors in London schools. His book also describes a programme developed at York in which, every year for the past 15 years, children attending volunteer summer schools for slower readers and ethnic minorities have been given their own individual tutors, recruited from undergraduates and graduates at the university helped by teachers and heads of local schools.

This kind of co-operation between universities and schools would be more readily accepted if the secondary school curriculum included a modest practical apprenticeship for older (fifth and sixth form) learners in helping younger children to develop their language skills.

Another rich source of 'adult time', found by committed teachers, is that of linking an infant school with a nearby old people's home. There was an excellent example in an area of Birmingham where the need for 'adult time' is pressing. Here the residents of the home volunteered to 'adopt' a particular child each for extra reading and talk. The volunteers were free to come in to school each day in their own time, by arrangement with class teachers. They had their own 'common room' with teapot, books etc. Each volunteer spent as much time as possible with the child he or she had 'adopted' at moments when the child was free from other activities. The adult simply listened, answered questions, motivated the reading and talked about it with the child in language directed to the 'here and now'.

Initiatives such as these might at least have been discussed if the Bullock Report had carried its own proposals to their logical conclusion and faced the realities of supplying the adults needed. In fact there is no mention of any such possibilities in Bullock. Nowhere is there any estimate of how many adults 'one-to-one' dialogue with slow readers would require, no thought as to where they might be found, no logistics or costing.

Not surprisingly Bullock's plea for 'adult time' fell on stony ground. Few commentators on the report even mentioned it. It awakened no echoes on the in-service courses that proliferated after the report was published. Failure to think through one of the most important proposals in the report robbed it of much of the credibility it might have had among practising teachers.

SPECIFIC STRATEGIES RULED OUT

The three radical proposals in Bullock that we have reviewed, namely:

(i) involving teachers in 'language across the curriculum'
(ii) giving all teachers training in language in education
(iii) restoring 'adult time' to children deprived of it

called for action at a number of administrative levels. All three proposals remain central to any serious attack on the problem of making equality of opportunity less of a sham in our system. Nothing that has happened since Bullock reported has reduced their importance. They form an essential background to the way forward that we are proposing. In the re-examination of these issues for which we are appealing, however, the hard practical questions that Bullock bypassed must be faced.

It is not only in matters of administration that there are nettles to grasp. Bullock also let down the classroom teacher by failing to set clear objectives. The report seems to suffer from a paralysis of the will whenever specific teaching strategies are called for. This can be seen if we examine two parts of the problem on which the Bullock committee was divided:

learning about language structure and pattern ('grammar'!)
learning the skills of listening ('education of the ear')

Learning about the structure of language

On the subject of learning how language works Bullock swings in successive paragraphs between, on the one hand, the realisation that grasp of structure (grammar) cannot be expected to develop spontaneously out of expressive use of language in the classroom, but that systematic strategies will be needed, and, on the other hand, a horror of language work that does not arise out of children's 'personal expressive needs'. Thus: 'We cannot accept that the development of language can be left to chance, on the principle that a "relevant moment" will occur' (p. 172). However: 'Is there anyone here who truly believes that it matters to anyone but the grammarian how you define a noun?' (an American opinion quoted with approval, p. 174).

To a majority of the committee the teaching of grammar was anathema because 'language is inseparable from the situation'. It is for this reason that they commended the Schools Council programme *Language in Use*. This was an imaginative scheme of work produced by the team of Doughty, Pearce and Thornton under the chairmanship of Professor Halliday of University College London. We discuss the programme later (p. 50 to 51) when we review some of the pioneering materials that have contributed to the teaching of awareness of language. The Bullock Committee welcomed the team's approach, for keeping language study rooted in 'language in use' and for recognising the need to start from the stage reached by the pupil. The committee were, however, dissatisfied with the *Language in Use* materials because they saw a danger. This was: 'the inevitable danger that teachers might work mechanically through the units [There was] the further criticism that [*Language in Use*] does not commit itself to fundamental values, that it remains in essence a training in techniques' (p. 175).

Pity the beginning teacher or the student in training reading Bullock. On the one hand: 'the development of language cannot be left to chance on the principal that a relevant moment will occur' and yet the humane programme, so carefully pupil-based, of the Schools Council team will not do because it 'does not commit itself to fundamental values' (!) and it 'remains in essence a training in techniques'. This was asking the teacher to tread a narrow tightrope indeed.

In the committee's opposition to anything that might be labelled 'training in techniques' it is possible to detect echoes of the argument of which more was heard when Bullock was reporting than (mercifully) is heard now. The underlying premise was that the whole school curriculum is a form of 'manipulation', by those with power (the 'middle class'), of 'working-class' learners. According to this argument any kind of planning of the curriculum was illegitimate, whether it was done by the school or by the Schools Council. (The latter, to its surprise, long accustomed to being reviled by its critics for ineffectiveness in curriculum innovation, suddenly found itself cast as enemy number one: the great manipulator; see Young, 1971.) If the whole curriculum was a form of manipulation of one class by another, it followed that the language in which teaching and learning were transacted was the manipulator's main tool. The teaching of English thus became the most sensitive area in the debate.

This view of the curriculum, and of the role of the school, as one of the means by which the authority of the state is maintained is, of course, an essential element of the political philosophy of anarchism. We must return to it when we discuss (p. 64) the 'cultural variability' hypothesis: the notion that there is a necessary conflict between middle-class and working-class culture in a democracy.

For the present we may note that though the anarchist argument, rejecting the right of school or of central government to plan the curriculum, gets no support in Bullock, yet the discussion of the sensitive area of language teaching does reflect some of the confusion that calls for 'deschooling' managed to create in the minds of conscientious teachers of English a decade ago. Meanwhile, the harsh facts showed that the gap between Class V and Class I children was widening, and that schools were failing the very children who could look only to the school for help. The parrot cry of 'manipulation' was allowed to paralyse the will of those who might have helped them.

Learning to listen

One of the most radical proposals in Bullock, as we have seen, was that all teacher training courses should include a module called 'language in education'. In the proposed model syllabuses for this new element in teacher training, Bullock included the study of 'ear language' (compared with 'eye language') and of 'auditory perception and discrimination'. Teachers had to learn, in other words, how to use their ears and how to improve their perception and discrimination of spoken messages. Was this something that children should learn also?

Here, again, the advice given by Bullock was muddled. On the one hand:

In our view listening ability cannot be regarded as something to be abstracted, remedied and returned.

On the other hand:

There may be no evidence to show that formal training procedures are lastingly effective, but there is an equal lack of evidence to suggest that the daily activity of the classroom is itself sufficient.

Nevertheless:

In our view the ability [of listening] can best be developed as part of the normal work of the classroom and in association with other learning experiences.

But, finally:

deliberate strategies may be required for it cannot be assumed that the improvement [in listening ability] will take place automatically.   (p. 151)

It is little wonder that teachers have not known how to respond to such a muddled call to action.

We must conclude that despite the imaginative proposals for restoring 'adult time' to children who need it and the suggested inclusion of a language element in the training of all teachers, the Bullock Report was a sad waste of a great opportunity to rethink the teaching of language. Its interpretation of the idea of 'language across the curriculum', a concept already widely discussed before the Bullock inquiry began, had the effect only of narrowing the concept, excluding any role for foreign language teachers.

Its chief defect, unforgivable in a national inquiry of this importance, was in failing to spell out clearly where the responsibility lay for initiating the changes called for. This avoidance of clear allocation of responsibility for decision making and curriculum planning may reflect the muddled theories of a school of sociology which enjoyed a brief popularity. Whatever the reason, the lack of clear guidance to schools and LEAs ensured that the imaginative proposals endorsed by a majority of the committee's members bore little fruit.

A NEW WAY FORWARD

Meanwhile a different response to the rethinking of language teaching called for by Crowther in 1959 was making headway, led by practising teachers, and with foreign language teachers to the fore. The movement had started before the Bullock Committee began its deliberations but it accelerated rapidly after 1975. Its aim was to introduce into the curriculum teaching about *language* itself and to make this a 'bridge' across the divide separating the different secondary school disciplines.

We have attempted (p. 4) to sketch the main lines of this alternative strategy. It sees all teachers who are concerned with language as equal partners and it offers a mechanism to bring them round the table to plan a common area of the curriculum. Where the Bullock

Report assigned to the teacher of, say, biology merely some ill-defined responsibility for the use of English in the biology laboratory, the alternative strategy invites the biology teacher to be a partner in planning *and teaching* the 'awareness of language' programme. Indeed there will be some parts of the 'awareness of language' syllabus that only the biology teacher will be qualified to teach.

The introduction of 'awareness of language' as an element in the curriculum thus gives to each discipline a specific task to do and makes a reality of 'language across the curriculum'. Moreover the alternative strategy does not rest on a purely horizontal model, epitomised by the phrase to which Bullock gave prominence. It proposes that 'awareness of language' must be set in the context of a series of measures beginning at the pre-school stage.

Three key elements in this programme, as our discussion of the Bullock Report suggests, must be:

(i) restoring 'adult time' to the many children who are currently cheated of it by the lottery of family circumstances, through no fault of their hard-pressed parents

(ii) seriously tackling the need of many pupils for progressive 'education of the ear', beginning with 'disembedding' the syntactic and phonological elements in verbal messages and learning confidence in 'listening for meaning' on which so much of foreign language learning, and the varied demands of the secondary school syllabus, will rest

(iii) providing an initial opportunity for pupils' curiosity about language to be quickened so that later in the secondary course it may be possible to build on this the essential language element in 'preparation for parenthood' courses (see p. 46)

There is, however, a further great advantage in the alternative strategy. It directly supports foreign language learning, by giving pupils the necessary verbal tools: 'education of the ear'; insight into pattern in language; confidence in disembedding new phonological patterns; practice in matching written to spoken symbols; relish for what is new and strange in language. When the learner is properly equipped the foreign language study itself becomes a valuable part of his/her growing awareness of language.

Only by getting outside the mother tongue and operating, even at quite an elementary level, in another language, can the mother tongue be seen objectively. The foreign language, however, must be taught, in the context of the 'awareness of language' course, with this in mind. It forms part of the new 'trivium' in the language curriculum of the 1980s: Mother tongue/Awareness of language/Foreign language, which we might liken to the trivium on which the mediaeval curriculum planners built their 'grammar school' course:

Grammar / Logic / Rhetoric

(This formed the introduction to the later quadrivium of science subjects and music studied at the university. Whatever its shortcomings the mediaeval curriculum aimed at coherence both horizontally and vertically!)

There is another reason why our foreign language syllabus should be planned as part of the trivium and as an apprenticeship in learning how to learn a foreign language, rather than as an end in itself, justified by an appeal to its future 'usefulness'. Unlike our European neighbours, who can predict that *all* their children will need English, whatever their future careers may be, we cannot possibly foresee, when our pupils are aged 11 or even 13, which one of a dozen possible languages they may later need for work or leisure purposes.

Schools may, most commendably, diversify their foreign language provision. They may even offer Chinese as a first language, as does Easthampstead School or include Arabic in the third-year options, as does North Westminster Community School. But the very pupil who chooses Chinese at age 12 may later find that his job takes him to Stuttgart, or the one who opts adventurously for Arabic at age 14 may find himself in his job conducting correspondence in Spanish or French. The secondary school foreign language course can only be justified as an apprenticeship, whose main object is to show how to learn, while giving confidence that the job can be done and is rewarding.

Such an apprenticeship, of course, must be followed at the post-16 stage, as adult needs and inclinations become clear, by a generous provision, *à la carte*, of languages to be studied by intensive techniques (as pioneered in the armed services) and wherever possible in 'reciprocal' courses, with teams of learners of matched languages giving each other individual tuition in their respective mother tongues.

In these first two chapters we have sketched the outline of our argument for the introduction into the curriculum of an element called 'awareness of language'. It offers both an effective way of achieving the goal of 'language across the curriculum', and a means of enriching the experience of language that has hitherto been lacking for too many children and future parents. At the same time it can make an important contribution to successful foreign language study. It is time now to examine some of the initiatives taken by teachers in this direction.

3 Initiatives in teaching and testing 'language'

A NEW KIND OF LANGUAGE DEGREE

It was at university level that the 'rethinking' called for by the Crowther Report began. The rapid expansion of universities in the 1960s gave the opportunity for several new approaches to language studies. It may be useful to describe one of those which was fairly typical of the new wave. This was the degree in 'language' created in York by the first head of the Language Department, Professor le Page, and his colleagues. Their task was made feasible by two decisions taken at an early stage in the academic planning of the new university. The first was to create a separate department for purely literary studies (at first 'English Literature', later expanded to include related, i.e. European, literatures). The second decision was *not* to set up traditional schools of, for example, French or German but to subsume all foreign language degree work, as well as work in English *language* (not literature), in a single department. This was the Language Department whose central core, common to all students, regardless of the language(s) in which they might specialise, was linguistics. A third decision, taken later, to cater for the obvious needs not met by the previously mentioned departments, was to create a department to serve the specialist function of teaching foreign languages, as well as to do research in foreign language acquisition and teaching methods, and to play a part in the training of graduate language teachers. This was the Language Teaching Centre.

Students in the York Language Department follow a four-year course. The first year is spent on an introduction to linguistics (which includes acquiring the tools a linguist needs, for example a thorough grasp of phonetics) and on an intensive study, partly in the Language Teaching Centre, of the student's main European language (French, German, or English). The second year is spent away from the university immersed in the French or German language (or, in the case of English specialists, teaching English as a second language). On their return to York at the beginning of the third year students face an oral test in their chosen language before embarking on the study of its history and structure in the remaining two years of the course. At the same time students are introduced to their second language, which must be either Chinese, Hindi or Swahili (i.e. one of the world's three most widely used languages, each serving a whole continent and each offering characteristics quite different from those found in the European family). The linguistic studies which predominate in the third and fourth years are informed and illustrated by the students' growing insight into the two contrasting languages chosen for study. (English specialists, it should be added, have to learn another European language – Swedish.)

Though York language students read widely in the literature of their foreign language, as they must, in order to deepen their command of the idiom, at no time in their examinations or seminars are they required to make value judgements about the *literary* qualities of the works read, unless they deliberately choose an optional paper to be studied in the Department of English and Related Literatures.

The course is flexible, in that it may be combined with other disciplines. Language and philosophy and language and education have been successful combinations. The York course has attracted students of the highest calibre from overseas (China, India, Africa, the Caribbean). The best of these, while studying English as their specialism, are well placed, as native-speaking informants, to help their British fellow students in the study of languages such as Chinese, Hindi or Swahili.

The York course has been described at some length because it represented, when the university opened in 1963, a radical break with the traditional approach both to English and to foreign language studies. Like other similarly radical courses elsewhere it has attracted sixth formers of high ability. The fact that, after 20 years, such a course no longer seems so revolutionary is a measure of the change that has taken place in expectations regarding language studies.

'LANGUAGE' AS A SUBJECT IN THE SCHOOL CURRICULUM

Bridging the space between L1 and L2

The sixth formers who applied to York and to the other new courses did not wish to restrict their interest in language to literary criticism.

They wanted to explore other equally important aspects of language, such as psycholinguistics (the relation of language to thought) or socio-linguistics (language studied as an aspect of social behaviour). The success of the new university courses in 'language' naturally led to the question: Should not the school curriculum offer *all* pupils the opportunity to explore some of these issues, at an appropriate level? The synthesis between English and foreign language studies achieved at York was made possible because the new discipline of 'linguistics' bridged the gap that had traditionally separated the two. This led to a further question: Might study of 'language awareness' do the same in schools?

The possibility was first discussed publicly at a national conference in Manchester in 1973, convened by George Perren, then director of the Centre for Information on Language Teaching. When he came to edit the conference papers for publication Perren took up a phrase introduced into the discussion by Jim Wight: 'the space between', referring to the different dialects met by pupils. Perren chose this as the title of the collected papers, giving it the wider sense of the space to be bridged between English and foreign languages and other ethnic minority mother tongues: 'all would be simpler in schools where no foreign languages were taught and where all children came with an acceptable form of English as their mother tongue. If rare today, such schools will be unknown in future' (Introduction to CILT, 1974).

The possibility of building this kind of bridge had been raised specifically in one of the conference papers: 'I would see the subject [the study of language] as linking the two supporting studies of mother tongue and foreign language ... which have hitherto, in nearly all schools, proceeded in completely separate departments' (Hawkins in G. E. Perren, CILT Reports and Papers 10, 1974, p. 62).

In later papers I have tried to develop the concept of the trivium (of 'Mother Tongue/Awareness of language/Foreign language') comparing it with the mediaeval trivium on which famous grammar schools such as Winchester were based. (At its foundation, Winchester was proud to call itself a 'trivial' school, i.e. it taught the trivium.) The three elements of our proposed new trivium would reinforce each other in much the same way that the elements of the early Winchester syllabus did. The new element in the curriculum, 'awareness of language', would help pupils in their attack on the foreign language, by strengthening their capacity for 'insight into pattern' and setting up correct expectations as to what patterns to look for.

At the same time the foreign language itself, if properly presented, could help to develop pupils' awareness of language and combat linguistic parochialism. This required, of course, that the foreign language teaching strategies used must encourage pupils to compare their emerging insights in the new language with their intuitions about their mother tongue. A mere drilling in simple dialogues to meet hypothetical 'survival situations' could not contribute very much to language awareness, nor offer that apprenticeship in 'learning how to learn' languages on which later acquisition, by intensive means, of the language(s) of adult need could build.

A SCHOOL SHOWS THE WAY

While the theorists were debating, the initiative of one enterprising school showed what was possible. In 1972 a new approach to language was introduced at Hessle High School, North Humberside. It was devised by Barry Laughton, head of modern languages there, who had already made his mark in the 1960s for his imaginative use of the new techniques of 'group work' in language learning. He had the advice of Dr D. Reibel (now at Tübingen), then a member of the Language Department of York University, who visited the school several times, discussed the programme with Laughton and his colleagues and suggested reading and projects.

The general aims of the course were to give pupils an idea of language as a whole, its evolution, history and structure, to help them to appreciate the similarities between their own and other languages, 'so that they might feel closer to them', and at the same time to give them confidence in manipulating their own language.

The course, called a 'language foundation course', had as its immediate aims to enable pupils to make more informed choices between foreign languages offered during their secondary education and in part to compensate for what was felt to be the neglect, or underemphasis, of overt structure and grammar in the new 'audio-visual' methods then in vogue in the foreign language classroom. It occupied one school year, with 4 periods per week, in addition to, but separate from, the pupils' normal English lessons. The topics explored during the year were grouped under the following heads:

(i) *beginnings of language*: language evolution, change, sources of English, languages in contact etc. Questions raised included: Why do we need a language? What similarities are there between languages? How has English changed? What has English borrowed from other languages?

(ii) *language developing*: the baby learning to communicate, role of the parent, invented 'family' words, children's 'mistakes', rhymes and superstitions about language etc.

(iii) *language in use*: dialects, styles, appropriateness etc.

(iv) *structure of language*: grammar, word order, intonation, ambiguity, including the activity of devising a questionnaire for use at the end of the course to discover what had been gained

Laughton found that among the most popular items in the course, as revealed by the pupils' questionnaire, was the discussion of the baby learning to communicate, and that in most cases the pupils' families were interested in the course.

One of the significant aspects of this pioneering initiative was that, from the beginning, it was a team effort, planned jointly by the head of the school and the head of the lower school, the heads of the foreign language and the English departments and the two teachers who undertook the initial classroom work, one a Latinist and the other a Germanist.

Experiments along these lines, in introducing 'language' as a curriculum subject, have continued, at Hessle and elsewhere, with growing confidence.

FURTHER INITIATIVES BY SCHOOLS

After the publication of the Bullock Report interest in the kind of course pioneered at Hessle High School quickened. A number of schools began to experiment with language courses for pupils about to begin their secondary education. It is significant that in nearly every case it was the modern language staff who took the initiative. Some courses depended on individual initiative and did not survive when staff were promoted to other work.

An example of such a course which attracted wide interest, despite being short-lived, was the 'linguistics module' introduced at Archbishop Michael Ramsey's School, London, by the head of modern languages, David Cross. This was a term's work intercalated in each of years one and two, alongside the 'taster' introductions to languages other than French pioneered by this school. French study proper began in the third year only.

Henry Box School

The language course developed (again by the modern language staff) at Henry Box School, Witney, Oxfordshire, became nationally known through the publication of the materials on which the course was based (Aplin et al., 1981) This first-year course became incorporated into a longer-term treatment of language in the secondary curriculum, including the pioneering of a course of language in child-care for pupils in the 15 to 16 age group which we discuss on p. 46. The first-year module itself was designed as a six- or seven-week introductory course for 11-year-olds about to start French. Experience has shown that the course has helped to create a more secure approach to the new language and at the same time to build a positive relationship between pupils and teacher. A summary of the course as designed in 1979 is as follows:

Aims
1 To create 'awareness of language'
2 To give practice in listening
3 To place the learning of a particular language in context
4 To create a positive relationship between pupils and teacher

Content
(i) *Language as communication*
  (a) Definition (message-sending, codes)
  (b) Animal language (visual, sound, scent)
  (c) Non-verbal communication (gestures, body-language)
  (d) Signs and signals (road signs, travel, politics, pictures)
  (e) Coded languages (smoke signals, semaphore, morse)
  (f) Speech (vocal apparatus, vowels and consonants)
  (g) Words (random collection of sounds)

(ii) *Acquisition of language*
  (a) How baby learns: follow progress of 0–5-year-old child with tape-recordings and video-cassettes, observing how the child develops linguistic ability
  (b) Lessons to be drawn
    (i) importance of understanding before response
    (ii) necessity of making mistakes
    (iii) why is language acquisition so rapid and effortless?

(iii) *Families of languages*
  (a) How many languages?
  (b) Idea of language 'families'
  (c) Most widely spoken ten international languages
  (d) European languages (Romance/Germanic)

(e) Similarities between languages
(f) History of languages (Romans, etymology, specialist lexis)

(iv) *Anatomy of language – Rules/Patterns*
    (a) Reference section – naming of the parts
    (b) Working together (subject–verb–object; tense; inflection; gender)
    (c) Differences between languages (uniqueness)

(v) *The golden rules*
    (a) Listen carefully
    (b) Spot the Rules and Patterns
    (c) Work hard in learning
    (d) Make mistakes
    (e) Watch for contacts
    (f) Keep trying!

North Westminster Community School

An interesting comparison with the Henry Box course is offered by the World Languages Project developed in the Inner London Community School, North Westminster, a school with a large number of ethnic minorities in its catchment area.

This lower school foundation course was designed by the modern language staff of the school. It aims to prepare pupils for learning a future foreign language, either European or non-European, by overcoming prejudices and encouraging motivation. It is organised as follows:

Aims
1 To develop the language learning skills of speaking, listening, reading and writing and to develop the skill of memorising
2 To strengthen awareness of grammatical concepts
3 To give an introduction to language variety, the development of languages and their interdependence
4 To encourage the comparison of structure, vocabulary and writing systems across languages
5 To break down intolerance and develop curiosity about language
6 To complement literacy skills in other subjects

The course attempts to achieve these aims as far as possible through direct experience of several languages.

Content

Years 1 and 2: Pupils study each of the main languages French, Spanish and German for 10 weeks (nearly one term) each. In addition they do one 'short unit' each term of 2 weeks' duration. These include several non-European languages and a unit on language awareness.
Year 3: Pupils embark on the study of their main language (they have a choice of one or two languages from French, Spanish or German). They continue with the 'short units' as in years 1 and 2.

The short units include Arabic, the Hebrew alphabet, the development of speech, the history of writing, Bahasa Indonesia, Bengali, language families (derivations of words, language comparisons, etc.), invented languages, Russian. It is envisaged that further units will soon be incorporated.

In the teaching of the main languages, links are made as far as possible with the short units. The latter are placed deliberately at points where useful comparisons can be made, for example, in year 2 the verb system of Bahasa Indonesia is compared with those of French, Spanish and German. In year 1 the Hebrew and Russian alphabets and study of the history of writing provide support and comparison in tackling reading skills in Spanish and German.

One teacher takes the class for the whole programme in order to ensure that the links and comparisons are made and that progress can be continuously monitored.

Language in a child-care course

While at Banbury School, Peter Downes developed, with Paul Baker of the Banbury Teachers' Centre, a course in language for child-care groups of pupils in their fifth year. This course was further developed and modified at Henry Box School, as part of the follow-up to the Introduction to Language module offered to the first years (cf. p. 43). The course was later introduced at Hinchingbrooke School, Cambridgeshire. It is organised as follows:

Aims
1 To create an interest in the language of young children
2 To develop a basic understanding of the way children learn to talk
3 To give opportunities for the practice of techniques in talking to children

The course attempts to keep direct instruction and transmission of factual or theoretical knowledge to a minimum, relying more on observation of children (at home, in playgroups, in school and on tape), on role-play, discussion and playing with children.

Content

(i) introduction to the acquisition of language and the crucial role of parents and other adults

(ii) observation of a child aged between 2 and 3 playing with teacher/parent in the classroom followed by simple analysis in the group

(iii) study of the stages of language development up to the age of 5 with help of tape-recordings, stressing variation from the average as no cause for anxiety

(iv) study of examples of parental interaction with children and their effects using recordings; practical role-play of use of everyday situations to develop language

(v) practical activities showing how language develops through play and how inexpensive toys can be used in promoting language development

(vi) language of control: discussion of the various ways of controlling children; role-play of alternative approaches

(vii) recollection of the rhymes, songs, stories learned by the pupils as children and discussion of their use in language learning

(viii) use of examples of picture books and simple readers brought into the class by pupils and discussion of their use for widening vocabulary and stimulating conversation

(ix) discussion of television output for the under-fives with recorded examples: emphasis on value of parents and children watching and listening together and talking about the ideas put over; teaching the use of the OFF switch!

(x) discussion of implications of the course: value of stable home relationship; the need for 'adult time'; social and financial implications; effect of size of family; role and responsibility of father

Some interesting lessons have already been learnt from this work. It has been found that watching films and listening to broadcasts are not helpful. It is better for teachers to select examples from broadcasts to develop in discussion. The experiment of pupils trying to use small tape-recorders to record children's language took far too long and did not work except with exceptionally able pupils. Pupils also found it very hard to observe children in playgroups and to report back. They did not know what they were meant to be listening for unless given specific guidance.

Downes sees a number of problems that might arise in a course of this kind:

(a) There is the danger, since child-care groups tend to consist of girls, of implying that fathers do not have an important role in language development – the father's role needs to be stressed.

(b) Pupils do not retain linguistic theory and the use of linguistic terminology can be counter-productive.

(c) Pupils are brought by the course to think about its relevance to their own experience at home; great sensitivity is, therefore, called for and the teacher must know the pupils, and their backgrounds, well.

(d) An initial reaction can be that pupils believe the aim of the course is to make babies 'talk posh', and this calls for sensitivity and perceptiveness in teaching.

(e) There is a danger of thinking of language as divorced from other activities; the role of language as the key to relationships and other activities must be emphasised.

Both in its imaginative sweep and in the sensitivity with which it is presented this course deserves to be a model for any school which seeks to prepare future young parents for their demanding role.

The success of the courses at Banbury, Henry Box and Hinchingbrooke cannot fail to influence the development of child-care courses and points the way to the introduction of the essential language element that hitherto they have lacked.

NEW MATERIALS FOR LANGUAGE TEACHING

The production of new language-teaching materials, meanwhile, both helped to focus the theorists' debate and to encourage schools to follow the example of pioneers such as Hessle High School.

Basic Linguistics for Secondary Schools

First in the field, by some years, was B. N. Ball, a lecturer at Doncaster College of Education, whose three-volume textbook *Basic Linguistics for Secondary Schools* appeared as early as 1967. This was an imaginative programme, to cover the middle three years of the secondary course and designed for average and less-than-average attainers.

It is probably impossible to quote an extract without being unfair to the course as a whole but the following may give some of the flavour of the material.

'Loaded' words

In Books 1 and 2 we saw that words themselves can be powerful. Skilled writers employed to sell commercial products know this. One extremely successful advertising man once drew up a list of the twenty most powerful words that could be used to sell goods. *NEW* and *FREE* were both high on the list.

How are these words powerful? Do you recall seeing them used in advertisements? How are these words usually printed or spoken – are they made to stand out from the background of the advertisement?

What other words are also used in this way?

The people who write advertisements use a practice of language that is common. We can see it at work in this piece of conversation:

'I hear your Fred's in hospital.'

'Yes.'

'What's the matter, then?'

'He's gone for psychiatric treatment.'

'The mental hospital!'

'Oh, he's not mad or anything like that. Don't go running away with the idea he's a nut-case!'

The words *psychiatric, mental, mad,* and *nut-case* are all concerned more or less with the same idea. Which are the 'loaded' words, in the sense that *NEW* and *FREE* were discussed as 'loaded'? What difference in meaning exists between these words? Why was the second speaker anxious to avoid the implications of some of them?

In another area, where again there is much fear and prejudice, there are various words in English that describe people whose skin pigmentation is not the pale colour of the Anglo-Saxon race. Probably the most 'loaded' of all such words is *black*. Why is this?

What other words of this kind exist?

Which are meant to be deliberately offensive?

Which are accurate as words describing these peoples?

Are there any words used to describe people with the skin pigmentation of the Anglo-Saxon peoples? Who uses them?

Are any meant to be deliberately offensive?

How are 'loaded' words concerned with colour avoided by speakers who do not wish to give offence?

Finally, there are 'loaded' words which are used – particularly at election times – by the political parties. Which are meant to harm an opposing party?

EXERCISES

1 Examine the pages of newspapers and magazines, hoardings, and television commercials. Complete the list of twenty 'loaded' words that are most used by advertisers. List them in order of effectiveness.

2 Some of the following are known by other words. Make a list of all the other terms, in descending order of politeness:

(a) private detective
(b) hire-purchase
(c) a patient undergoing psychiatric treatment
(d) an employee who refuses to join other employees in a strike
(e) a public-house.

Explain how any one of (a) to (e) consists of 'loaded' words when a certain point is reached in the descending order of politeness.

3 Some of the most abusive language that appears in the daily news consists of exchanges between countries who resent one another's policies. Collect examples from news broadcasts and from newspapers, where a country, or its leaders, are referred to in uncomplimentary terms. Explain how any speaker of these examples uses 'loaded' words to attack the persons or country he is talking about.

Language in Use

The Schools Council programme worked out by the team of Doughty, Pearce and Thornton under the chairmanship of Professor Halliday, and published in 1971, broke quite new ground. Whereas Ball had offered an approach to 'linguistics' appropriate for secondary school pupils, Halliday, in his introduction to *Language in Use*, came close to arguing for the kind of 'awareness of language' approach that we are advocating:

Each one of us has this ability [to use language] and lives by it; but we do not always become aware of it or realise fully the breadth and depth of its possibilities. . . There is no place for language in the division of knowledge into arts and sciences – this is no doubt a principal reason for its neglect in our educational system, which depends on boundaries of this kind. . . There should, however, be some place for language in the working life of the secondary school pupil; and, it might be added, of the student in a College of Education.   (p. 4)

The units of work in the Schools Council programme are grouped into three main aspects of language use:

(i) the nature and function of language
(ii) its place in the lives of individuals
(iii) its role in making human society possible

The aim of the units is: 'to develop in pupils and students awareness of what language is and how it is used and, at the same time, to extend their competence in using it'. The authors thus accept that 'awareness and competence are linked'. We shall return to their argument on p. 73. The material in *Language in Use* is not offered as a course to be worked through but rather as a resource bank from which each teacher will select units to suit pupils' interests.

ALPINE

The set of teaching materials which came to be known as ALPINE was produced by a working party of teacher trainers and teachers based in Norwich which began work in 1975. The convenor of the group was the county language adviser, Ray Whiley. The acronym stands for 'A Language Project In Norfolk Education'. The ALPINE materials have not been published nationally but are distributed within the LEA schools.

The Norfolk initiative was originally, in part, a reaction to the set-back to primary French. After the publication of the NFER Report *Primary French in the Balance* (Burstall et al., 1974) it was felt useful to rethink the place of language education for the 10 to 12 age group. A set of worksheets was produced offering materials for a one-year course conceived as an alternative to beginning French. Some schools, however, have used the materials with pupils who have started French, so that the two studies run in parallel.

The multi-media materials, which it was hoped teachers would not treat as a course but use to build their own courses to suit their and their pupils' interests, were divided into units of work and grouped in four areas:

(i) language as system
(ii) language in action
(iii) language across cultures
(iv) language as change

SUPPORT FROM TEACHER TRAINERS

At teacher training level interest in 'awareness of language' in the curriculum has grown rapidly. Initiatives in promoting discussion of the new courses have mainly been taken by tutors in modern languages. Teacher training institutions which have already made significant contributions to the development of this area of the curriculum include: King's College London, Department of Education; Durham University, Department of Education; Ealing College of Higher Education; King Alfred's College, Winchester; Homerton College, Cambridge; Brighton Polytechnic; Department of English, University of Birmingham; Language Teaching Centre, University of York.

Although tutors in modern languages have been most active, specialists in English studies have also shown a growing interest in this development in the language curriculum. Teacher trainers who have travelled, in countries such as the United States and Australia, have become aware of the extent to which, in those countries, the kind of curriculum development we are advocating has, for over a decade, been actively discussed and developed in many schools.

THE NATIONAL CONGRESS ON LANGUAGES IN EDUCATION

NCLE was set up in 1976. It was the outcome of several years of discussions among some 40 national associations concerned with English, linguistics and foreign language teaching at school, university and polytechnic levels. Its purpose was to fill an obvious gap. There existed no national forum where teachers, researchers, examiners, advisers, publishers and others interested in all aspects of language in education could meet and discuss their common problems. The Congress seeks to meet this need through its working parties and its biennial assemblies. The assemblies are prepared for by detailed discussion in working parties. These publish their discussion documents for consideration by the constituent associations prior to each assembly. At the first assembly of the Congress in 1978, at Durham, I was invited to write a paper on 'Language as a Curriculum Study' (Hawkins, 1979). Summing up the argument of my paper I suggested that: 'study of language in the curriculum could be the place where mother tongue acquisition makes contact with foreign languages and with the languages of immigrants. As it is there is no meeting ground.'

There followed, at the next assembly (1980), a working-party report, *Issues in Language Education*, 'Language Policies in Schools with Special Reference to Co-operation Between Teachers of Foreign Languages and Teachers of English'. The working party found (not surprisingly) very little evidence that the approach which had come to be called 'language across the curriculum', following Bullock, had made any headway at all in schools. While the 1980 working party reported that they could not come to an agreed policy about the alternative strategy to Bullock, namely offering 'language' as a curriculum subject, they did recommend that carefully monitored experiments in this direction would be justified.

Accordingly the standing committee of NCLE set up in 1980 a small working group chaired by John Trim, director of CILT, who was succeeded in the following year by Professor John Sinclair of Birmingham University, to co-ordinate and monitor the pilot schemes in 'awareness of language' which by now were proliferating in the schools. The first task of the group was to summon a national conference in Birmingham in January 1981. Here it was decided to attempt to map the variety of new courses (estimated to number well over 150) and to try, by questionnaires and visits, to arrive at some judgement of their objectives, their content and (if possible) their degree of success.

The third Assembly of NCLE, held in 1982, authorised the working group to proceed to the next stage of its work: the close observation by members of the group of the most interesting of the experiments, followed by their description in a series of case studies. These would be valuable in assessing the extent to which the experiments were fulfilling their stated aims and would facilitate the production of teaching materials and the planning of initial and in-service training courses. It was hoped that the schools might also gain from making contact with other pioneering schools, and by widening their own experience.

To launch this stage of its work the working group convened a second national conference at Leeds University in January 1983 at which six schools which had made particular progress in developing 'awareness of language' in the curriculum gave accounts of their work. The conference was attended by some 100 teachers and language advisers, publishers and examiners.

NEW EXAMINATIONS

University of London Board: GCE 'A' level – 'Varieties of English'

Reference was made earlier (p. 12) to the recommendation of the Secondary Schools Examinations Council in 1964, in its last report to the Secretary of State, that an optional paper in 'language' should be available for sixth formers reading 'English' at GCE 'A' level. Nearly 20 years later this dream has come nearer to reality with the introduction by the University of London Board of an 'A' level paper called 'Varieties of English'. This is an optional alternative to the paper 'Comprehension and Appreciation'.

The aims and objectives of the new paper are as follows:

Aims: The aim of the alternative paper . . . is some study of the forms and uses of a wide variety of different kinds of spoken and written English, both literary and non-literary. A theoretical study of language is not intended, but candidates will benefit from some understanding of the sound, word and sentence structure of English, in order to identify and describe the textual features of the language. (This paper is unlikely to be suitable for candidates for whom English is a second language.)

Objectives: To demonstrate some awareness and understanding of:

      the nature of language variety and change

      the sound and sentence patterns of present-day English

      factors affecting the styles and uses of English – social, regional, situational, historical

      the differences between spoken and written English

      the differences between a descriptive and a prescriptive attitude to language usage and between notions of 'correct' and 'appropriate' language use

      how to make a simple descriptive analysis of a text or a contrastive analysis of two or more texts, in order to relate their linguistic features to their function and context of situation

Some 42 candidates from three centres took the paper in the first year, 1981. In his report the examiner noted significantly that the results:

showed no correlation between the marks for the literature and language papers.

He also made an interesting comment on the prevalent attitude to the teaching of grammatical terminology:

Although the provisional syllabus for the pilot scheme does not call for a technical knowledge of language, it is difficult to see how a candidate can make perceptive and accurate remarks about varieties of English without a metalanguage selected from language study. It was evident that the candidates had been taught to use linguistic terminology, and therefore to perceive the features that the terms represent. I think the time has come to stop apologising for this. If the need for linguistic technical terms is accepted, then the scope of the paper might be extended or varied.

Schools Council 16 to 19 English Project

This challenge, to rethink the terms in which language can be discussed by pupils who have not previously been given the requisite vocabulary, is one that has exercised the Northern Joint Working Party of the Schools Council 16 to 19 English Project. The working-party is elaborating proposals for an 'A' level English language examination which promises to take the *language* and not its literature, as the stuff of study.

Oxford and Cambridge Board: 'OA' level

A third initiative at sixth form level is the new Oxford and Cambridge Board's paper at 'OA' level, called 'Principles of Language', approved by the Board's English Language Awarding Committee and first set in 1982. This paper was set at the request of The Oratory School, Reading, where a one-year 'pilot' course for the lower sixth form, called 'Principles of Language' had been developed by a modern language teacher, Tony Tinkel. The course occupied three 40-minute sessions per week for one year. It was seen as following on from traditional 'O' level English. The 1982 examination paper took two and a half hours, in which time candidates answered 3 questions out of a possible 12, with complete freedom of choice.

Each of the 12 questions deals with a different aspect of the course followed during the year. In 1982 the 12 aspects were as follows:

1 Signs: designing suitable emblems for an international conference to represent places such as: a car-park; a silent meditation room etc.
2 Communication without language: how to communicate by visual means only. For example, trying to show the difficulties of communicating the question: 'Where did you go yesterday?'
3 Phonetic transcription: transcribing a short dialogue passage into broad phonetic script.
4 Intonation and stress: marking tonetic stress on a dialogue passage and proposing five different intonation and stress patterns for the sentence: 'We'll have a bottle of champagne instead.'
5 Morpheme analysis: defining some common prefixes and suffixes and commenting on the problems facing the compiler of a traditional dictionary who wishes to include these minimal units in his work.
6 Syntactic structure: analysis of short sentences, using tree diagrams if desired OR distinguishing 'sentence adverbs' from adverbs of time, manner and place in a given list.
7 Syntactic and semantic ambiguity: distinguishing deep structure meanings from surface structure similarities in sentences such as: 'They were drinking friends'/'They were drinking tea' and explaining different meanings in ambiguous sentences such as: 'We dispense with accuracy.'
8 Contextual ambiguity: suggesting three different contexts in which remarks such as 'no duck' or 'pen lines' might have been made.
9 Regional dialect sounds: choosing for given dialects (11 being listed) one

vowel or diphthong that is typical and differs from RP, writing the sound in phonetic script, plotting it on quadrilateral etc.

10 British and American English: giving ten examples of lexical and syntactic differences, comparing acceptability in British English of given American usages.

11 Styles of language use: suggesting what a policeman might say on finding his car stolen, if he were speaking to a fellow officer or a tiresome young boy, and commenting on the lexical and syntactic changes involved.

12 Register: suggesting probable contexts for a number of extracts with lexical and syntactic reasons for choice.

In addition to this written paper each candidate submits an extended essay of some 2,500 words on a subject of his choice approved by the moderator. This carries one-third of the total marks.

Our summary of some of the questions in this pioneering paper certainly does not do justice to it, but it will be clear that sixth formers who have followed the one-year course will have had to think hard about some interesting aspects of language. As the author of the course modestly claims, 'by increasing students' awareness of the nature and functioning of language the course aims to make them more sensitive to their own and other people's use of it'.

A point of special interest is that the course is taken by a mixed group of specialists in science as well as in arts. It offers both sides a rare opportunity to discuss together a subject that concerns them both but to which they bring different expectations. 'Awareness of language' in the sixth form might thus help to bridge the gap between the 'two cultures' in the way that, in the French *lycée*, the common course in *philosophie* provides a meeting ground for students following very different routes to the *baccalauréat*.

The intiatives in teaching and examining language that we have looked at were motivated by the experience of teachers. In trying to help their pupils the teachers have proceeded largely by trial and error. What we have been seeing is a kind of 'action research': finding out by doing, rather than being content to split hairs in dispute in the journals. It is action research in a good tradition and need make no apology. There are, however, some theoretical issues involved which have been blurred rather than clarified by recent socio-linguistic debates. It is to these issues that we turn in the next section.

4 Awareness of language and school learning

'RESTRICTED' CODES?

It is necessary to clear away a possible misunderstanding at the outset. We are not seeking to revive debate about the theory that certain languages (or dialects, or 'codes') used by some children are in some way intrinsically deficient, and that the children who use them are therefore in some way 'deprived'.

The theory that certain children speak a 'restricted' form of language is generally associated in the UK with the name of Basil Bernstein, though Bernstein has, since 1969, emphatically denied that he ever proposed a 'verbal deficit' theory. Bernstein's successive formulations of his position are not easy to follow. In his early papers he contrasted 'public languages' (of which there might be several kinds) with 'formal languages'. Public languages were used by working-class speakers while only the middle class had access to formal languages.

A 'public language' was defined, *inter alia*, as a language of 'implicit meaning'. That is, the speaker expects his hearer to share common expectations which enable meanings to be transacted with minimal, purely linguistic signals. A perhaps simplistic example of implicit meaning might be this. Imagine a husband and wife whose routine on going to bed is unchanging; when the husband rises from his chair at 11.0 p.m. and goes towards the kitchen he may say 'Hm?' or 'Time?' For his wife, the monosyllable carries the implicit, quite complex, meaning: 'Shall I fill the hot-water bottle now and lock up?'

Formal language, by contrast, is a language of 'explicit meaning'. It relies much less on shared expectations but explicitly spells out its meaning so as to be understood by a wider variety of hearers. The interesting hypothesis that children from certain kinds of background might be less at home in language of explicit meaning (the language of teaching and of textbooks) aroused widespread discussion. But even before the theory had been fully worked out, and certainly before rigorous analysis of children's language had proved the theory, Bernstein changed his ground. The notion of 'code' was substituted for 'language'. Language was defined as words actually spoken whereas a 'code' was rather a system of rules or principles, 'verbal planning activities, at the pyschological level' (1965, p. 131).

At the same time the terms 'restricted' and 'elaborated' code replaced 'public' and 'formal' language. The suggestion was that while middle-class children can switch between these two codes, the working-class pupil has access only to the restricted code.

It should be said that it is very difficult to find in any single one of Bernstein's papers a fully worked out, integrated definition of the two codes. Nevertheless the notion that working-class pupils had access only to a restricted code caught popular attention and, whatever Bernstein's later papers said, it was with this notion that his name was linked by most teachers, and especially by those recently graduating from the colleges.

If Bernstein's formulations were imprecise and sometimes contradictory, it should be remembered that the field was new and knowledge was expanding rapidly. Nothing should detract from the brilliance of some of his insights in areas that had been little explored. His formulations were certainly more subtle than some of his detractors have made out or than the essays written by generations of college students might suggest.

By contrast, what has been called the 'classical verbal deficit theory', developed in the USA, was both less subtle in its formulation and easier to attack. The classical theory, which lay behind much of the Head Start programme in the USA, might be summarised as follows (Gordon, 1981):

There are two varieties of speech: a high and a low variety; the low variety lacks the necessary ingredients for learning in school; . . . it is the low variety that is spoken by working-class children and by most black children; . . . if such children are to succeed in school they must be helped to acquire the high variety as soon as possible.

After reviewing the corpus of 'classical verbal deficit' writings Gordon offers a judgement on the controversy that, he suggests, most linguists would now accept. It is worth looking at closely:

Probably no linguist would deny that language plays a significant role in many cognitive processes – in particular, categorisation, planning, self-monitoring and abstract reasoning . . . What linguists do not accept are notions that any one variety of speech is intrinsically superior to another for the purpose of cognitive development . . . If one dialect were superior in cognitive terms to another, then the same would be true in an even more striking form in respect of differences between languages, and there is no evidence that speakers of any particular language are cognitively more developed by virtue of their language than speakers of any other language . . . any language can adopt or create new lexical items as and when conditions require. (p. 62)

The catch phrase here is 'cognitively more developed'. There may be two ways of thinking about the usefulness of a particular language for 'cognitive development'. The linguist may have in mind the potential capacity of any given language to serve as support for thinking or learning by providing symbols for concepts and a syntactic structure in which to manipulate the concepts. The language allows (or does not allow) the user to define concepts precisely, to discriminate concepts that differ, to group concepts into categories, to compare them, and to form new concepts by deduction, or induction.

Now it may well be that the linguist can show that for cognition, as defined above, all languages are potentially equal. (The claim that any language can adopt new lexical items as and when conditions require might be seen as begging an important question. It may be true in theory, but how long would it take for, say, the Eskimo language to 'adopt or create the new lexical items' required for discussion of atomic physics? And can the young Eskimo student *now* in school wait so long?) But leaving aside this quibble, and assuming that the linguist is right (though it is not easy to see how his claim could be proved), the argument that all languages are potentially equal as vehicles for thinking may not help the teacher in the classroom or the pupil who wants to learn.

For there is another aspect of 'cognitive development'. This is the extent to which cognition depends on book learning: on getting access to the stored wisdom of one's community, or that of other communities. Here, as Orwell might have said, some languages are decidedly more equal than others.

There is, first, the obvious distinction between those languages which have a written form and those (the majority) which do not. Transmission of experience from generation to generation in a community without writing is limited by the span of human memory. If 'cognitive development' is to mean anything, the child who is limited to a language with no written form is clearly at a disadvantage compared with the speaker whose language can offer him access to books and libraries.

But there is a difference, also, between a language that can give access to *particular* ideas and knowledge and one that cannot. For example, the number of languages that can give the advanced student direct access to modern linguistic theory is quite limited. Reliance on translation of ideas of great complexity must put the learner at a disadvantage.

It does not help the discussion to make untenable claims that no language can *ever* be superior to another, *for certain purposes*. What is helpful is to accept, as most socio-linguists do, that languages do *differ* greatly. The consequences of substituting the notion of difference for deficit are considerable. If we think in terms of deficit we denigrate a child's language or dialect. If we accept difference the remedy may be to change our teaching and educate ourselves to overcome linguistic prejudice and parochialism.

To put across the notion that difference can be interesting and enriching may require effort. It calls for the re-education of our community, not least of parents and teachers, in linguistic tolerance. It is a strong argument for the kind of 'awareness of language' with which this book is concerned. As Gordon (1981) puts it: 'open discussion in schools of attitudes towards linguistic diversity could form a useful basis for discussion of other, equally harmful stereotyped attitudes and even of the mechanisms of stereotyping in general'.

Once we accept a 'linguistic variability hypothesis', it becomes possible to examine dispassionately the ways in which some languages may be less useful than others as learning tools in school and to consider, equally dispassionately, whether what is true of languages may also be true of dialects. It then becomes easier to discuss the real problems facing teachers in schools.

REALITY OF THE LANGUAGE OF EDUCATION

The African writer Camara Laye has described movingly in his autobiography (translated by Kirkup (1959) as *The African Child*) a brilliant boy's journey out of his tribal culture and language as he seeks an education in his native (francophone) country. The tribal language into which the boy was born had no written form and was not used in the secondary school open to him. Only through the French language could the boy qualify in the examinations that would take him to France and the higher education he sought. For his 'cognitive development' the tribal language and French were far from equal.

The same case may present itself nearer home. The London schoolboy of immigrant parents who speaks Gujerati at home cannot hope to be educated in Gujerati in London beyond the nursery level, if only because teachers, examiners and textbooks in secondary subjects are not available in his home language. No university in Britain will accept him unless he has good English and has studied his 'A' levels in English. Clearly, therefore, English and Gujerati are not merely 'different'. For practical learning purposes in London, one language is greatly 'superior' to the other. The linguistic richness, antiquity, subtlety, value as a tool for expression of thought or emotion of Gujerati are immaterial in this assessment. It is important not to muddle the two sets of considerations.

We cite these obvious cases to illustrate the way in which the linguist's humane insistence that all languages are potentially equal for cognitive development may seem in practice, to the teacher trying to help the pupils in front of him, not very helpful or meaningful. (In a later section, p. 160, we suggest some ways in which the 'linguistic variability hypothesis' might be given practical form and propose some activities for the multi-lingual classroom, designed to bring out the interest and richness of linguistic diversity.)

Children of West Indian origin

A more controversial case is that of the child of West Indian origin whose home dialect is or has features of a Creole. The difficulties faced by the West Indian child in school epitomise, perhaps to an extreme degree, those faced by pupils who do not use standard English. How can the teacher best help? Peter Trudgill (1974) in an informed and sympathetic analysis distinguishes three possible approaches.

The first is to try to eliminate the non-standard speech, by preventing the child using it and correcting non-standard features as 'wrong'. Linguists, Trudgill comments, consider this approach to be mistaken psychologically and socially; but above all, they consider it mistaken because it cannot succeed.

The second approach is 'bidialectalism' and it is supported by most linguists. It accepts that non-standard forms are rightly used at home, with friends, and, in certain circumstances, in school. It treats the two varieties objectively as separate forms, both legitimate for certain purposes, and encourages 'code switching'. It requires that the teacher have some knowledge both of language teaching and of the child's dialect, and that he or she respect the child's language. This approach, Trudgill thinks, is likely to be successful only with *writing* since children will adopt the *speech* of another group only if they wish to become economically and socially accepted members of that group.

There is a third approach described by Trudgill as 'appreciation of dialect differences'. Teachers adopting this approach would teach children to *write* standard English but beyond that would try to educate opinion to accept non-standard dialects as valid systems. Trudgill admits that critics have called this approach hopelessly utopian. It would require education towards tolerance in the schools by teachers who were themselves free from linguistic prejudice: 'In the short run we may not be able to afford to abandon the bidialect-alism approach' (Trudgill, 1974, p. 83).

Part of the case for the 'awareness of language' programme for which we are arguing is that it may provide the essential background against which teachers might develop the 'bidialectalism' approach to non-standard forms of English described by Trudgill. In the long run, too, the only hope we have of achieving his ideal solution, the ultimate 'appreciation of dialect differences', is by a sustained effort at developing language awareness in the schools, in teacher training and among parents.

The challenge to teachers and teacher trainers is formidable. It is not confined to the UK. In all the great industrial democracies teachers are facing the same challenge: how to offer more equal opportunity in the school system to speakers of minority languages and non-standard dialects. The contributions of William Labov, a socio-linguist in the USA, have greatly helped to illuminate the problems. In a recent paper (Labov, 1982) he reviewed a celebrated court case: the 'Black English Trial at Ann Arbor'.

The case turned on the question: What is the school called on to do when some of the pupils speak a 'non-standard' form of the language, in this case 'Black English'? The further question raised was: What exactly is the linguistic status of 'Black English'? Prior to the trial linguists were not in agreement but Labov claims that the trial concentrated their minds and they reached a consensus which was excellently expressed in the summing up of Judge Joiner:

All of the distinguished researchers and professionals testified as to the existence of a language system, which is a part of the English language but different in significant respects from the standard English used in the school setting, the commercial world, the world of the arts and science, among the professions, and in government. It is and has been used at some time by 80 percent of the black people of this country and has as its genesis the transactional or pidgin language of the slaves, which after a generation or two became a creole language. Since then it has constantly been refined and brought closer to the mainstream of society. It still flourishes in areas where there are concentrations of black people. It contains aspects of Southern dialect and is used largely by black people in their casual conversation and informal talk.

Judge Joiner delivered his opinion on 12 July 1979. He found for the plaintiffs (the parents) and directed the Ann Arbor School Board to submit to him within thirty days a plan defining the exact steps to be taken to help. These steps would include:

(i) identifying children speaking Black English
(ii) using that knowledge in teaching such students how to read 'standard English'

Labov comments:

In his decision, Judge Joiner expressed the view that there were no barriers to communication in the classroom. According to his observations, teachers could understand children and children could understand children. Rather, he believed that the language barrier that did exist was in the form of unconscious negative attitudes by teachers towards children who spoke Black English, and the reactions of children to those attitudes.

The plan submitted by the School Board was for in-service training for teachers that would include: twenty hours of instruction on the characteristics and history of Black English; methods for identifying speakers of the dialect; ways of distinguishing mistakes in reading from differences in pronunciation, and strategies for helping children to switch from Black English to standard English.

Labov continues:

My own view ... is that operations on attitudes alone will not be enough to make a substantial difference to the reading of black children. What is needed is a set of additions to the day-to-day reading curriculum, in order to show the teachers how to deal with students in the classroom who have a different linguistic system than that assumed in the curriculum. No such materials exist as yet, but some linguists have been working at putting their knowledge to use in this way.

The 'awareness of language' programme that we are advocating can claim to provide at least the essential background of knowledge and of attitudes without which the strategies for which socio-linguists like Trudgill and Labov are pleading have no chance of succeeding. Trudgill's 'bidialectalism' approach and still more his '[ideal] appreciation of dialect differences', like Labov's re-education of teachers, will only be possible as part of a sustained effort to raise standards of 'awareness of language' in schools, in training colleges and among present and future parents.

THE CHARGE OF 'MANIPULATION'

The linguist's acceptance of the need to teach at least the *written* form of standard English, for all its humane consideration of the child's learning difficulties, has, however, been condemned in some quarters. The argument, often stridently expressed, is that those who would try to teach children the standard forms (the 'language of education') are guilty of foisting on them an alien culture (which might be referred to as 'mainstream', 'middle class' or 'elitist'). Gordon (1981) considers this argument and rejects it in forthright terms. He refers to those critics who

see traditional curricula as largely alien and meaningless to the cultural values of working-class communities [and as] the bourgeois values of the school. [What they overlook is that] all children in Britain, and their parents, live in one and the same nation state, under one and the same political, economic and social order ... it is very much open to question how many schools are actually located in identifiable communities with clearly defined cultures of their own ... In general, much of the discussion about conflicts between middle-class and working-class (and also mainstream and non-mainstream) cultures is based on very simplistic concepts of culture in a complex society.

(p. 106)

Acceptance of linguistic differences, and the creation in school of a climate in which language differences can be discussed without prejudice, need not imply the denigration of the culture of any group, but need not carry with them any denial of the values that, in a democracy, all children should learn to share. Yet some critics would characterise even the teaching of the standard forms of English, the language of education, as 'manipulation' of pupils. The argument is mischievous and has muddled and confused many young students and teachers exposed to it on training courses.

There must be a sense, of course, in which any decision by the community to set up a school system, or to design a curriculum, indeed to teach a child anything, can be described as 'manipulating' the child. All attempts to give children the means to lead fruitful lives within the context of the community and the state of which they are citizens must be seen by the convinced anarchist, who does not believe in the state, as 'manipulation' of children. For this reason the philosophical anarchist demands that society be 'deschooled', because schools are one of the state's most powerful agencies. The doctrine of the anarchist has a long intellectual history. Within its own terms it presents a logical critique of all authority (though its philosophers have never satisfactorily answered the question: *At what age* are adolescents supposed to put off childishness and assume the maturity to dispense with the hateful authority of the state?).

The believer in democracy is bound to take a very different view of the purposes of schooling. Fundamental to the theory of democracy is the concept of the 'autonomy' of the individual. Every citizen, which means every *voter*, must be presumed to be independently capable of exercising the vote. This notion of the autonomy of the individual determines the main role of the school, which is to make people as *free* as they have it in them to be.

If the purpose of education is to make individuals free, we have to ask: What are the hindrances to freedom? The 'long march' of compulsory state schooling since 1870 has been a sustained attempt to push back the threats to children's freedom. The threats include ignorance, prejudice, the sway of fashion, the lure of the market and the 'hidden persuaders' of the media. Equally limiting to freedom, of course, is a lack of the skills needed to survive in the environment, such as the means (or opportunity!) to earn a living: or, more basically, lack of the sheer knowledge needed to understand what is happening in one's community.

If the democrat is asked: what are schools for? he must answer that at their best they must be *refuges* within which freedom from outside pressures can be guaranteed and within which the *apprenticeship in autonomy*, which is vital for a democracy, can be learned. Those who plan the curriculum have a heavy responsibility and the best of them will never lose sight of the main objective which must be to help children to learn how to exercise freedom.

It is against this concept of the school that proposals for the reform of language education should be judged. Those who oppose the reform on the grounds that teaching 'language' is 'manipulation' of children must be challenged to answer two questions. First, are they arguing that the whole curriculum is 'manipulation' and therefore that schooling itself stands condemned? And, second, why, having had the good fortune themselves to acquire the language of education, do they feel justified in arguing that the same opportunity to learn should be denied to the children now in school?

FAILURE TO MASTER THE MOTHER TONGUE

We have perhaps said enough to justify giving greater attention to fostering the right attitudes to language among pupils, teachers and especially parents, who are often the most linguistically prejudiced.

This in itself would make a strong case for the kind of 'awareness of language' courses whose development in schools we have traced earlier.

By bringing round the table, in the planning stage, teachers of English (both mother tongue and ESL), of foreign languages and of ethnic mother tongues, and speakers of Creole, they have begun a dialogue 'across the *language* curriculum' that has not hitherto taken place in schools.

Discussion in such boards of language studies may help to put into perspective two aspects of language learning which some recently fashionable views in linguistics have confused rather than clarified. The issues can be put in the form of questions:

(a) At what age can normal children be assumed to have 'learned' their mother tongue (whether they learn a standard or a non-standard version)?
(b) Do all children reach a comparable level of competence in their mother tongue or are there some children (and if so, how many?) whose competence is markedly different from the norm?

One recently influential school of linguistics in effect answers both questions quite dogmatically. Thus, in Noam Chomsky's words, towards the end of his famous excoriating review of B. F. Skinner's *Verbal Behavior* (Chomsky, 1959):

this task [learning the mother tongue] is accomplished in an astonishingly short time, to a large extent independently of intelligence, and in a comparable way by all children. . . Any theory of learning must cope with these facts . . . all normal children acquire essentially comparable grammars of great complexity with remarkable rapidity.   (p. 57)

If we are to take this to mean anything more than that all speakers of English learn comparable versions of the grammar of English, that is, if it means that all speakers learn the grammar to comparable stages of *mastery*, then the claim is seriously misleading to teachers. Yet many linguists follow Chomsky in assuming that the child's acquisition of syntax is virtually complete by the age of 5.

It was this assumption that Carol Chomsky set out to investigate in a famous study (1969) which prompted many subsequent studies. She followed the progress of a group of forty children aged between 5 and 10, testing their ability to understand sentences of the form: 'John is easy to understand' and 'complement constructions' with verbs: 'see', 'promise' and 'tell'. She found that some pupils had not mastered these constructions by the age of 9 and one was still unsure of the form 'John asked Bill what to do', at the age of 10.

Other investigators have questioned the general application of some of Carol Chomsky's conclusions but in the light of her study it is difficult to maintain the assumption that the acquisition of syntax is complete by the end of the pre-school stage. It is an assumption that would find little support from practising teachers, accustomed to correcting the written work of adolescents, or even of university students!

Nor does the notion find support from psychology. Research on children's memory shows that clear notions of time are slow to develop. Without them it is not clear how a child can be said to operate the tense system within the syntax of English. I. M. L. Hunter, Professor of Psychology at the University of Keele, describes children's notion of time in these terms:

> The observations of Stern and others suggest that the performance of recalling is not achieved until early in the second year of life and does not appear with any great frequency until around the age of three. But even when experiences are recalled, there is little question of their being referred to any definite point of past time, *for the simple reason that the child has yet to develop a clear notion of time* [our italics]. Even the 4-year-old has little more than an indefinite notion of 'long ago' and a broad distinction between 'earlier' and 'later'. He cannot refer an event to 'the day before yesterday' or to 'last week' with any probability of accuracy... Sometimes he can accurately locate a recalled experience as having happened 'today' or 'not today', but he can scarcely use 'yesterday' as a more exact location for experiences from the less immediate past. So far as he is capable of making temporal distinctions between his recollected experiences, he does so by reference to places: 'That was at so-and-so's house', or 'That was at such-and-such a town'... he simply seems to place one event in the context of a more outstanding event without any clear reference to its location in a temporal order of events... and it is not until after the age of six years that he acquires an awareness of his own past as a historical sequence of events.   (Hunter, 1964, p. 54)

Any description of the kind of syntax acquired before the age of 6 (if we may borrow Chomsky's forthright challenge) must take account of Professor Hunter's evidence concerning the absence of a notion of time.

If language acquisition must be seen as a long-term process (for most learners continuing over a lifetime) what of our other question: Do all children reach a 'comparable competence' or progress at comparable speed? The evidence is that they do not and that this is due partly to innate and partly to environmental factors.

First, as to innate capacity, the precocity of girls in acquiring language is well attested. With any of the accepted tests, the evidence (summarised, for example, in G. Miller's classic *Language and Communication*, 1951) shows that girls, on average, begin to outstrip boys from the age of 2. By the age of 11, girls' verbal competence is so far ahead of that of boys that special measures were always taken, in the days when boys and girls took a common selection examination for places in the selective 'grammar' schools, to scale up the marks of boys in English tests, in order not to allocate a disproportionate number of girls to the scarce selective places.

The superior verbal aptitude of girls (of which some neurologists now claim to find indications already present in the unborn foetus brain) was confirmed in an interesting study by the National Foundation for Educational Research. For the purpose of their evaluation of French in the primary school (Burstall et al., 1974) the NFER team tested large cohorts of children not only in French but *inter alia*, in English comprehension and in certain aspects of formal English grammar. The girls at age 11 scored consistently higher than the boys in all the tests of English.

The consistent superiority of girls over boys when tested (as above) for *production* of language is also demonstrated, though to a less marked degree, in scores for *reading*. In the series of measurements of national reading scores (at ages 10 and 15) carried out by the NFER for the Department of Education between 1948 and 1971, girls scored consistently higher than boys, the difference generally reaching the 'significant' level. The results are summarised in *The Trend of Reading Standards* by K. B. Start and B. K. Wells (NFER, 1972).

In this connection the anthropologist Gordon W. Hewes in *Language Origins*, 1973, p. 115 comments:

No one seriously supposes that the consistent precocity of girls in acquiring speech and their lower incidence of speech defects can be attributed to cultural learning differences... The point is that [the observed differences between girls and boys] are compatible with our reconstruction of early hominid behaviour, in which males would have been the principal hunters, trackers and protectors of the group – with a survival premium on ability to analyse environmental noises as well as spatial and constructional abilities – whereas females, as the main transmitters of speech to infants as well as the sex with the greater need to detect the emotional overtones of vocal messages, could be expected to be more precocious in language learning and less prone to speech defects.   (Quoted in Bolinger and Sears, 1981, p. 195)

Bolinger, in the same study, cites the fact that females are almost never dyslexic as suggesting that they have a more stable genetic equipment for language.

If there are clear indications that aptitude for language learning, both of the mother tongue and of foreign languages, may be partly innate, it is equally clear that aptitude is also strongly affected by the environment. The NFER study referred to above (Burstall et al., 1974), which confirmed the superiority of girls at both French and English, also found a linear correlation between test scores in English and *parental occupation* (p. 41). This merely confirmed the findings of a long series of studies (whose results are usefully summarised in Bullock, 1975) which show conclusively that home background correlates closely with test scores in both spoken and written language.

One obvious environmental variable is *extent* of reading. One of the more interesting off-shoots of the research by Carol Chomsky referred to earlier was her finding that the rate at which her subjects mastered the rules of syntax correlated closely with the amount of reading that each one did at home. It is not only to young children that this applies. Very much of the imagery and metaphor which is the common currency of our language was coined first and set in circulation over the centuries by great writers. Speakers of the language differ greatly in their mastery of this linguistic inheritance. It is only by thoughtful reading that competence in this area of usage can be won. The reader whose experience is limited to writing that is of little insight and reliant on borrowed cliché will simply be less competent in the use of the language at its most effective than the reader more familiar with the linguistic inheritance.

It does no service to children to pretend that, though in every other cognitive area there is a long apprenticeship to be served, somehow, in language learning, the rules are different and there is no need for apprenticeship, no difference between the precision and integrity of some language, and language that is slipshod and imitative. As in other areas of learning, genetic and environmental factors may work together so subtly that it is impossible to disentangle them. However it may be explained, the fact is that by the time they reach the age of 5 children differ widely in their acquisition of their mother tongue. Yet, curiously, the extent to which speakers of any given dialect, whether it be London Jamaican or 'received standard', may differ in their competence *in their home dialect* has had little place in the discussions of socio-linguists.

In order to talk about 'language' (or 'langue' as Saussure termed it) as an abstract concept it has been convenient to pre-suppose an 'ideal speaker/hearer', equipped with something called 'adult mastery' of the language. Teachers, faced with flesh and blood pupils exchanging acts of speech (Saussure's 'parole') are daily reminded that all individuals do not enjoy an equal competence. (The very use of the phrase 'ideal speaker/hearer' pre-supposes this difference.) The picture of the speech community that the teacher sees is one of a long road along which the speakers are strung out, as they advance at very different speeds, towards a goal of an ideal competence *which none will ever reach*. The linguistic distance along this road separating the front runners from those who trail behind, limping and breathless, is immense.

Once we substitute this real picture for the linguist's abstraction we are compelled to rethink two related issues which some linguists have declared closed. They are:

(a) The debate about the meaning of 'correct/incorrect' language use.
(b) The need to reformulate the discussion of 'language deficit', using the term not in the 'classical' sense of the deficiency of certain 'codes' or dialects *in themselves*, but in the new sense that some, possibly many, speakers (of whatever dialect) travel less far along the road into the usage and awareness *of their own dialect* than others.

'LANGUAGE IS WHAT I SAY, NOT WHAT YOU SAY I OUGHT TO SAY'

It is an axiom in linguistics that 'language is what people say, not what some people [teachers, for example] think they ought to say'. There is an obvious sense in which this must be true. The linguist takes as his raw material current usage of the language. But it does not follow that all speakers to whom the linguist listens are *using* the language with equal authority. Each individual's usage has to be learned over a long period, even over a lifetime. Many speakers never cease improving mastery of their own language. Also one speaker's usage will be more 'authoritative' than another's in the sense that the speaker has mastered more completely the usage of his/her own speech community (as the adult is more competent than the child, from having listened to more language).

We can see this clearly if we consider one, admittedly narrow area, namely, mastery of vocabulary. In a discipline such as physics, language usage has developed in step with the discoveries of the laws of the discipline itself. Learning physics therefore is, in large part, learning the 'correct' matching of concepts to linguistic symbols. Matching is 'correct' when those who have made the discoveries and done the experiments to prove the concepts are in agreement. It is the discipline of physics that has established the 'correct' matching of language to such concepts as 'mass', 'latent heat' and 'gravitation', which the aspiring physicist is not at liberty to vary. The aspiring physicist's usage of language is thus less *authoritative* that that of his tutor, *within that discipline*.

But it is the same story wherever we look at language in use. The student learning the law seeks to learn the 'correct' usage of words such as 'evidence'. The young musician is not free to vary the usage of the vocabulary of music. If the medical student hopes to qualify as a doctor he would be wise not to call the 'femur' the 'tibia' in front of his professor, nor the budding cook decide that 'grilling' and 'frying' are interchangeable terms. Of course the 'front runners' are busy creating new language as the discipline advances. But, even for them, in every other area of language usage there is a long apprenticeship to be served.

Each individual's use of language will reflect how far his particular apprenticeship has taken him. But the speaker who is more competent can say, not simply what concept a given word does evoke for him (the point at which his own usage has arrived) but also, within the areas of the language which he has truly mastered, what concept the word *ought* to evoke. His authority for the 'ought' is simply greater acquaintance with usage in that particular area.

DEGREES OF COMPETENCE

There is, then, a valid distinction, which has been blurred by some recent discussions, between what people say and what they would say if they were more informed. Competence and 'intuition of the native speaker' may be useful concepts in linguistics, so long as it is remembered that they are relative terms.

If we were discussing the competence of English-speaking pupils in, say, French, German or Spanish, the point would scarcely be worth making. The pupil just beginning the foreign language does not use it with the same authority as his teacher. He cannot claim that 'French is what I say'. Yet it may not be very different in the mother tongue classroom. Of course linguists will always be interested in language 'as she is spoke'. But they must remember that many of the speakers to whom they listen will still be learning the language, whatever their age.

The researcher in child language distinguishes a series of steps along the road to 'adult' language use. What is often overlooked is that the road does not suddenly end at an arbitrary point (age 5, or 11 or 16). Language acquisition is a life-long apprenticeship. Much of

ry education and of university study is a matter of
ıg competence in the mother tongue in defined areas,
ıg, with increasing discrimination, new language, or old
language used in more precise ways, to new concepts of great
complexity.

This gives a different gloss to loosely used phrases such as
'verbal deficit'. The debate about 'restricted' varieties (codes, dialects) is seen to have been peripheral and unhelpful. It is not a
question of certain dialects or codes being 'disadvantaged' in themselves, nor of implied comment on any social or racial groups. We
are concerned, as teachers, with individual children, whatever their
dialect. The crucial difference between some of our pupils and
others is that some achieve a greater competence than others *in
their own dialect*.

LANGUAGE AND THOUGHT

To argue that individuals differ in important ways in their linguistic competence and in their intuitions concerning the language
usage of their own group is not to suppose any simple causal relationship between language mastery and cognition. The question of
the link between language and learning is complex and controversial. In the course of his apprenticeship in the language usage of his
community the learner's progress in the language must, to a great
extent, *depend* on his cognition. In the early stages especially language 'waits upon cognition'. Equally, language learning may later
take the lead and make possible certain cognitive steps that would
otherwise be impossible. As the school process develops language
increasingly leads in the interplay with cognition. Crucial ways in
which the language of school seems to take the lead and facilitate
cognition are:

(i) 'signposting' concepts not yet met, pointing to the fact that they exist
and should be explored, much as a signpost shows that the road leads
to a town not yet reached
(ii) allowing concepts to be stored in the filing cabinet of the memory in
such a way that they can be retrieved economically
(iii) using language to control one's own behaviour, a phenomenon observed in young children but more common in adults. Consider the
example, quoted by Cook (1979), of the aircraft pilot running through
a verbal checklist of precautions before take-off
(iv) enabling the speaker/hearer to be emancipated from the here and now
and to think of, and refer to, events distant in time and space

(v) enabling concepts to be distinguished from one another, and for hierarchies to be built as in: ANIMAL includes
DOG includes
TERRIER includes
KERRY BLUE

In sum, language makes possible the process of 'categorisation': that is the arrangement of concepts in 'sets' or 'categories' which belong together (they share 'criterial attributes'). As suggested above, in the earliest stages the process that takes the lead is cognition, that is the child's recognition of the 'categories' of concepts into which the initially haphazard sense impressions received from the chaotic universe fall. As the child grows older it is language that increasingly takes the lead and makes possible the complex categorisation which Bruner (1966) called 'the calculus of thought'.

It is significant that all these processes become increasingly essential as the exploration of the school disciplines unfolds. Whether the child is learning to solve problems in geometry, or to distinguish 'mixtures' from 'compounds' in chemistry, the 'categories' which the language allows the child to distinguish and compare become the building blocks of future learning. The quality of the learning – the strength of the building – will depend on the clarity with which one conceptual 'set' is distinguished from the other, the sharpness of their outlines, and the speed and dexterity with which they are handled. This depends on precision in matching concepts to language.

CAN 'AWARENESS' AFFECT 'COMPETENCE'?

The advocate of giving an important role to 'awareness of language' has a further question to answer, however. Granted that language provides the building blocks of school learning, is it the case that deepening pupils' *awareness* will lead to greater *competence*? Are the two causally linked?

Professor Halliday and his colleagues, in the Introduction to *Language in Use*, answer the question in this way:

there is ... a crucial relationship between the two [awareness and competence]. The long argument over the teaching of 'grammar' in schools really concentrated upon the effects of a certain kind of explicit knowledge of the language, such as classification of words and parsing, on pupils' use of language. When teachers discovered that there seemed to be no observable effect of the one on the other, they rejected teaching about language, because they could see no justification for it. It was unfortunate that the study of language came to be identified with a rudimentary and inadequate type of knowledge about language, and that its validity was judged solely upon its power to increase competence.

Language in Use offers a form of language study which can be valued as a rewarding end in itself, namely the development of awareness. However, a basic premise of the volume is that *the development of awareness in the pupil will have a positive effect on his competence* [our italics], though this effect is likely to be indirect and may not show up immediately. A second premise is that what is well-rehearsed through being talked out in discussion, especially where the discussion involves groups of three to five, will have a similar oblique, delayed but quite positive effect upon pupils' command of the written language...

... Whatever their potential, pupils often find themselves unable to handle the language which the processes of explicit analysis and impersonal comment require, and it is the use of language of this kind that makes up so large a part of the working lives of most pupils. The development of awareness has a marked effect upon a pupil's ability to cope with the whole range of his work, because he comes to see that many problems are not so much problems in grasping the content of what he studies, but problems in handling the language appropriate to it.   (p. 10)

The reference in this passage to the effect of discussion in small groups on acquisition of the *written* language is extremely interesting (cf. our argument for 'adult time', pp. 81 to 88). It is exactly the point made by Professor Margaret Donaldson (1978):

the preparation for reading should include, as a most important component, attempts to make children more aware of the spoken tongue. It is not just a matter of helping them to use speech more effectively, it is a matter of helping them to notice what they are doing.   (p. 97)

In an earlier passage Donaldson reminds us how difficult the breakthrough to reading is for some pupils:

As literate adults, we have become so accustomed to the written word that we seldom stop to think how dramatically it differs from the spoken one. The spoken word ... exists for a brief moment as one element in a tangle of shifting events – from which it must be disentangled if it is to be separately considered – and then fades. The written word endures... We may return to it tomorrow. By its very nature it can be quite free of non-linguistic context... So the child's first encounters with books provide him with much more favourable opportunities for *becoming aware* of language in its own right than his earlier encounters with the spoken word are likely to have done.
                    (p. 90)

Short Term Memory

A point that is implicit in what Donaldson says, but which is not developed in her argument, is that learning to read sets the learner free from the severe restraints of the Short Term Memory. Processing of the spoken message is entirely dependent on being able to hold it in the STM for long enough to identify its components and recognise the pattern(s) which determine the meaning. The listener cannot control the speed at which the message arrives and must process the components strictly in the order in which they arrive. By contrast the components of the written message can be scanned repeatedly *and in any order*. Research on the rapid eye movements made by practised readers as the text is scanned show how important this facility is.

It is this that explains one great difference between listening and reading, namely the *speed* with which messages can be taken in. Mattingley (Kavanagh and Mattingley, 1972) estimates that the maximum speed for reading with meaning is 2,000 wpm against a mere 400 for listening. The breakthrough to reading clearly means a change of gear in learning.

It is relevant to remember that the capacity of the STM has, since the early days of IQ tests, been known to be systematically related both to age and to IQ measures. Testing the number of digits that could be retained in the STM was one of the devices used in early intelligence tests such as the Stanford–Binet and the Wechsler batteries. The STM span increases on the Stanford–Binet scale from two digits at age 30 months, to three digits at 36 months, and four at 54 months and stabilises in adulthood at about seven digits (plus or minus two).

However it has been demonstrated (Olson, 1973) that there is no systematic relationship between STM span and language learning. To explain this Olson goes back to an observation by Miller (1956) that STM capacity can be increased by imposing *pattern* on the incoming message. This ability to impose pattern (or to recognise patterns as old friends as the message arrives) is *learned*: 'The performance deficits we find in younger children's remembering are due to failure to organise, plan, monitor and integrate their information processing' (Olson, 1973). It is not that children cannot process incoming messages so that they retain more of them in the STM: 'children as young as 3 or 4, if not younger, can employ many of the strategies they will later use routinely in remembering. But unless prompted they do not' (p. 151). Olson concludes: 'language presents the earliest and most acute challenge to the child's ability to handle information in real time'. The irony is that though the mastery of reading sets the child free from the restraints of the STM on processing messages, yet the breakthrough itself comes only *after* the processing strategies have reached a certain level.

This brings us back to the need for one-to-one dialogue with an adult (Bullock, 1975) and the need for 'adult time' in the home (Donaldson, 1978), in order to allow the processing strategies to be practised, upon which, in due course, the reading skill can be built.

To sum up: much recent discussion of the relationship of language and learning, like the debate about 'verbal deficit', has seemed to assume that language learning is a single, all-or-nothing, process. It has overlooked the fact that acquiring the mother tongue is a process in two distinct stages. The second stage, mastery of the written language, seems to depend on a high degree of 'awareness' of, and hence the ability to 'process', the spoken form.

Far more children than is commonly imagined never achieve the degree of awareness that is called for and so never master written language with confidence and relish.

In the next section we examine what failure or partial failure to read can mean.

5 Reading and the effect of 'adult time'

FAILURE TO READ THE REAL DEPRIVATION

Failure to read has been bypassed in much of the discussion of verbal deficit. As Harold Rosen commented in the *TES* (9 April 1982) reviewing the book *Verbal Deficit – A Critique* by J. C. Gordon to which we referred on p. 58: 'The discussion of verbal deficit almost ignores the critical question of literacy and the extent to which ... development of it occurs in circumstances which handicap the working-class child.'

Whatever the differences found by research in children's *spoken* language the teacher in the classroom knows that it is reading that is the great divider. No assurance from the linguist that the child's home dialect is potentially a medium of great expressiveness and subtlety can compensate the child for failure to master reading in the school dialect, to the point where the activity is relished and is intrinsically motivating.

Many educationists have argued that our school system is excessively verbal and that too little attention is given to mathematical and mechanical skills, to planning and creating, to arts and crafts. The present curriculum, it is suggested, encourages the observer and the analyst, rather than the designer and the producer. Whether or not the critics are fully justified, it certainly seems to be true that the prizes go to those who are proficient in the written language. Given our largely written examination system, to be a quick reader and writer and to have a good memory is the passport to success. We have, for example, made little use of the viva examination, common in some of our European neighbours' systems. Yet to face cross-examination on one's subject from a jury of tutors can be a more searching test of real understanding of difficult issues than the written answer which may rely on a faithful memory of what others have said.

In an earlier section (p. 13) we suggested that the numbers of pupils who achieve only a partial literacy may be far higher than is commonly imagined, while schools have proved unable to help those pupils who do not bring from home the essential verbal tools.

It is time to examine more closely the implications of failure, or partial failure, in the first, decisive intellectual test that all children face. In particular we should look at two aspects of language acquisition each having interesting links with learning to read: acquiring the vocabulary and learning the syntax.

VOCABULARY AND READING

Among linguists it is now less unfashionable than it was to study vocabulary. Fashions in linguistics change rapidly, as J. S. Bruner has pointed out: 'While vocabulary was becoming unfashionable, grammar was becoming all the rage. Young psychologists who in earlier decades might have studied the acquisition of vocabulary were now captivated by the arcane mysteries of grammar acquisition... The primacy of syntax may be a valuable axiom for linguistics, but the primacy of semantics is a better axiom for psychology' (1975, p. 65).

One aspect of the acquisition of vocabulary that has been neglected is the way in which children categorise their conceptual experience and match their new-found categories to the language offered by their community. An insight into this was given by L. S. Vygotsky (1962, p. 109) in his discussion of the two kinds of concepts that children acquire, which he called 'spontaneous' and 'scientific'. The spontaneous concept ('brother', for example) is unconscious; the ability to define the concept in words comes long after the concept has been acquired. The child knows what it is to have a brother, from sharing his parents, his meals, often his bed with him. Only after the concept is well established is the *word* 'brother' met and matched to the idea.

Vygotsky's example of a scientific concept was 'exploitation'. (The choice of example helps to explain why the book was banned in Stalin's Russia in the 1930s. It circulated only in typescript until 1962.) Scientific concepts must be matched with language in exactly the reverse way. The child first hears the *word* 'exploitation' (perhaps by listening to the talk of adults round the table in the evening) and at first attaches no clear concept to the word. The word is like a signpost at a road junction, pointing to the fact that a concept exists, but is not yet known. Only gradually, as Vygotsky says, 'in the course of further school work and reading', or in other words, if the child goes along the path to which the sign points, do the attributes of the concept, little by little, become clear. If it is a complex concept, the outlines are only slowly filled in with detail. The mere *word* is easy to say and to remember. The *concept* can be very subtle and hard to grasp. The match between concept and word may take long to effect with discrimination.

Vygotsky goes on to speculate that the second of these processes of vocabulary acquisition is analogous to the effect of learning a foreign language: 'a process that is conscious and deliberate from the start'. He was probably thinking of the old 'construe' methods of the classics classroom rather than of the more communicative methods of today, but the insight is interesting because some recent work on the effect of learning Latin (referred to earlier, p. 12) links provocatively with Vygotsky's distinction between scientific and spontaneous concepts.

David Corson, researching at the London Institute of Education, studied the language of pupils aged 12 to 15, in social classes I/II, and IV/V (which included children of parents of West Indian origin) in schools in London, in Yorkshire and in Sydney, Australia. He observed a qualitative difference (a 'lexical barrier') between pupils who had studied Latin and those who had not. Lack of Graeco-Latin words in the pupils' vocabulary correlated with social class. The lexical barrier, he suggests, closes doors to whole conceptual areas, leads to 'bypassing' 'hard' words and hence to school failure. In a study of children's reading Corson has observed: 'There is a descending percentage of Graeco-Latin words in children's fiction that matches the descending reading ages of that literature' (Corson, 1982).

However it is at secondary level that the lexical barrier is greatest. Whereas there were no oral differences observed between the two broad social groupings at age 12, the differences at age 15 were 'massive': 'Upper middle-class children show great development in oral and written use of Graeco-Latin words between 12 and 15 while poorer, working-class and West Indian children show only slight development in oral use' (Corson, 1983).

It is, of course, a commonplace observation, though an oversimplification, that there is a dualism in English vocabulary reflecting the Norman French and the Germanic roots of the language. The modern lexicon dates from the period when Norman French and the dialects of Old English were in use side by side in the years following 1066. The lexicon that emerged contained a frequently used stock of short words of Germanic origin and a 'learned' vocabulary of longer, mainly polysyllabic words derived from Latin via French. Fresh import-

ations of Graeco-Latin roots came with the scientific and tech-
nological discoveries of the Renaissance.

The importation of words from Norman French came in two
waves. In the first wave, roughly in the two hundred years after 1066,
the words imported (some 900) were words learned by the English-
speaking lower classes from contact with their masters, the largest
single group of words in this case being associated with the Church.

In the second wave, after about 1250, when people of French
origin were increasingly speaking English, a far greater number of
French words were imported. The borrowings were mainly of words
carried over into English by the upper classes, accustomed to
speaking French, and now using the French words to eke out their
English vocabulary. They are words associated with government and
administration, the law, the army, fashion, learning, and medicine. The distinction is, therefore, partly one between 'popular' and
'learned' words:

loved	enamoured
death	mortality
motherly	maternal
to make sure	to ascertain
to make believe	to pretend
to do again	to repeat
to do well	to succeed

The dichotomy, which Sir Walter Scott skilfully exploited in
Ivanhoe (chapter 2) reflects the different perceptions of the French-
speaking master and the English-speaking servant:

from Norman French	*from Old English*
master (*maître*)	shepherd (*scēaphirde*)
farmer (*fermier*)	workman (*weorcman*)
beef (*bœuf*)	cow (*cu*)
veal (*veau*)	calf (*cealf*)
mutton (*mouton*)	sheep (*scēap*)
pork (*porc*)	pig/swine (*picga/swingan*)

Less frequently quoted is the interesting duality in the way that the
passage of time is measured in English. Thus time that is measured by
the sun and moon, accessible to all, is referred to by Old English
words (day/week/month/year) while measures of time that require
expensive machinery such as hour-glasses or clocks use a French
vocabulary (hour/minute/second).

The distinction 'master/man' soon merged into the distinction 'reader/non-reader' as the school system developed. It is no accident that Corson's research shows that the big difference between the vocabulary of his two social groups developed in the early secondary years. This is the time when the pupil following an academic course meets reading in a range of specialised areas.

Corson's lexical barrier is therefore a barrier between pupils who have the lexicon of the written language and those who do not. He refers to work in America which seems to show amazing progress made by pupils who were taught Latin. One might doubt whether it was the acquisition of a limited number of Latin roots that greatly affected the pupils' progress. On the other hand the experience of working in the foreign language, and especially the experience of constantly coping with new words which at first convey no meaning, and having to search for and conceptualise their precise meaning, may change attitudes both to language and to learning in important ways. The process is subtle and has been little discussed.

THE EFFECT OF LEARNING A FOREIGN LANGUAGE ON ENGLISH VOCABULARY

Let us return to Vygotsky's observation that some 'word–concept' pairs present themselves to the child in the order *concept* first, as in 'brother' while others are learned *word* first, as in 'exploitation'. It will be clear that children will not differ very much in their stock of spontaneous concepts. Most children share a common experience and the words concerned with this common experience (play, meals, clothing, family etc.) will be transacted daily and learned, in Vygotsky's terms, 'spontaneously'. The acquisition of scientific concepts, however, will depend on the lottery of family circumstance, on the availability of adults to talk to and on access to reading, for these are the sources of scientific concepts.

The child who enjoys little one-to-one dialogue with an adult and who reads little, or only within elementary limits, will seldom be challenged to match concepts to new, unfamiliar words. Such a child may have a quite extensive vocabulary but it will be mainly of one kind. It is not simply that the vocabulary may lack Vygotsky's scientific concepts. What the child will miss is the special kind of intellectual challenge (to be faced in school many times a day) of meeting words for which initially there is no clear meaning, but which 'signpost' meanings, and then 'consciously', in Vygotsky's terms, seeking out their meanings.

The case for Latin (or any other foreign language studied in school) may not simply rest on the argument that it gives a qualitatively different vocabulary. More important may be the effect of daily practice in seeking meanings that have been signposted by language. The expectation of having to do this, the confidence that practice of the techniques brings, the positive relish of the exercise, may be not the least of the by-products of an apprenticeship in foreign language learning. The reason is that reading the signposts that language offers is the key to much of school learning. The greater part of many forms of higher education (for example, legal studies) consists essentially of this activity.

There is a further dimension to Vygotsky's insight. As he observed, the child's scientific concepts will at first be 'schematic, lacking the rich content of personal experience'. The concept 'exploitation' will only acquire depth and precision as instances of exploitation are met and as 'exploitation' is compared with related concepts ('slavery') or contrasted with others ('freedom', 'democracy'). This will depend on the *quality* of the adult dialogue (and ultimately the reading) available to the child. To enjoy undisturbed dialogue with an adult who has learned to match concepts accurately to words in a home where books are to be found will obviously be a great advantage.

The process of acquiring the stock of scientific concepts on which education builds is a long one. The vocabulary makes a number of spurts of growth. In the junior school, given encouragement and a successful breakthrough to reading, there should be a great leap forward. Another spurt comes in the secondary school as the new disciplines of science, history and geography are met and when the adventure into the foreign language begins. A third spurt takes place at the level of specialist training or higher education. Take, for example, legal training. To study the law is largely a process of matching clear concepts to new legal vocabulary, distinguishing 'hearsay' from 'evidence', 'slander' from 'libel', 'torts' from 'offences that are not torts'. It may take the young lawyer many months of hard study before the criterial attributes that make an offence a 'tort' in law are fully mastered.

Whatever some linguists may claim about the learning of grammar rules, it is certain that our vocabulary is not learned 'in an astonishingly short time'. And in most of this learning it is the 'signposting' role of language that predominates.

ANALYTIC COMPETENCE AND READING

Mother tongue competence can differ from one learner to another in a different way. A valuable pointer has been given by Bruner (1975). He suggests that the capacity to use language for everyday purposes, so long as it is closely tied to events and people, does not differ markedly from one child to another. He calls this ability 'communicative competence'. He distinguishes it from 'analytic competence' which is not so widely shared but has to be learned. The school process makes heavy demands on analytic competence: 'What schools do is to decontextualise knowledge and to demand the use of analytic competence', or, in other words, the 'ability to turn language in upon itself'.

This is very similar to the analysis of two 'levels' of language proposed by I. G. Mattingley (Kavanagh and Mattingley, 1972). He describes speaking and hearing as 'primary' language activities, for which we seem to be innately programmed. Reading, however, is a 'secondary' activity. It is not innate. The secondary activity, he suggests, can only be mastered if the primary level is fully developed and if the learner is 'aware' in his use of the language. To this extent the secondary activity can be described as 'parasitic' upon the primary.

Speaking and hearing have a high level of redundancy since cues to meaning are carried in many ways: facial expression, intonation, gesture, stress, pauses etc. Meaning in the written form is carried at the levels of semantics and grammar. The secondary activity, Mattingley argues, is not innately programmed (unlike speaking) and does not develop by maturation (as, say, walking on two legs does). It is, therefore, far from evenly distributed across the population. This is in contrast with the primary activity of speaking which is relatively consistent across the whole community.

Mattingley argues further that different writing systems make greater or lesser demands on the learner. To learn to read or write in an alphabetic system a certain level of 'linguistic awareness' is called for which a logographic or a syllabic system might not demand. The learner has to make, in alphabetic writing, a complex matching of grapheme to phoneme, which is particularly complex in English, for example, as compared with languages such as Spanish, German or French. This calls for more than simply understanding speech. Ability to recognise the patterned nature of speech, to which the match of the written forms must be made, is needed. It is this recognition that Mattingley calls 'awareness'. English spelling, as we argue in a later section (p. 117), is designed for those who know the language but is a sore trial for those of limited 'language awareness'.

An analysis very similar to this has been offered by Margaret Donaldson (1978). She argues that reading requires that the purely linguistic elements of an utterance (its syntax, recognition of the segments of which it is composed and of the pattern in which they are arranged) must be 'disembedded' from the complex of signals of a non-linguistic kind that accompany the message and which are often, for the immature listener, the salient part of the message. To accomplish the breakthrough to reading the child must first be 'aware' of the patterns to be looked for:

the first step is the step of conceptualising language – becoming aware of it as a separate structure, freeing it from its embeddedness in events... Some children come to school with this step already taken, or at least with the movement already begun. They come with an enormous initial advantage ... in some homes awareness of the spoken word is greatly encouraged. Some parents talk *about* words to their children, play word games with them and so on. But most talk only *with* words. Indeed a great many children come to school not even aware that separate words exist – that the flow of speech can be broken up into these units.   (p. 88)

It seems that as children move out of the familiar childhood world of concrete objects, the 'enactive' universe of babyhood, into the 'symbolic' environment of the written language, everything turns on the lottery of their home background. Striking confirmation of this has recently come from two important research studies.

PARENTAL INVOLVEMENT IN READING

Two research studies

We have referred earlier (p. 29) to the work of the Thomas Coram Research Unit of the University of London. The research team, led by Jack Tizard (whose death in 1979 was such a loss for all who work in the field of children's learning), set out to study the effect on the reading performance of children aged 7 and 8 of involving their parents in hearing them read regularly at home.

An earlier study (Hewison and Tizard, 1980) had shown that children encouraged to read to their parents (and to talk with parents about their reading) had markedly higher reading attainments than children who did not get this opportunity. But, as the team saw, this study left important questions unanswered: How far could parents who did not ordinarily hear children read be persuaded to change their habits? Could teachers get *all* children to take reading books home (and bring them back)? How many parents would put children off by unsatisfactory, perhaps punitive, ways of being involved? Could non-English-speaking (or illiterate) parents help in this way? The follow-up project reported in Tizard et al. (1981) tries to answer some of these questions. With the collaboration of six schools in the London Borough of Haringey the team set out to find out if there was a causal relationship between active parental help and reading performance. The effect of parental involvement was measured against that of extra tuition in school by specially qualified teachers. The families involved were almost all in the Registrar General's manual worker category. The experiment lasted two years. A check was made on children's further progress one year after the cessation of the experiment. At each of the 'parent involvement' schools (1 and 2) and the 'teacher help' schools (3 and 4) one top infant class was randomly selected for 'intervention' and the remaining classes of that year become 'within-school controls'. The year-groups concerned were not streamed, and at the start of the experiment there was no statistical difference between the reading performance of the experimental and control groups. In schools 5 and 6 no intervention other than annual testing took place, and these schools became controls only.

The co-operation of parents was sought by a letter from the Chief Education Officer followed by meetings at school (individually) and visits to homes by appointment. The parents also agreed to allow researchers to visit them at home two or three times each term to observe the child reading and to give advice on good practice. Parents were, on the whole, eager for advice and suggestions. Books were sent home three or four times a week in schools 1 and 2. The book used was either the class reader, a book chosen from the reading scheme, or a library book. Later, other material, including the child's own written work, was used. Very few books were lost or damaged. The tests used were: Southgate Group Reading Test (word recognition); Carver Word Recognition Test (Haringey LEA); NFER Test A (comprehension); NFER Test BD (comprehension) and the Spooner Group Reading Assessment (word recognition, comprehension and phonics). The conclusions from the experiment may be briefly summarised:

1 In the inner city it is feasible to involve nearly all parents in formal educational activities, even if some of the parents are non-literate or non-English speaking.

2 Children who receive parental help read much better than children who do not.

3 Parents express great satisfaction at being involved; children are keener and behave better.

4 Teachers found involving parents worthwhile and went on doing so after the experiment had ended.

5 Small group instruction by highly competent specialists in school time did not produce improvements in attainment comparable with those obtained by parental involvement.

6 Parental involvement was effective with children at all initial levels of attainment, including those who at the start of the study were failing to read.

7 The fact that some parents could not read English or could not read at all did not prevent the children improving or the parents collaborating with the school.

The findings of the Tizard study are interestingly confirmed by a study carried out at the University of Manchester, by M. Beveridge and A. Jerrams (1981). It set out to study the effect of parental involvement in language development through an evaluation of a school-based 'Parental Assistance Plan' (PAP).

To summarise: the researchers selected four groups of 10 children (matched for language development) in nursery school and designed a PAP to help parents to work on their children's language development for 20 minutes a day. Two of the groups received parental help. One of these groups also received help from a formal language intervention programme DISTAR (Englemann and Osborn, 1969). A third group received only the DISTAR programme while the fourth group received no intervention but played with toys in the presence of the teacher for an equivalent period.

The school's catchment area is mainly unskilled working-class families in one of Manchester's first housing complexes. It is now a social priority area quoted as having the highest crime rate in Europe. Psychiatric illness is relatively common, many mothers being treated for depression and neurotic symptoms. Yet those parents who participated in the project, and many others who wished to become involved, showed concern for their children and wished a better future for them.

Parents' comments on the PAP were positive: they found it interesting and enjoyable, while their comments on the formal DISTAR programme (like the teachers' comments) were distinctly negative. The children receiving the benefit of the PAP clearly made better progress than the pupils who had DISTAR only. The latter did make some improvement but it was not significant. The children's general ability was not related to the gains made by the intervention. When the children were tested 18 months after the experiment both the groups who had had the parental involvement showed significantly greater increase in language development.

The children in this study were, of course, much younger (ranging from 3 years 5 months to 4 years 5 months) than those in the Tizard study. Also the study lasted for only twelve weeks as compared with the two years of the other project.

Its chief interest is that it shows that parents in a social priority area will involve themselves, given a suitable lead, guidance and resources, in helping their children to improve their language skills, and that the children make real progress as a result.

EVIDENCE FROM CHILDREN DEPRIVED OF INDIVIDUAL DIALOGUE

Further light is thrown on the need for 'adult time' by work with:

(a) deaf parents' children learning their mother tongue
(b) children who have heard adults speaking a foreign language among themselves but have not been spoken to individually by adults in that language

In their study *Psychology and Language* (1977) the psycholinguists Herbert and Eve Clark ask whether exposing children to 'any kind of language' will enable them to acquire it. They comment:

Experiments on these topics are difficult if not impossible to devise, but occasionally a naturalistic situation presents itself in a way that provides a glimpse of the answers to these questions. For example, the hearing children of deaf parents who only use sign language sometimes have little spoken language addressed to them by adults until they enter nursery school. The parents' solution for teaching their children to speak rather than use sign language is to turn on the radio or television as much as possible. Sachs and Johnson (1976) reported on one such child. At 3.9, Jim had only a small vocabulary that he had probably picked up from playmates plus a few words from television jingles. His language was far behind that of other children of his age. Although he had *overheard* a great deal of adult-to-adult speech on television, no adult had spoken to him directly on any regular basis. Once Jim was exposed to an adult who talked to him, his language improved rapidly. Sachs and Johnson concluded that exposure to adult speech intended for other adults does not necessarily help children to acquire language.

Exposure to a second language on television constitutes another naturalistic situation in which children regularly hear adults talking to each other. However, Snow and her colleagues (1976) reported that young Dutch children who watched German television every day did not acquire any German. There are probably at least two reasons why children seem not to acquire language from radio or television. First, none of the speech on the radio can be matched to a situation visible to the child, and even on television, people rarely talk about things immediately accessible to view for the audience. Children therefore receive no clues about *how to map their own ideas onto words and sentences* [our italics]. Second, the stream of speech must be very hard to segment: they hear rapid speech that cannot easily be linked to familiar situations. All this suggests that one ingredient that might prove necessary for acquisition is the 'here and now' nature of adult speech to children.   (p. 330)

'Here and now speech' is what we mean by one-to-one dialogue of the kind demanded by the Bullock Report and of whose importance the studies in Haringey and Manchester gave impressive confirmation. What seems undeniable, in the light of these studies, is that parental involvement is the key factor in the difficult transition from the 'primary' to the 'secondary' (written language) stage.

Our conclusion, in summing up this section of the argument, must be that failure to master the written form of the language of education with confidence, whatever the child's apparent communicative competence in its native dialect, and whatever the potential richness of that dialect, far from being a 'myth' to be dismissed by the theorists, is the cruellest form of language deficit, and that deprivation of 'adult time' in the critical years is the cruellest kind of deprivation.

LEARNING A FOREIGN LANGUAGE IN SCHOOL

The role of insight into pattern

An important dimension in this discussion, for the teacher of foreign languages, is that just as 'awareness of language' seems to underlie learning to read the mother tongue, so insight into the patterned nature of language seems to be called on when children begin to study a foreign language under school conditions. Evidence for this comes from three sources:

(i) aptitude testing
(ii) research on Short Term Memory
(iii) cloze testing

1 Aptitude for foreign language learning

Work on aptitude testing (Pimsleur, 1966; Carroll, 1971; Green, P. S., 1975) shows that a key factor in success is 'the individual's ability to demonstrate his awareness of the syntactical patterning of sentences' (Carroll, 1971, p. 7). Green found that success in learning German in school among boys aged 11 to 15 correlated consistently with the capacity quickly to accomplish two steps:

(a) to spot the pattern or regularity ('rule') in sentences of a language never met before
(b) to invent new, analogous items to fit the perceived patterns (creating by analogy)

For Pimsleur (1966) one of the key components of foreign language aptitude is the 'ability to reason analytically about verbal materials' (p. 182).

Confirmation of the importance of insight into pattern in foreign language learning comes from work on Short Term Memory (STM).

2 Short Term Memory and foreign language learning

The limited capacity of the average adult to hold in the STM at any one time only some seven 'bits' of information (i.e. seven randomly chosen digits or seven syllables of a totally unknown language) is clearly a great restraint on learning. The 'echo' of the verbal message held in the STM lasts only a few seconds. In those few seconds the hearer must either attach some meaning to the message, in order to store it away in the long term memory reservoir, or lose the message. Researchers have shown that the surface features of the message (the actual words heard) are only retained momentarily; it is their *meaning* that must be stored away. Listeners begin purging their memory of verbatim content immediately after a sentence is received in the STM. It follows that the hearer must impose some meaning on the message very quickly. If some pattern can be identified in the incoming string of sounds, more items in the string can be held in the STM and there is a greater chance of the meaning being spotted. Thus 'processing' of the message depends on identifying the set of patterns to which the message belongs and on grasping how the pattern differs from (or resembles) previously learned patterns.

The important point that emerges from recent work on processing messages is that it is a skill that has to be learnt. Gary Olson (1973) has argued that children's difficulties in language performance are due to their failure to learn how to process information: how to organise, plan, integrate and monitor what comes in via the STM. It is not that they cannot do it, but many children need prompting and encouraging to do it. The processing of messages that he has described comes very close to the 'insight into pattern' identified by Pimsleur, Carroll and Green as essential components of language aptitude. It is also very close to the 'awareness of language' that is our present concern.

3 Cloze tests

We have seen that the processing of an incoming verbal message, held momentarily in the limited STM, is a learned process. It calls for decoding, organising and monitoring, none of which can begin until the items composing the message are identified and the pattern to which they belong recognised. These two processes in fact interact with each other.

Rapid recognition of pattern in language, however, is crucial not only in understanding *spoken* messages. Work on cloze testing shows how the same insight into pattern is called on when *reading* a text. When the subject is presented with a text from which, say, every seventh word has been deleted, and is asked to fill in the blanks by guesswork, the ability to insert acceptable answers has been shown to correlate with scores in *listening comprehension* of the language. In other words, a purely pencil and paper gap-filling test seems to call on the same capacity as processing an incoming *spoken* message. J. W. Oller, who has worked on cloze tests for many years in the USA, has called this capacity 'a grammar of expectancy' (1973). The subject who can successfully fill in the gaps in a written text has the capacity to spot the pattern in the words which precede the missing item and, from the evidence, form a hypothesis as to the missing item which can be confirmed (or disconfirmed) by reading on a little further.

In fact work on children's reading difficulties shows that this is precisely the procedure followed by the skilled reader. It is the reader whose guesses are not reliable, and who constantly has to check back and guess again, who stumbles.

Oller's 'grammar of expectancy', Olson's 'processing strategies' and the 'insight into pattern' identified by Pimsleur, Carroll and Green all point towards the same explanation for learning failure. Learning to read in the infant school, like learning French in the secondary school, is one aspect of a wider problem: the fact that the *processing* of language, both spoken and written, is a learned strategy which some children never learn confidently.

It is this conclusion that encourages us to believe that, by helping pupils to strengthen the vital processing capacity at the outset of their difficult secondary course, we shall be giving them the best preparation possible for further work in English, in foreign language learning, and in the whole range of learning across the curriculum. The secondary school timetable calls on the rapid processing of verbal messages, delivered in a variety of language registers and specialist contexts by many different teachers, to whose classrooms pupils are 'summoned by bells' in a bewildering succession of lessons. The sheer variety of learning met in a given day in the secondary school would bewilder most adults if they had to sit through it. Yet we launch our troops into this verbal Armageddon without preparation and with the weapons for learning lacking or sadly mishandled.

A POSSIBLE MISUNDERSTANDING

Our insistence on insight into pattern in language should not be taken to mean that we do not appreciate the importance of other language experience. In the mother tongue it is, of course, vital that children should learn to use language in several modes, not least *expressively*. We fail our pupils if they leave school unable to use English with accuracy, discrimination, force when necessary and, above all, integrity. Expressiveness must have an important place, though in giving exclusive rein to expressiveness some teachers have seemed to encourage pastiche and imitation rather than precision and integrity in self-expression.

Our suggested stress on insight into pattern *accompanies*, but does not replace, other kinds of English work. It comes in to reinforce what teachers of English are already doing, often with great imagination.

An equally important disclaimer may be needed regarding foreign language teaching, lest it should be concluded that we are trying to put the clock back and return to the 'grammar grind' of the inter-war years.

THE ROLE OF 'INTENTION TO MEAN' IN FOREIGN LANGUAGE LEARNING

Foreign language acquisition is now generally recognised as a dual process going on at two levels simultaneously. One level is insight into pattern; here the learner is concentrating on the 'form' of the language. No less essential is the second level of language activity; here the learner is concentrating on the 'message'. To appreciate the importance of the second level we should go back to the philosopher's notion of the 'total speech act'.

The notion of the 'total speech act' was first developed by the Oxford philosopher J. L. Austin in *How to Do Things with Words* (1962). His pupil, the American John Searle, further developed the theory that the 'speech act' and not the Chomskyan sentence (in written form) is the basic unit that the linguist must study if he is to discuss 'serious' language. The 'illocutionary' speech act (that is the speech act considered from the standpoint of the speaker) has two components. It has 'propositional content' (the part that may be submitted to grammatical analysis) but it also has 'force', that is the *intention* to achieve some objective, to change the world in some way. Without 'force' there is no speech act but only a 'non-serious' string of words which is not suitable as a unit of analysis by the linguist because real human communication does not consist of such strings.

The interest of this for the foreign language teacher is that it is precisely this element of 'force' or 'intention to mean' that makes new language 'stick'. Carl Dodson, working with bilingual children in Welsh schools, has noted that the children who make most progress in learning their second language are those who move constantly between two levels of language, one level at which they concentrate on the 'form' of the language itself, and the other at which their whole attention is given to 'doing things with words'. This is the level of the true speech act, that has 'intention to mean'.

In the traditional foreign language classroom we are constantly asking pupils merely to imitate our utterances, or to show that they understand other people's meanings in a text or an examination paper, with no expectation of their expressing any meaning of their own. The whole of the 16+ examination consists of such 'transmission' of other people's meanings (except for the trivial 'oral' test). This is why John Searle, giving examples of what he calls 'non-serious' language, cites foreign language teaching.

The idea that language is acquired most effectively when the learner's attention is distracted away from the *form* of the language onto the *meaning* is not new. Harold Palmer (1917) made 'subconscious assimilation' the foundation of his programme: 'Of the vocabulary possessed by any one person proficient in the use of a foreign language a very small proportion has been acquired by conscious study, probably less than 5 per cent; the bulk of his vocabulary has been acquired by subconscious assimilation.' The claim was made quite explicit by Otto Tacke (1923): 'a will to mean must always underlie the learning of expressions in the foreign language, otherwise the foreign expressions do not stick'.

In the last few years Stephen Krashen has refined this hypothesis. In his 'monitor theory' (1981) he distinguishes between 'acquisition', which can only be subconscious, and 'learning', which is conscious: 'Acquisition is the most effective and central means of internalizing language for adults as well as children.' On the other hand the consciously learned system which concentrates on form cannot initiate utterances but can only serve to 'monitor' (correct, revise) them. The learner must 'acquire' enough of the target language to initiate utterances.

In *Modern Languages in the Curriculum* (Hawkins, 1981) the discussion is taken a little further with the attempt to devise a taxonomy of levels of 'force' in the language used in the foreign language classroom. Four levels are analysed, ranging from dialogue in which pupils concentrate entirely on 'form' to language in which the whole attention is given to the meaning of the message, with no thought of any ulterior language-learning 'pay-off'. It is suggested that teachers should know at any one time at what level of 'force' they are asking pupils to perform. Only by doing so will they be able to ensure that a balance is kept between the different uses of language. It may be noted that these four levels are not levels of difficulty. Levels 1 and 2 may be difficult enough; they aim at strengthening insight into pattern. Levels 3 and 4 help the new language to stick.

This helps us to see more clearly the value and the limitations of the work on 'functional' syllabus design. There is no doubt that the study of adult 'needs' in foreign language use, and the design of syllabuses which aim to provide the vocabulary and the structures to meet such needs, can economise in time and effort by the learner. Some adult needs are no doubt predictable. However some 'needs', such as adult leisure needs and especially the needs of children, are much less predictable. As the late Julian Dakin asked, how could one possibly predict the language needs of the 8-year-old who told the interviewer: 'My guinea-pig died with his legs crossed'? We can never be certain what a learner will do ultimately with the language we teach.

This is not the only limitation of the functional syllabus, however. There are good pedagogical reasons for selecting learning units and determining the order in which the grammar is introduced. Coulthard (1977) asks: 'In a syllabus that is structured communicatively, where the students . . . acquire at any one time only those aspects of grammar necessary for the realisation of a particular act . . . how can the student be assisted to relate a particular structure to the overall framework of the language?' (p. 139). Any 'functional' syllabus is an inventory of items. It only becomes truly functional if the items are used in real 'speech acts', that is if the user utters them with intention to express *his own meaning*, to 'change the world' in some way. It would be perfectly possible to take the items of the most strictly functional syllabus and incorporate them as mechanical drills in an exercise devoid of any communicative intent. The challenge to teachers posed by recent research is to find ways of engaging the learner in true 'speech acts' in the foreign language in classrooms at whose door the 'gale of English' blows.

The ESL teacher is in a happier position. His pupils can go from the ESL classroom and be immersed at once in the English language both in other lessons and outside school. Teachers of Latin in the Tudor grammar school saw the need to mix formal classroom work on 'grammar' (insight into pattern) with use of Latin outside the classroom. They could do this in a world where Latin was the lingua franca. Their school charters made sure that this advantage was exploited to the full. A typical injunction in such a charter said: 'any boy who has been at the school for 3 years must speak nothing but Latin at all times and if found speaking English in the playground he must be beaten by the headmaster' (King James, Knaresborough, 1657). Again: 'boys must speak Latin to each other as well in the school as coming and going to and from the same' (Oundle, 1556). Learning the grammar (in class) was reinforced by active use outside the classroom.

The foreign language teacher is less fortunate than the teacher of Latin in the Tudor grammar school or the ESL teacher. How can he turn the dialogue in his classroom into Searle's 'serious language'? There seem to be three obvious strategies:

1 Greatly increase the ratio of native speakers to learners
2 Develop intensive courses, and especially 'reciprocal' courses, which build a wind-break against the 'gale of English'
3 Adopt a new approach to 'reading for meaning'

The need for native speakers

The scheme for the exchange of foreign language assistants has done more than any other single innovation to bring authentic dialogue into classrooms. It is a tragedy that just as research was proving beyond doubt the need for such dialogue a number of LEAs should have so betrayed their responsibilities as to withdraw completely from the scheme and denude all their schools of foreign assistants. The Parliamentary Select Committee for Education, Science and Arts in its second report to the House of Commons (1981) saw this as a disaster:

it is absolutely vital that pupils should have access to native speakers of the foreign languages concerned. For this reason we recommend that the DES should take on responsibility for the Foreign Language Assistants programme and should make arrangements for this to be funded centrally, since

without such a measure we believe that the number of FLAs will diminish
below an acceptable level ... we are also concerned to see an increase in the
number of pupils who have an opportunity to exchange with pupils from
other countries, and we recommend that the DES should explore means of
funding such provision centrally.   (p. 39)

The Select Committee went on to suggest that the EEC might have a
role to play in this. In fact the EEC record in this field is dismal. What
might we have expected? Let us suggest a quite modest initiative.
Suppose that the EEC offered scholarships for selected teams of, say,
a dozen pupils from any one school, 3 each from the third, fourth,
fifth and sixth forms. They would go to France, Spain or Germany for
six months, in exchange for a similar team from the other country.
The presence in our classrooms of such teams of selected native
speakers would give life to the dialogues in the foreign language,
while outside the classroom our pupils would enjoy real conversation
with children of their own age and interests, concentrating on the
message. The various levels of language use would interplay with each
other in the way that research shows that they should. And the effect
of our own teams returning from their six months abroad with
near-perfect native pronunciation and fluency would greatly
strengthen the expectations of the rest of the class and of their
teachers.

Intensive and 'reciprocal' courses

The value of the intensive course in avoiding interference from the
'gale of English' was shown by the wartime crash-courses run by the
armed services. It has since been shown, by intensive teaching
techniques at university level, that highly motivated students can
reach, in no more than two or three weeks of concentrated effort,
levels that secondary school pupils normally take four or five years to
attain.

The 'reciprocal course' is a development of such work. Such a
course brings together matched teams of students from two countries
who teach each other and learn from each other in alternate sessions.
By this means each learner acquires an individual tutor, attentive to
his or her individual needs and progress. Dialogue between the
partners is, of necessity, 'serious language' in Searle's sense. The
potential of the reciprocal course for adult learners is clear. If
specialists (lawyers, engineers, accountants, salesmen) are to learn
the functional language of their trade they need tutors who have

learned the highly specialised concepts that are transacted. No generalist language teacher can expect to know the meanings that, say, the lawyer attaches to the vocabulary of the law. Yet it is these very fine meanings that the foreign lawyer will wish to have explained. Who better to do this than the British lawyer who, in return, expects to be taught the legal language of the foreign country?

In a similar way it should be possible to arrange reciprocal courses for school pupils. Experiments at York with teams of sixth formers in reciprocal teaching/learning courses have proved the potential of such *enseignement mutuel*.

A new approach to reading

Reading has been called the 'forgotten skill'. It seems clear that if we wish to restore to the classroom what Dodson has called 'message-orientated' language use, one way, at least so far as receptive skills are concerned, would be to encourage pupils to read for meanings that matter enough to distract their attention from the 'form' of the message. The challenge to teachers is to find reading matter that genuinely interests young learners, from the very first weeks of their course. As the course progresses the need for such reading becomes steadily greater. Beyond the age of 16 reading for meaning (learner's meaning, not meanings of interest only to teacher or examiner) should form the staple of the course.

A PROBLEM SHARED

In both English and foreign language teaching, then, we can distinguish two levels: insight into pattern and use of language to express personal meanings effectively. The two levels are mutually supportive and the interplay between them is constant. The two kinds of teachers thus face a common problem. The use of language with 'intention to mean' in their two classrooms may be very different but at the other level of language activity, that of 'insight into pattern', they can make common cause. It is here that we see exciting possibilities for co-operation where hitherto the two kinds of language teacher have worked in total isolation.

The pioneering initiatives that we have discussed earlier sprang from the wish to make the child's whole language experience a more coherent, less fragmented business. One of the most hopeful features of the new approach to teaching language is that teachers who previously worked in isolation have come together to plan and teach the new courses. Actually getting round the table to agree the new syllabus and allocate teaching roles has begun to achieve what the Bullock Committee hoped for but what its incompletely worked-out concept of 'language across the curriculum' failed to promote. Now teachers can be given a precisely outlined job of work and they are responding with enthusiasm.

This alone would have justified the new programmes. But there has been another gain. For the first time the school timetable offers all children, whatever their mother tongue or their home language experience, the chance to discuss on equal terms the mystery that unites them. They have all acquired language; they can all look forward to the responsibility of passing on language to their own children.

Instead of allowing language to be a divisive element in their education the new programme reminds them, and their teachers, that they all share a great deal. The 'awareness of language' programme brings out this shared experience and encourages each child to offer a personal contribution to the discussion. It thus makes a virtue of linguistic diversity while at the same time challenging preconceived ideas and laying foundations for the acceptance of difference as interesting not threatening. This is to build constructively on the linguist's concept of 'linguistic variability', which ceases to be a nebulous concept, only read about on training courses. It becomes a central theme in the classroom and a powerful means of combating unconscious linguistic prejudice, which underlies much racial misunderstanding.

'AWARENESS OF LANGUAGE' – NO PANACEA

Our discussion has, perhaps, gone some way towards justifying the following two claims that may be made for 'awareness of language' in the curriculum.

1 The new courses are ending the isolationism of teachers of English, foreign languages and ethnic minority mother tongues.
2 Scope is being found in the curriculum for the first time for discussion of the phenomenon of language itself: its rule-governed structure, its variety and at the same time its universals, its acquisition, and its place in society etc. Moreover the discussion is such that all children, no matter how diverse their linguistic experience, can make a contribution.

Can the new courses go beyond this and help children whose insight into pattern in language is unsure? We must avoid oversimplifying the problems and making exaggerated claims. 'Awareness of language' is no 'panacea'. The fundamental need is to give back 'adult time' to young children deprived of it. This was first suggested, as we have seen, by Vygotsky's observation that in order to categorise the intellectual universe and to match his emerging concepts to the language symbols offered by the speech community, the child needs adult dialogue and, later, encouragement to read.

Lack of 'adult time', as Tizard's work has shown, leads directly to reading failure and this equation holds regardless of the dialect used in the home. The only long-term solution is to give back 'adult time' to the children (possibly as many as 50% of group V children) who have been cheated of it, and this must begin in the pre-school stage and continue throughout the junior school and even beyond.

No curriculum innovation or organisational arrangements at secondary level can make up for lack of 'adult time' for such children. For them the 'awareness of language' programme can only be complementary to longer-term strategies. For all children, however, practice in sharpening the tools for verbal learning will be beneficial and a determined attempt by the secondary school to develop awareness of the role of language in society may be the surest way of creating a climate in which teachers and parents will come to accept their responsibilities in the way that the Bullock Report advocated.

Part 2

Awareness of Language: Topics

This section of the book is divided into the most likely topics that teachers will want to include in any treatment of 'awareness of language'. The topics are also those chosen for the series of books, 'Awareness of Language', published in association with this book.

The 'Awareness of Language' topic books are intended for pupils in the age range 10 – 14. They can therefore be introduced at the top of the junior school, in middle schools or in the first years of secondary school. Although they introduce a wide range of language themes, they do not form a sequential course. Each book is self-sufficient; it is not necessary to cover all the topics. Each topic book can, if desired, provide work for one term with two to three lessons per week or for two terms if only one weekly lesson is available.

The order in which the topic books are used will vary from school to school or class to class, depending on teachers' judgement and interests, though it may be found convenient to begin with *Get the Message!*, so that pupils start thinking about the uniqueness of human language by comparing it with animal and other non-verbal forms of communication.

Who teaches the new subject? There is no cut-and-dried answer. In some schools the English staff have taken the initiative and introduced the subject as part of a revised syllabus, finding the time from the English timetable. In other schools the initiative has come from the modern linguists, with 'awareness of language' being introduced either as a preparation for learning the foreign language, whose start is delayed appropriately, or in step with the introduction of the foreign language, spread over the first two years.

The ideal solution is for the two departments to form a joint board of studies to plan and teach the syllabus. One advantage of this arrangement, particularly if the head of the school throws his or her weight behind the work, is that other specialist teachers (e.g., of biology, history, geography, music, drama, art) may be brought in to strengthen the team with their special skills. One lesson learned from the schools that have pioneered 'awareness of language' courses is that the subject, once launched, however modestly, brings teachers together and promotes co-operation across subject boundaries by suggesting interesting themes to colleagues who may not previously have thought of taking part in language teaching.

The topic books are:

> *Get the Message!*
> *Spoken and Written Language*
> *How Language Works*
> *Using Language*
> *Language Varieties and Change*
> *How do we Learn Languages?*

The suggestions for further reading given at the end of each of the following sections are no more than suggestions, depending very much on teachers' time and interests and access to good libraries.

The cassette accompanying the series includes listening material relevant to the six topic books (full details are given on cassette liner) in addition to the listening games outlined on pages 191–208.

Get the Message! (Non-verbal communication)

This book is about some of the ways in which messages are sent and received: in other words about communication. It deals with: communication by animals; human communication without words; signals and signs; symbols and made-up languages.

The subject is one that all children find interesting. It lends itself to wall displays and project work. Children can readily find out more for themselves from the many encyclopaedias and magazines published on the animal world and on individual species which communicate in interesting ways (bats, dolphins, whales, spiders, bees, chimps etc.). They can also learn from television programmes and from their own observations of their pets, farm animals and visits to the zoo.

Although the study of animal communication is intrinsically worthwhile it is hoped that it will start pupils thinking about the question which underlies much of the 'awareness of language' programme, namely: what has 'homo loquens', the 'articulate mammal', got that is so unique?

WHAT IS SO SPECIAL ABOUT HUMAN LANGUAGE?

A straightforward way into this question might be to take some of the functions that are clearly served by human language and look for evidence of their having any part in animal communication. Possible functions to consider might be:

(i) *directive* use of language: the use of language to produce or prevent action by others (No smoking! Fasten your seat-belts!)

(ii) *expressive* use of language: the spontaneous outgoing in words of personal feelings such as joy or sorrow, or reaction to the experiences of others in expressions of sympathy or gratitude etc.

Pupils may possibly suggest that it is easier to find in animal communication instances of the first of the above functions than of the second. But why exactly does the cock crow in the morning? (For a discussion of a philosopher's and a linguist's account of 'function' in language see p. 155.)

HOCKETT'S 'DESIGN FEATURES' OF HUMAN LANGUAGE

For language teachers who wish (perhaps in collaboration with science colleagues) to examine the question further the most complete 'taxonomy' of the characteristics of human language has been offered by C. F. Hockett. In *The View from Language* (1977) he listed 13 'design features' shared by every known language (see table 2). Some of these, but not all, are found in animal communication and in non-verbal forms of language. They are:

1 *Use of the vocal–auditory tract*: most mammals possess vocal chords, the only exception being giraffes; an example of non-vocal communication is the bee-dance.

2 *Broadcast transmission and directional reception*: human speech carried on sound waves can travel round corners; nevertheless *hearing* is directional.

3 *Rapid fading*: sound waves rapidly fade, hence the great importance of writing; note, too, repetition as a characteristic of bird calls.

4 *Interchangeability*: humans, unless deaf, both send and receive.

5 *Total feedback*: human speakers, unless deaf, hear everything they themselves say.

6 *Specialisation*: human language serves biological needs only indirectly; it can be motivated by such needs at levels such as 'I'm hungry!'

7 *Semanticity*: the language items must have a clear meaning known to both sender and receiver. Bee-dancing is semantic in this sense.

8 *Arbitrariness*: human language is not 'iconic'. i.e. 'dog', 'Hund', 'chien', 'perro' do not look or sound like what they represent (see p. 106). Onomatopoeic words (splash, ding-dong, bang) are faintly iconic, though cross-language comparisons show a degree of arbitrariness: English 'bang'; French 'pan'; German 'päng'; Spanish 'pum'. Traces of iconicity are found in the way increased volume in speech matches anger or mounting excitement, as in a sports commentary.

9 *Discreteness*: slight variations can lead to misinterpretation, for example, 'ship' for 'sheep'.

10 *Displacement*: message can be removed in time and space from event and thus involves memory and foresight. Bee-dancing is displaced in this sense.

11 *Productivity or openness*: humans can say things never heard before; animal calls are predictable.

12 *Duality*: perhaps the most important characteristic, not shared by animal communication. Human language contains a finite number of 'phonemes', the smallest discrete sounds that can affect meaning, and that combine to make thousands of 'morphemes', the smallest bits of language to carry discrete meaning (see discussion on p. 144). (Note: some experts

Table 2

	1 Some Gryllidae and Tettigoniidae	2 Bee dancing	3 Stickleback courtship	4 Western Meadowlark song	5 Gibbon calls	6 Paralinguistic phenomena	7 Language	8 Instrumental music
1 *Vocal-auditory*	auditory not vocal	no	no	yes	yes	yes	yes	auditory not vocal
2 *Broadcast*	yes	yes	yes	yes	yes	yes	yes	yes
3 *Rapid fading*	yes (repeated)	?	?	yes	yes (rep.)	yes	yes	yes
4 *Interchangeability*	limited	limited	no	?	yes	yes (largely)	yes	?
5 *Total feedback*	yes	?	no	yes	yes	yes	yes	yes
6 *Specialization*	yes?	?	in part	yes?	yes	yes?	yes	yes
7 *Semanticity*	no?	yes	no	?partly?	yes	yes?	yes	no (in general)
8 *Arbitrariness*	?	no	—	if semantic, yes	yes	in part	yes	—
9 *Discreteness*	yes?	no	?	?	yes	largely no	yes	partly
10 *Displacement*	—	yes, always	—	?	no	in part	yes, often	—
11 *Productivity*	no	yes	no	one, or both, yes	no	yes	yes	yes
12 *Duality*	? (trivial)	no	—		no	no	yes	—
13 *Tradition*	no?	probably not	no?	?	?	yes	yes	yes

Source: C. F. Hockett, *The View from Language* (1977)

suggest that some forms of bird-song exhibit a degree of duality. This is still being debated.)

13 *Cultural or traditional transmission*: human language has to be learned over a number of years; animals and birds use their calls almost from birth. Human genes are not specific to any one language. Bird-song does have to be learned and separation from the parent does affect the learning but there is no evidence that birds can learn songs of other species otherwise the cuckoo would probably long since have learned a less boring song! The human baby can learn several languages simultaneously, and over half of the world's population are bilingual. Some learners even manage to learn a foreign language in school!

There is a fourteenth characteristic to add to Hockett's list: perhaps half of the world's population speak languages which have a *written* form. The implications of this for cultural evolution are immense. After this characteristic of language, Hockett's 'duality' and 'tradition' (nos. 12 and 13) are perhaps the most important, and unique to the human race. They are discussed further in the section 'How Language Works' (p. 144). One other of Hockett's characteristics, the fact that language is not iconic, has important consequences.

SYMBOLIC v. ICONIC REPRESENTATION

A drawing of a dog looks like a dog and can be recognised at once (though very young children cannot do this). If words represented their meanings in this way then would not all languages have to have the same or very similar words to represent the same things? Clearly they do not. It may be useful to carry out a classroom survey of the languages within the experience of the class. What is a dog called? – 'chien'/'Hund'/'perro'/'canis' etc. Of course the survey may show some similarities – 'bread'/'Brot'/'brød' etc. – but this is because these languages are members of the same family (see p. 163) and not because the words are iconic.

Another group of words may be found by the survey which are partially iconic. These are the onomatopoeic words whose sound imitates their meaning. Even here the iconicity is only partial as we saw earlier from our example of 'bang'. Drawing a wall chart of such words with the help of pupils from the ethnic minorities, including as many languages as possible, would bring this out. This might be followed by a similar chart plotting the words for, say, 'water' in all the languages represented. As new pupils came to the school they should be invited to add to the chart.

The lesson to be brought out is that words can only convey meaning if their meanings have been learned. They are not self-evident, like the meanings of 'signs'. A word is a 'symbol' whose meaning is agreed by the community. It may help pupils to grasp the meaning of 'symbol' if it is contrasted with 'symptom' (a symptom is technically a sign of something *of which it is itself part*): 'The difference between a symbolic and a symptomatic act may be illustrated by contrasting the intentional genuflexion of a suppliant with the emotional quaver in his voice. There is a convention about the former but not about the latter' (Susanne K. Langer, 1942).

SIGNALS, SIGNS AND SYMBOLS

The signals (or messages) that we get from the outside world can be of two kinds: signs or symbols. For the philosopher a sign is in a one-to-one relationship with the thing or event that it points to. The relationship is fixed and unchanging. It is a logical relationship and therefore readily learned or can easily be 'conditioned'. (This is how Pavlov was able, by simple conditioning, to make a bell tone become a sign of food.) Examples of signs in this sense could be:

> a wet road – a sign that it has been raining
> a scar – a sign of a previous wound or cut
> a ring on the doorbell – a sign that someone is calling
> a bell tone – a sign that the typewriter carriage is at the end of its run
> red spots – a sign of measles or chicken pox

Note that some of these signs are natural, such as the wet road or the scar. Others are artificial, such as the doorbell or the typewriter bell. The artificial signs need a little more learning than the natural ones. But all share the characteristics of one-to-one relationship with what they represent, and fixed, unvarying significance.

Animals respond to signs. The animal gets a signal (say the scent of an enemy) and soon learns (partly by copying adult behaviour) to read the signal as a sign of danger and to take appropriate action. As the philosopher Susanne Langer says: 'The interpretation of signs is the basis of animal intelligence.'

Humans share with animals the power to interpret and act on signs and to exchange them, with gesture and looks. Humans, however, have the extra power to respond to symbols. For Langer the essential difference between a sign and a symbol is that whereas the sign evokes an object or an event a symbol evokes the 'conception' of an object or event. And the connection between the symbol and the idea it represents *has to be learned*; it is not self-evident.

To give some examples of this definition of the symbol in Langer's terms: the union flag is a symbol of the political union of the countries of the United Kingdom; a flag flying at half-mast is a symbol of mourning for some national figure; the red cross has become a symbol of a hospital or first-aid post; a red flag might be a symbol of danger (as when it is flying at the entrance to a firing-range or being carried in front of a motor car in the early days of the internal combustion engine) but at a political meeting it would symbolise something quite different.

Some road signs, according to Langer, would be signs in the sense described above, while others would be symbols. For example, the modern sign warning that there is a school ahead is a drawing of children running. It points to the children who may be ahead and logically signals 'Look out – children!' It replaced an older picture showing a burning torch. This was a symbol ('the lamp of learning') representing the *idea* of a school. It only represented the idea of a school, however, for those motorists who knew about the lamp of learning or who had learned the meaning of the symbol.

Now the essence of language is that words are symbols for the most part, not signs. It is true that occasionally a word is used as a sign and little more. Thus a label on the lid of a box is not much more than a sign. It is in a one-to-one relationship with the contents, unvarying, pointing to the object inside, not to the *idea* of the contents. Most commonly, however, words evoke conceptions. Language serves to transact the conceptions that we retain from our experience of the world. It is not necessary for the events or experiences to be present. The idea of them persists in our minds and it is these ideas that are represented by the symbols, or words that we learn to apply to them. This is the essence of human thought, which, though it does not begin with language, and can go quite a long way without language, yet is greatly facilitated by the learning of the linguistic symbols. These represent ideas and enable us to relate one to another, to compare and contrast them, to distinguish very small differences, to group ideas into categories, draw conclusions and make plans etc.

It is worth spending some time on the symbolic nature of language because it has important consequences.

Symbols take longer to learn

Human language cannot be learned nearly as quickly as, say, bird-song. It is true that young chicks have some learning to do. Take, for example, chaffinches. They are genetically programmed to learn the chaffinch song very quickly but they need a model. If taken away from the mother soon after hatching, and kept away for a critical number of days, they never learn to sing like a chaffinch. They will sing, but not the authentic chaffinch song. The environment does matter for the chaffinch. But the learning does not take long. And the chaffinch cannot learn the song of any other bird. The human baby can learn any language. For the human baby the learning of symbols takes much longer, however, and the environment is all-important. Learning new symbols for complex conceptions will continue into adult life. The 'grammar' of English (the 'formative' symbols for the ways in which the 'lexical' or 'content' symbols relate and combine) will not be mastered until adolescence and even then there will still be much to learn.

Symbols can carry more complex meanings

Though learning the meaning of symbols takes longer than reacting to signs, the symbols once learned can be used in many contexts. They do not stand in a purely one-to-one relationship with what they represent, but evoke ideas. The only way to react to a sign is to take action (avoid the danger, put out the cigarette, fasten the seat-belts, slow down in case the road is wet and slippery). A symbol invites reflexion, comment, response with another symbol etc.

Symbols can represent abstractions

One of the most important ways in which thought is set free by linguistic symbols is by enabling abstract concepts to be transacted. How, for example, could a sign represent 'courage' or 'yesterday'? But language goes beyond mere representation. It is not simply that symbols *refer to* experience. They may come to *replace* it. As Edward Sapir put it in a seminal discussion (1921): 'language may not only refer to experience, but it also substitutes for it in the sense that in those sequences of interpersonal behaviour which form the greater part of daily lives, speech and action supplement each other and do each other's work in a web of unbroken pattern'.

Learners differ greatly in their mastery of symbolic meanings

Another characteristic of language that follows from its symbolic nature is that some learners will master it more thoroughly than others. The learning which takes so long can be done precisely or in a haphazard, approximate way; differences between concepts can be vaguely grasped or sharply distinguished; complex concepts may be fully grasped by some, left unexplored by others.

Symbolic meanings may change

Again, as a consequence of the learned, symbolic nature of language, the meanings attached to the symbols at any point in time may change. Language is fluid, unlike bird-song, which does not develop. Note that this characteristic of language is so marked that it resists attempts by governments to prevent change, whether by fixing the meanings of words or by preventing borrowings from other languages. (The recent history of the French language and the government's attempts to hold back the tide of borrowings from English illustrate this.)

Teachers may wish to explore with pupils the changes of meanings that have taken place in English in their own parents' lifetime or over longer periods. (See Further Reading suggestions for information on this area.)

'Correct' v. 'incorrect' language

Another consequence of the symbolic, learned nature of language may seem to contradict the previous one: it is that because language has to be learned there has to be something to learn: a 'correct' as opposed to an 'incorrect' form. This sometimes leads to muddle and acrimony in discussion. Learning a language is not a matter of learning something which is immutable and will never change but it *is* a matter of learning the current usage of the speech community and especially the usage of the sources from which one wishes to learn (e.g., the media, textbooks, original documents). In this sense there is a 'model' to be mastered just as when one wants to read texts in a foreign language.

The role of schooling

A final characteristic of human language is that, because many of the symbols to be learned and the concepts which they match are complex and specialised, language needs *schooling*, in our culture. It could not be learned without the help of specialists, who have explored particular areas of the conceptual field in depth. Language cannot be learned simply in the family or the market-place or from the peer-group, though each of these has an important part to play. The most difficult areas of language remain closed without the intervention of adults and access to dictionaries and libraries where the concepts and their matching language are stored. The language is in a real sense 'in the keeping' of those who have most and best experience of it. In language learning it is not true that 'Jack is as good as his master.'

A point that may be made in discussion with pupils is that language is not the only symbolic activity we learn, though it is the most complex. Much of children's play is symbolic. The dance rituals of many societies are full of symbolism. Many aspects of the way we dress, rituals connected with meals, public ceremonies, and much of our art, music and entertainment have symbolic meanings for us which they would not have for members of another culture who had not been brought up to it, that is those who have not learned the symbolism. One way to approach this subject in class, suggested in *Get the Message!*, is to discuss the question of school uniform. What symbolism is involved? How do the issues raised touch on other kinds of symbolism in dress? What is the effect of passing fashions and how much symbolism is there in changing notions of what is acceptable, for example, in the dress thought suitable for men and women?

FURTHER READING

1 As a general introduction to the themes in *Get the Message!* (and indeed to all the topic books):
D. Bolinger and D. A. Sears, *Aspects of Language* (3rd edn, revised) (Harcourt Brace Jovanovich, 1981). This scholarly yet readable book answers most of the questions that pupils will ask and suggests many more for the interested teacher to pursue.

2 On animal communication:
E. Linden, *Apes, Men and Language* (Penguin, 1981)
National Geographic Magazine (October 1978) for attractive pictures and readable text about Koko the gorilla.

3 On non-verbal communication:
T. Brun, *International Dictionary of Sign Language* (Wolfe, 1969)
M. Argyle, *Bodily Communication* (Methuen, 1975)
D. Morris, *Manwatching* (Jonathan Cape, 1977)
D. Morris et al., *Gestures: Their Origin and Distribution* (Jonathan Cape, 1979)

4   Books for pupils on flags:
The Pocket Book of Maps and Flags (Usborne, 1980)
W. Crampton, *The Observer's Book of Flags* (Frederick Warne, 1979)

5   On words which have changed their meaning:
S. I. Tucker, *English Examined: Two Centuries of Comment on the Mother Tongue* (CUP, 1961)

6   A valuable essay on symbolism in language is:
'Language' in S. Langer, *Philosophy in a New Key* (Harvard University Press, 1942, 1957). Langer argues persuasively that the origins of human language should be sought in the essentially human faculty of symbolism, manifested in many forms of behaviour, rather than in the human animal's need to *communicate*: 'Language is the acquired ability to symbolise'.

Spoken and Written Language

This topic book aims to start pupils thinking about spoken and written language: how they are alike and how they differ and where the kind of writing that we use came from. The contents cover: learning to speak and learning to write; early kinds of writing; the alphabet; some other ways of writing; printing and spelling; spoken and written language – are they the same or different?; test your Short Term Memory.

Teachers may well wish to tackle this topic with their pupils after *Get the Message!* for two reasons:

1 It raises interesting problems to challenge the more able pupils while offering slower learners the chance to revisit, without the stigma of 'remedial work', the mysteries of writing and spelling. The practical exploration of different kinds of writing can increase pupils' confidence and bring them back to their own alphabet ready to see more 'system' in English spelling than they had suspected, and more aware of the pleasure that writing can offer.

2 It offers pupils whose mother tongue is not English the opportunity to take the lead in some parts of the discussion and to bring examples from home (involving their parents whenever this can be encouraged) of writing in other languages.

THE MYSTERY OF WRITING

Pupils whose own confidence has been shaken by their initial engagement with the technical problems of writing may be encouraged to reflect that throughout history writing has seemed to be a threatening mystery to those who could not read. The ancient Egyptians believed that the god Thoth invented the hieroglyph. Writing was 'the speech of the Gods'. Hindus thought it was Brahma who had given knowledge of letters to man. The Norse sagas attributed the invention of the runes to Odin. Only in ancient Greece was writing widespread. Legends about the divine origins of the alphabet were not needed. Literacy was the handmaid of democracy.

Again pupils whose own handling of the pen has let them down in the past may be helped by exploration of the history of writing implements. Discussion might start from the meaning of the word 'to write'. In most languages the word either meant to cut, incise, scratch or else to paint. The implements used determined the shape of the letters. This can be seen if we compare the runes and ogams, with their straight cuts made with a knife in wood or bone, and the cursive Chinese characters painted with a brush. The vocabulary of the different languages reflects this:

Old Norse   *rîta* – to incise (cf. modern Scandinavian *rita* – to draw)
Old English   *wrítan* (cognate with Old Frisian *wrîta*) – to score, cut, write (cf. modern German: *reissen* – to tear, scratch)
Latin   *scribere* (German: *schreiben*) is cognate with Greek: *skarisphasthai* – to incise, scratch.

On the other hand many languages 'paint' when they write:

Old Gothic   *mēljan* (to write) is cognate with modern German *malen* – to paint.
Slavic   *pisati* originally meant 'to paint', now, 'to write'.

Chinese children are still taught in school to use a brush to 'write' the characters.

In this initial exploration of writing methods a valuable classroom activity which pupils will enjoy is to practise cuneiform writing. (Latin: *cuneus* – a wedge.) The story of the discovery of one kind of cuneiform writing is itself a detective story. It happened in 1928 when a peasant at Râs Shamrah, near Latakiya in Syria, discovered a subterranean tunnel which led to the excavation of the lost town of Ugarit. Here a long lost kind of cuneiform writing was discovered. It consisted of 30 symbols in which a Semitic language, dating back to the fourteenth century BC, was written. Technically it was not an alphabet but a 'syllabary', the forerunner of the alphabet as we know it.

Typical examples from this cuneiform syllabary are:

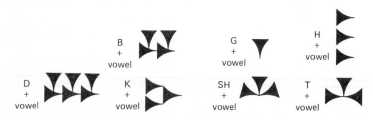

(For the complete syllabary see Gelb, 1963, p. 130.)

It is not necessary for pupils to learn all the symbols of this cuneiform as this would entail discussion of the highly technical question of how the syllabary differs from the modern alphabet. (Usually in a syllabary each consonant stands for its own sound plus any one of the five vowels. In the Râs Shamrah syllabary there are three additional signs expressing vowels.) Pupils can work out their own simplified 'cuneiform alphabets', with a symbol for each letter, including vowels, and then practise writing their names, inscriptions for the classroom wall, etc. To do this they will need to make their own wedge-shaped stylus and to use smooth tablets of Plasticine or clay.

THE ALPHABET WE USE

The two key questions that call for discussion are:

1 How do the spoken and written forms of English relate to each other and is the matching of the two any more consistent in other languages within the experience of the class? (For example, in French, German or Spanish or the mother tongues of pupils from ethnic minorities?)
2 Where did our alphabet come from and how does it differ from the kinds of writing known to members of ethnic minorities in the class?

HOW DO SPEECH AND WRITING RELATE?

Linguists distinguish three ways in which speech and writing relate:

> chronologically
> socially
> logically

Chronological relationship

In the history of the human race and in the life of each individual it is speech that comes first. Literacy is comparatively recent. 'Homo loquens' may be 1 million years old yet the earliest writing system dates only from about 3500 BC. Of the total world population today more than 40% cannot read or write and some 65% are 'functionally illiterate', that is they can decipher words but cannot read well enough to 'function' in society. In Shakespeare's day it is calculated that perhaps one-third of his potential audience could read. One hundred years ago probably half of the population of Britain was still illiterate.

At the present time it is estimated that there are 2 million functionally illiterate adults in Britain. K. Gardner (1968) even claims that 1 in 4 of all school-leavers in the UK is functionally illiterate. In the largest English-speaking country, the USA, the situation seems to be even more serious. A study in 1975 sponsored by the US Office of Education at the University of Texas at Austin, showed that 21.7% of adults in the USA between the ages of 18 and 65 (some 23 million people) could not read well enough to understand a job application form, the label on a medicine bottle, or a safety sign at their work place. Of these 23 million some 19 million had had at least four years' schooling.

Is there some special difficulty about learning to read *in English*? It is claimed that in Spanish-speaking countries, whenever schooling is freely available, illiteracy is not found on the same scale as in the UK and in the USA, despite the effort put into schooling in these countries. We return to this question later.

Social relationship

Although speech comes first chronologically, society gives the written form priority. In school it is writing that counts most, especially in examinations. In the laws of our society it is writing that carries most weight. This 'social priority' arises partly because writing gives permanence to otherwise ephemeral words. But the written form of language is not simply a transcription of speech. It has a life of its own, distinct from spoken forms.

One example of this is the way in which spelling, instead of being a way of representing the sound of words, comes to affect pronunciation. This can be seen clearly in American English. Modern American English developed at a time when immigrants were flooding into the country and spreading across the West. They learned their language (and especially their pronunciation) largely from two sources: the early spelling primers of Noah Webster (read aloud in class) and the regular readings from the Bible by the preacher. These two kinds of experience tended to fix a 'visual' pronunciation of words met for the first time on the printed page. This influence of the written form on speech is one important way in which American pronunciation differs from British English.

Another difference between American and British pronunciation is that in British English the 'model' of pronunciation tends to be the 'accent of authority' (at one time the Court, the aristocracy, the 'county' or the great schools; more recently the BBC or prestigious individuals in popular entertainment). In America the model at a formative period of mass immigration was a more democratic one: the teacher or preacher reading from the Book, often working out the pronunciation of words by guesswork from their written form. One specific sign of this in American pronunciation is the tendency to give fuller value to unaccented syllables. (Other important aspects of the social relationship of writing to speech, which apply in America just as in Britain, are discussed when we consider varieties of language on p. 169.)

Logical relationship

Speech and writing are not simply representations of each other. The earliest examples of writing that have come down to us are not representations of things people *said* but rather lists of equipment for armies, inventories of supplies etc. What then is the logical relationship of writing to speech? To answer this we must turn to a consideration of English spelling. (Here, as in much of this section, we should acknowedge our gratitude to Michael Stubbs' book *Language and Literacy* (1980), an indispensable guide to this topic.)

THE SPELLING OF ENGLISH

There are two main kinds of writing system:

(i) *logographic*: in which symbols represent the *meanings* of words or parts of words (morphemes). Examples would be: the logo '£' which means 'pound sterling' and the logo '&' which means 'and'
(ii) *phonological*: in which *sound units* are represented by symbols

The phonological system itself can have two forms:

(a) *syllabic*: in which each written symbol represents a syllable
(b) *alphabetic*: in which each written symbol represents a phoneme

Stubbs (1980, p. 48) sets this out diagrammatically:

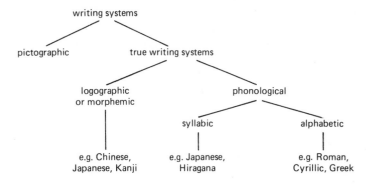

Clearly English spelling has most in common with a phonological system. There are very few logographic symbols in English, unlike, say, in Chinese. As Stubbs points out, however, it is important not to oversimplify the way in which sounds relate to symbols in the writing of English. English spelling does indicate pronunciation but in addition it gives lexical and syntactic information. An example quoted by Stubbs is '-ed' in final position ('he walked') which is a marker of the past tense and does not signal the *sound* of 'walkt'. This economises comprehension for the practised reader but does not help the beginner or the foreigner learning English. English spelling works very well for those who have a good knowledge of the spoken language. The language underlying English spelling is the adult language and the system is maintained by adults who have mastered the language, that is by educated adults with a good knowledge of the derivation of words, and the families to which they belong. This is reflected in the spelling. The educated reader knows the derivation of 'debt' from 'debitum'. He accepts the 'b' in 'doubt' equally readily, or the 'c' in 'science'. For him the differences in spelling of 'where', 'were', 'wear' and 'ware' (both meanings!) make for more rapid comprehension *once reading is mastered*. They also make the hurdle of initial literacy so much harder for the beginner who does not know the language well.

Stubbs quotes the estimate that it takes English-speaking children, on average, one or two years longer to learn to read than it takes speakers of the other European languages which use the Roman alphabet. He dismisses the superficial conclusion that this is entirely due´ (as Bernard Shaw thought) to an 'antiquated' or 'irregular' spelling system.

Nobody would be likely to deny that the system is irregular. There are at least nine spellings for the sound of the vowel [i:] (believe, receive, people, key, leave, machine, quay, be, see) and nine for the sound of the vowel [ɔ:] (jaw, floor, bore, caught, bought, broad, all, always, water). We use a dozen or more different spellings for the consonant [ʃ] (shoe, sugar, issue, mansion, mission, nation, suspicion, ocean, conscious, chaperone, schist, fuchsia – and Shaw's own 'pshaw'!). There is, however, more system than there might appear to be in some aspects of English spelling. Stubbs shows that Shaw's famous suggestions that a logical English spelling for 'fish' might be:

  ghoti

('*gh*' as in enou*gh*, '*o*' as in 'w*o*men', '*ti*' as in 'fic*ti*on') is based on a misunderstanding: '*gh*' cannot represent the sound 'f' in *initial* position in any word in English spelling. Similar limitations apply to the other letters of '*ghoti*'.

There are, in fact, a number of sub-systems operating in English spelling and the problem is that children do not get clear explanations of these systems. They may be taught that letters correspond to sounds, which is true only some of the time, or they may be taught that words have to be read as 'wholes', which is only partly true.

The most hopeful way forward, as we have argued earlier (p. 98), is by *individual* dialogue with a sympathetic adult to strengthen the slow reader's competence and awareness in the primary language activity of speaking/listening on which the secondary activity of reading must build.

SOME ASPECTS OF ENGLISH SPELLING TO EXPLORE

The notes on spelling in the Schools Council materials *Language in Use* (referred to on p. 50) suggest some helpful areas for teachers to explore which will both interest pupils afresh in a topic that has often caused them trouble and at the same time strengthen their grasp on the sub-systems underlying English spelling.

Language in Use recommends the classroom activity 'Shannon's Game' in which pupils challenge each other to guess, letter by letter, words that they have thought of. One feature of English spelling that emerges from the game is that the written form often makes clear distinctions that the spoken form does not make. An example of this is the spelling of common words which are sometimes used as surnames:

car	Carr
pen	Penn
boil	Boyle
smith	Smyth(e)
low	Lowe
hawk	Hawke
cook	Cooke
cross	Crosse

Another activity will usefully draw attention to the large number of 'homophones' in English: that is, words which sound alike but are distinguished by their spelling. Examples:

night	knight
where	wear, ware
there	their

main	mane
him	hymn
week	weak

The number of 'homographs' (words that are written alike but sound differently) is much smaller. One group is formed by words (usually of Romance origin) that serve as both verb and noun, in which the noun is commonly accented on the first syllable and the verb on the second:

a contract	to contract
an intern (in hospital)	to intern
the desert	to desert
his conduct	to conduct
a construct	to construct
a concert	to concert (measures)
the refuse bin	to refuse

This rule governing the change of stress seems to apply even to recent colloquialisms:

> Did you get an invite?   to invite

However there are numerous exceptions:

a bargain	to bargain
the control	to control
the forecast	to forecast

A different rule applies to words carrying dual stress:

the replay	to replay
a rewrite	to rewrite

In such words only the verb seems to carry the dual stress. A sometimes confusing example of a homograph is the word 'read':

> I read (when I have time)
> I read (when I was on holiday)

Similarly with 'lead':

> This lead is made of lead;
> this lead should give us a lead;

It may be worth noting that in French, when pairs of words are written (and often pronounced) alike, their grammatical gender often helps to differentiate them:

le livre	*la livre*
le tour	*la tour*

This illustrates one way in which grammatical gender aids comprehension. There are, of course, homophones in French:

le signe   le cygne

whose grammatical gender does *not* help to distinguish the meaning, but they are rare.

Another aspect is the effect of gender in 'labelling' the groups of words (article, adjective, noun) which form 'wholes' or noun phrases. Thus the 'agreements' that are such a bugbear to the English student doing a *dictée* may be most helpful to those who know the language in seizing the meaning quickly when it is heard or read. Spelling can help if you know the language! Discussion in class of these aspects of written and spoken language can lead naturally to the question of spelling reform.

SPELLING REFORM

It may be helpful to distinguish three kinds of reform that have been proposed for improving the spelling of English:

(i) use of diacritics
(ii) omission of 'useless' letters
(iii) invention of new letters to represent particular sounds

Diacritics

One of the earliest reformers to propose the use of diacritics was Richard Mulcaster, the teacher of Spenser and headmaster of the Merchant Taylors' School. His *Elementarie* (1582) was the most important treatise on spelling in the sixteenth century. Mulcaster was a very moderate reformer. He saw no chance of purely phonetic systems being accepted:

> But sure I take the thing to be to cumbersom and inconvenient . . . where no likelihood of anie profit at all doth appear in sight [every such attempt] hath alwaie mist, with losse of labor . . . (quoted in Baugh and Cable, 1978, p. 211)

He advocated one diacritic: the use of the sign '˘' to show the short 'a' in:

'babble' (which he would spell 'băble')
or
'dabble' ('dăble')

Another diacritic (proposed in 1634 by Charles Butler) which, like Mulcaster's suggestion, was not followed up, was the use of an accent '`' to show the pronunciation of the long 'a' in:

'hate ('hat`') as distinct from 'hat'
or
'mate' ('mat`') as distinct from 'mat'

The modern spelling of 'hate' and 'mate' is directly owed to Mulcaster whose suggestions for simplifying spellings had more success and we return to them in the next section.

Diacritics never commended themselves to English printers or schoolmasters (except perhaps for 'i' and the apostrophe). The other European languages which use the Roman alphabet make much more use of diacritics. An interesting class project might be to compile a wallposter showing the diacritics used in all the languages within the experience of the pupils, including the languages of members of the ethnic minorities.

A good example to study, perhaps, would be the use of the written accent in Spanish to show the tonic stress on the accented syllable. The rule in Spanish is:

(a) all words ending in a consonant (except 'n' or 's') are stressed on the last syllable, e.g., Madrid
(b) all words that end in a vowel (or 'n' or 's') are accented on the next to last syllable, e.g., Sevilla, Burgos.

Whenever this simple rule is broken a written accent shows the departure from the norm. Examples:

Málaga, Córdoba, Irún, Cádiz, Cordobés
or
(*yo*) *diré*
but:
(*nosotros*) *diremos* (no written accent on '*e*')

The teacher might then pose the questions: Would diacritics help us to read English? Would they help the foreigner struggling with English stresses?

Pupils might be asked to invent their own diacritic rules. They might first need to practise hearing where the stress falls (main stress only). They may then consider the problem facing the dictionary maker who has to show how English words are normally stressed. (By writing the stressed syllable in italics? By underlining the stressed syllable? By marking the stress with a diacritic as in Spanish?) Several dictionaries may be studied by pairs of pupils working together, and reports prepared on the solutions found by the compilers of the dictionaries. The merits of the different solutions can be discussed. It may be pointed out to pupils that in our most authoritative guide to pronunciation, the *Oxford English Dic-*

tionary, the accent is shown by a diacritic placed immediately *after* the stressed syllable, thus:

> transmigra'tion
> sympathet'ic
> imposs'ible
> arch'itecture

On the other hand the *English Pronouncing Dictionary* (Everyman) places the accent *before* the stressed syllable.

Pupils might perhaps be asked where they would put the accent on words that are often not pronounced as shown in the *OED*, such as:

> kilometre

shown in *OED* as:

> ki'lometre

in line with other words ending in '-metre' such as:

> cent'imetre
> mi'llimetre

but which is often wrongly equated with the group of words ending in '-meter' such as:

> gaso'meter
> milo'meter

and hence pronounced:

> kilo'metre

Other doubtful words such as 'controversy' may be explored and pupils asked to listen (to BBC news bulletins, for example) to check for discrepancies between the pronunciation shown in the dictionary and what they hear. Pupils might discuss what advantages and disadvantages they see in diacritics.

The history of the French circumflex accent may be told. This began when printers realised that many words traditionally spelled with 's', such as 'maistre' (from Latin 'magister'), were commonly pronounced without the 's' sound. They began to print the unspoken 's' above the line: mai^{s}tre, and later formalised it into a circumflex accent on the preceding 'i': 'maître'. (Compare ' ˆ ' on words such as 'école' with Spanish 'escuela', English 'school' etc.) While discussing the lack of diacritics in English spelling it may be useful to draw attention to the lack in English of letters found in languages like Danish, French and German such as: ø, å, œ, æ, ß which were not in the Roman alphabet.

Omission of 'useless' letters

Mulcaster was probably the most influential of the many advocates of simplified spellings. He printed at the end of his *Elementarie* a list of some 7,000 spellings for the commonest words in English. Most of his spellings were adopted. For example, he got rid of double consonants at the end of words like 'putt', 'grubb', 'ledd' 'and a thousand such ignorant superfluities'. To distinguish 'mat' from 'mate', he adopted the regular form of an added 'e'. Thus, in the same way, 'hat' became 'hate'. Some of his simplifications were not followed, however. For example, his spelling of 'guide' as 'gide', or 'guest' as 'gest' had no success. Mulcaster may have reflected closely the lines along which English spelling was tending. It seems that, by about 1650, 'our spelling in its modern form had been practically established' (Baugh and Cable, 1978, p. 213).

Simplification was taken much further in American English in the nineteenth century. Here the story is largely that of the success of Noah Webster's dictionary. Noah Webster (1758–1843) began as a lawyer, after education at Yale, but was forced to turn to teaching to earn a living. He had to write his own textbooks, and, between 1783 and 1785, published a spelling book, a grammar and a reader. The spelling book had great success and was republished as *The American Spelling Book*. In the next century more than 80 million copies were sold and even with a royalty of less than one cent a copy Webster lived on the sales for the rest of his life. The book had enormous influence. It led to his great work, *An American Dictionary of the English Language*, published in 1828. The successors to this book have grown into the authoritative dictionary which is for modern American English what the *OED* is for British English. Webster at first had no use for 'simplified' spellings (as Baugh and Cable, pp. 342–99, show in the discussion to which this section is indebted). It was Benjamin Franklin who converted him. Franklin had, in 1768, published *A Scheme for a New Alphabet and a Reformed Mode of Spelling*. Whereas Webster had, in 1783, scorned those who 'write the words favour, honour etc. without the "u"' and deplored the omission of the 'e' in 'judgement' as it is 'the most necessary letter in the word', Franklin's arguments had, by 1789, convinced him: 'I now believe with Dr Franklin that such a reformation is practicable and highly necessary.' So the changes were made:

music, logic *for* musick, logick
honor, favor *for* honour, favour
theater, meter *for* theatre, metre

check, mask *for* cheque, masque
woolen, traveling *for* woollen, travelling
defense, pretense *for* defence, pretence

He also proposed the spelling:

determin, examin *for* determine, examine

but this was not generally followed in America. Other changes suggested by Webster were also rejected as too radical:

bred *for* bread
karakter, korus *for* character, chorus

Invention of new alphabets

Suggestions for new letters are not new. One proposal made in 1634 by Charles Butler was for a new letter 'ɿ' (like a 't' upside down) to represent the sound 'th', as in 'both', and the voiced 'th' as in 'without'. More recently, reformers have proposed not simply new letters but whole new alphabets for improving what Coleridge, anxious about his own child's progress in reading, called 'our lying alphabet'. These proposals have had two main purposes:

(i) To help foreigners to learn English so enabling English to become the accepted international language
(ii) to help English-speaking pupils to learn to read

'Anglic', the invention of a distinguished Swedish philologist, R. E. Zachrisson, professor at Uppsala, is an example of a proposal of the first type. In 1930 he published his proposed alphabet, of which the following is an example (it will be seen that he retains about 40 of the commonest words in English in their traditional spelling, and that he uses the Roman alphabet throughout):

Lincoln'z Gettysburg Speech

Forskor and sevn yeerz agoe our faadherz braut forth on this kontinent a nue naeshon, konseevd in liberti, and dedikaeted to the prophozishon that aul men ar kreaeted eequel.

Now we are engaejd in a graet sivil wor, testing whedher that naeshon, or eni naeshon soe konseevd and so dedikaeted, kan long enduer. We are met on a graet batl-feeld of that wor. We hav kum to dedikaet a porshon of that feeld as a fienl resting-plaes for those who heer gaev their lievz that that naeshon miet liv. It is aultogedher fiting and proper that we shood do this.

But in a larjer sens, we kannot dedikaet – we kannot konsekraet – we kannot halo – this ground. The braev men, living and ded, who strugld heer, hav konsekraeted it far abuv our puur pour to ad or detrakt. The wurld will litl noet nor long remember what we sae heer . . .

Zachrisson inspired a number of others, including his fellow Swede Axel Wijk who also had an interest in English as an international language. He produced in 1959 his 'Regularized Inglish'. Here is an example:

> Traditionally wun ov the first taasks ov the infant scoole woz to teach children to read. It iz still, quite rightly, a major preoccupation, since reading iz a kee to much ov the lerning that will cum later and to the possibility ov independent studdy. In meny infant scooles, reading and writing ar treated az extensions ov spoken language. Thoze children hoo hav not had the opportunity at home to graasp the part that they play ar introduced to them by the everyday events and environment ov the claasroome.

Another move influenced by Zachrisson was the 'New Spelling' put forward in 1940 by the British Simplified Spelling Society. It was a 'systematic' alphabet using the Roman letters. It came close to receiving government approval. A spelling reform bill was narrowly defeated in Parliament in 1949 and a similar bill was actually passed in 1953 but was withdrawn in the face of opposition from the Ministry of Education (Baugh and Cable, 1978, p. 328).

ITA, the 'Initial Teaching Alphabet', is an example of the second type of proposal. This is probably the best known of the 'reformed' alphabets. It is estimated (Plowden Report) that in its heyday in the 1960s it was used in some 5% of primary classes in the UK and in some 10% in the USA. It is strictly an *initial* alphabet. Children transfer to traditional orthography (TO) after some three years of reading in ITA. Though researchers differ as to the efficacy of the alphabet, there seems to be a clear increase in the pupils' motivation and in their attitude to reading outside the classroom. In *Spoken and Written Language* activities introducing pupils to ITA are suggested. Here is an example of the alphabet:

> tradiſhonally wun ov ſhe first tasks ov ſhe infant scꝏl woſ tꝏ teeɕh ɕhildren tꝏ reed. it iſ still, kwiet rietly, a mæjor pre-occuepæſhon, sins reediŋ iſ a kee tꝏ muɕh ov ſhe lerniŋ ſhat will cum læter and tꝏ ſhe possibility ov independent study. in meny infant scꝏls, reediŋ and rietiŋ ar treeted aſ ekstenſhons ov spœken laŋgwæj. ſhœſ ɕhildren hꝏ hav not had ſhe opportuenity at ·hœm tꝏ grasp ſhe part ſhat ſhæ plæ ar introduest tꝏ ſhem bie ſhe everydæ events and envieronment ov ſhe classrꝏm. messæjeſ tꝏ gœ hœm, letterſ tꝏ sick ɕhildren, læbelſ tꝏ enſhuer ſhat mateerials and tꝏls ar returnd tꝏ ſhær proper plæs; aull caull for reediŋ and rietiŋ.

An even more 'systematic' alphabet is the phonetic transcription used by scholars to represent accurately the sounds of speech. The phonetic transcription now used worldwide by scholars is IPA (International Phonetic Alphabet) developed by the International Phonetic Teachers' Association. This was founded in 1886 by a group of distinguished phoneticians from several countries, including the Oxford scholar Henry Sweet. The latter was a great friend of George Bernard Shaw whose passion was spelling reform and who left his entire fortune in trust for this purpose. Shaw's character Professor Higgins in *Pygmalion* was based on Sweet, as he tells in the foreword.

Here is an example of IPA in Daniel Jones' 'simplified' transcription (it is possible for a phonetic transcription to be a 'broad' representation of the sounds of speech or to attempt an exact representation of every minute detail):

> trədiʃənəli wʌn əv ðə fəːst taːsks əv ði infənt skuːl woz tu tiːtʃ
> tʃildrən tu riːd. it iz stil, kwait raitli, ə meidʒe priokjupeiʃn, sins
> riːdiŋ iz ə kiː tu mʌtʃ əv ðə ləːniŋ ðət wil kʌm leitə ənd tu ðə
> posibiliti əv indipendənt stʌdi. in meni infənt skuːlz, riːdiŋ ənd
> raitiŋ aː triːtid əz ekstenʃnz əv spoukən laŋgwidʒ. ðouz tʃildrən
> huː həv not had ði opoːtʃuːniti ət houm tu graːsp ðe paːt ðət ðei
> plei aːr introudjuːst tu ðem bai ði evridei ivents ənd
> envaiərənmənt əv ðə klaːsruːm. mesidʒiz tu gou houm, letəz tu
> sik tʃildrən, leiblz tu enʃuə ðət mətiəriəlz ənd tuːlz aː ritəːnd tə
> ðeə propə pleis; oːl koːl fə riːdiŋ ənd raitiŋ.

Some teachers have suggested that pupils beginning the study of a foreign language should be taught a phonetic transcription from the outset. This would both enable them to write confidently from the start, and so record in their notebooks the words they meet, and at the same time establish the correct pronunciation at once, avoiding the 'interference' of the sound associations that the ordinary English alphabet carries for them. This is not the place to rehearse the arguments for this suggestion which were first cogently put by Sweet in his now classic book *The Practical Study of Languages* first published in 1899 and reissued in 1964 by Oxford University Press.

It may be valuable to discuss with pupils, however, the merits of a modified suggestion, namely that they should learn enough of the IPA symbols and the sounds that they represent to be able to discover from the dictionary exactly how new words sound in the foreign language. This may also be a way of helping pupils to make distinctions between sounds that are phonemic (i.e. effect the meaning of words) in French but not in English. Such an example is the difference between the three 'e' sounds:

1 [e] as in *é, et, ez, ai, ied, er, es.* E.g. [me] *mes*
2 [ɛ] as in *è, ê, elle, ette, ais, aît.* E.g. [mɛ] *mais*
3 [ə] as in *me, te, le, se.* E.g. [mə] *me*

The three different sounds can also be heard in a single word:

Hélène; élève
1 2 3   1 2 3

It is certainly difficult to see how a student of modern languages can progress very far without a basic grounding in phonetics. Discussion of dialect differences in English must surely also be of limited usefulness or precision if pupils have no knowledge at all of how sounds are produced or of how the different sounds can be accurately represented on paper. Teachers of English and of foreign languages might well agree on a common programme and decide together when would be the best time to introduce their pupils to an aspect of language study that concerns them both equally.

PUPILS' OWN PHONETIC ALPHABETS

Rather than teach pupils IPA some foreign language teachers favour a classroom activity which may be the most useful of all, namely encouraging pupils to work in pairs to construct their own simplified spelling system in which to transcribe the words they are learning in their foreign language. It was Otto Jespersen in his *How to Teach a Foreign Language* (1904) who first advocated the use of such simplified scripts. He estimated that it was possible to make an adequate phonetic alphabet for transcription of the main European languages by adding between five and eight new symbols to the conventional English alphabet. Class discussion and work in pairs on the foreign language sounds that call for symbols not offered by the English alphabet is an excellent way of focusing attention on the sound contrasts between the mother tongue and the foreign language. A simplified script allows pupils to write down everything they hear in their new language with confidence from the start. Transfer to traditional orthography takes place, as with ITA, when pupils are ready. A specimen simplified script, using as few new symbols as possible, in which English, French and Spanish can be transcribed, is suggested in *Modern Languages in the Curriculum* (Hawkins, 1981).

SHORTHAND AND WORD PROCESSING

Shorthand in its various forms also offers an interesting area to be explored and one that will appeal to pupils who have any interest in its applications in journalism, the radio and television or the office. If the subject is taught in school it may be possible to arrange for a demonstration followed by discussion. If not, an instructor may be invited in from a nearby college.

Another topic that teachers may wish to explore is the modern development of word processing machines with their own memory banks, correcting mechanisms, copying facilities etc. It should be possible for teachers to collaborate with their colleagues responsible for commercial courses in arranging useful demonstrations and discussion of this aspect of written language.

INFORMATION FROM THE SPEAKER'S VOICE

One aspect of the comparison of spoken and written language that pupils will enjoy exploring is the way in which the speaker's voice can give information that the written word cannot convey.

In *Spoken and Written Language* the signals given by the two forms of language are compared. It is suggested that the voice can give the following information:

> approximate age of speaker
> whether man or woman
> if foreigner and from what country (or region of UK)
> whether the speaker is in a good or a bad temper
> state of the speaker's health
> whether the speaker is interested or bored by the subject
> whether the speaker is shy, nervous or at ease
> (sometimes) whether the speaker is telling the truth

At another level, possibly with abler pupils, it may be possible to explore the way in which the grammar and the speaker's voice manage to make allowance for what the hearer already knows. This feature of dialogue, the 'thematic structure' of the give and take of information, seems to have three main functions:

(i) To distinguish between the statement of information that the speaker assumes the hearer already knows, and new information. This can be done either by the structure of the sentence or by the intonation and stress on certain words or parts of words.
(ii) To state a subject about which something is then said (subject/predicate).
(iii) To set up a 'frame' and 'insert' some information in the frame.

Let us give an example. In the sentence

> It was your UNCLE who stole the money

the new information is not that money was stolen (you knew that already) but that it was your uncle who did it. When spoken, the word UNCLE carries the *focal stress*; when written, the order of words shows what is 'old' and what is 'new' information.

A class exercise suggested in the topic book is to speak sentences of the type:

MARY said that HENRY'S PARTY was on FRIDAY EVENING

putting the focal stress on each item in turn and possibly adding phrases to explicate the meaning.

MARY (not Jane) said...
Mary said that HENRY'S (not Bill's) party...
Mary said that Henry's PARTY (not his birthday) was...

A further useful classroom activity, best engaged in by pairs of pupils working together, is to invent a new system of written punctuation which might enable more of the information that the voice conveys to be carried by the printed page.

COMPARISONS ACROSS LANGUAGES

In *Spoken and Written Language* it is suggested that pupils should explore different kinds of writing. Classroom activities are proposed involving Greek and Russian (Cyrillic). Easily recognisable words that are cognate with English are given, to be deciphered. Then, as a problem-solving game, the pupils are asked to work out from the evidence provided how to write, in Greek or Russian (Cyrillic), suitable English words chosen so as not to offer too much difficulty.

This activity, when combined with the suggested construction of phonetic alphabets for the transcription of the sounds of, say, French, Spanish or German, helps to focus pupils' attention on the precise differences between the sounds to which they are well accustomed in English (in the pupils' particular dialect of English, which may not be the teacher's dialect!) and those of the new language.

One point that emerges from the discussion is that although the spelling of English may not match the sound system consistently (as, say, Spanish spelling does) there may be advantages in the English spelling. The difference between 'principal' and 'principle' signals the meaning at once to the reader. The hearer must rely on the context to tell which is which. Another point is that the same spelling may represent a variety of different pronunciations. Consider the regional differences in the sound of the letter 'a':

northern [a] } as in bath, castle
southern [ɑ:] }

Pupils might be asked to consider whether our spelling should make a distinction between the northern and southern sounds. Or whether it would help if the American word 'tomato' were spelled differently from the British word, since the sound is quite different. Another point to make is the one noted in the sixteenth century by Mulcaster: pronunciations change. Should spellings constantly be altered to keep in step?

Perhaps the most important point for pupils to grasp, in discussing spelling, is that English spelling is a 'mixed' system. It does not simply transcribe the sounds of words. Spelling tells (for those who know the language) both the history of the word (its etymology) and the language family to which it belongs. The spelling also gives clues as to the grammar of the sentence. This greatly economises comprehension (again for the reader who knows the language). This may partly explain why reading, for practised readers, is so much faster than listening.

A glimpse of Chinese

Chinese writing is 'logographic'. This enables it to be read all over China, despite the fact that the dialects of Chinese differ from each other as much as, say, Dutch does from Swedish or English from German. Pupils may be asked to consider what the advantages might be if all the European countries enjoyed a common (perhaps logographic) form of writing.

In order to investigate this the best way is to learn a little Chinese and practise writing it. This is what *Spoken and Written Language* encourages pupils to do. In trials of the materials with 12-year-old pupils of quite moderate ability it has been found that they enjoy seeing how a totally different kind of writing works. They also enjoy the satisfaction of making the characters themselves.

A good way to begin is with the ubiquitous Chinese word: *hau*, meaning 'well' or 'good'. It occurs in the daily greeting: 'Ni hau?' ('Are you well?') and the reply: 'Wo hau. Ni hau ma?' ('I'm well. Are you?') It is also found in compounds such as: *haukan* ('good to see', or 'handsome'). Originally, in old Chinese writing, the idea of *hau* was shown by two drawings side by side. One represented a mother and the other her baby.

Old Chinese characters:

mother

child

The relationship of mother and child spelled 'goodness'. In modern Chinese the character is written like this:

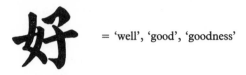 = 'well', 'good', 'goodness'

Similarly the character meaning 'not' (*bu*) is written as follows:

This drawing originally represented a seedling prevented from growing above the ground – a graphic way of saying 'no'!

Children are readily interested in exploring this totally different way of conveying meaning in writing. It is recommended that they are equipped with chisel-edged felt pens or with brushes. They should draw squares neatly in pencil before beginning to attempt to copy the characters set out in the topic book. It may be helpful to explain that Chinese children spend many years in school learning to draw the characters and that artists who can draw them really well, making their pages into works of art, are greatly honoured. Chinese children practise first standing up facing the teacher, making sweeping gestures with their arms to imitate the brush strokes of each character. When they are ready to write they must sit straight-backed, square to the table. Each stroke has its correct order which must be carefully followed. The first strokes to be drawn are those nearest to the top left-hand corner of the square, moving towards the bottom right-hand corner, the brush lightly lifting off the paper at the end of each stroke, giving the strokes their characteristic tapering effect.

DEAFNESS AND BLINDNESS

The discussion of speech and writing can lead naturally to a comparison between the ear and the eye as pathways by which information can reach the brain, while helping pupils to see how much of learning, and especially language learning, is a 'dialogue between the ears and the eyes'.

By comparison with some members of the animal kingdom the human ear and eye seem, in some ways, to be limited. Compared with the dog's, for instance, our ears are insensitive. The dog can hear sound waves at a frequency well above that which the human ear can detect. This can be shown by experiments with a high-frequency dog whistle. Pupils can also observe their own pets reacting to sounds before they themselves hear them.

The human eye, also, has limitations compared with, say, the eagle's, hence 'eagle-eyed'. The human eye, however, has great flexibility. It can focus over short and long distances. The eyes working together can measure the speed of an approaching object with such accuracy that, for instance, a cricket ball can be caught at exactly the moment it reaches the hands, or a tennis ball can be struck in the centre of the racquet. The sensitive and flexible human eye, able to turn in its socket without our turning our head, is well protected, moistened and lubricated by the tear ducts, equipped with a fine filter against dust.

How significant is it that the human eye is also equipped with a lid to shut out unwelcome sights, or to let us get to sleep more easily, whereas there is no 'ear-lid'? Do we learn, in self-defence, to 'shut off' our hearing inside the head? Do some of us have difficulty in learning when to switch on again? The most important point, perhaps, for pupils to understand here is that, as a result, we only hear what we expect to hear. Learning to listen, therefore, is largely learning what it is that we have to listen for. Setting up appropriate expectations may be the main function of the teacher. The 'learning' may then proceed under the powerful stimulus of curiosity and the 'will to learn'.

The discussion of learning by ear and by eye should lead to consideration of our own immense good fortune in possessing good sight and hearing. Our pupils will naturally empathise with those who are less fortunate, the deaf and the blind, but, more importantly, will have much to learn from them.

Sign language

In the topic book *Get the Message!* there is an account of the use of British Sign Language (BSL) and of American Sign Language (ASL) as used by the Gardners in their attempt to teach their chimp Washoe to communicate. It may be possible to develop this theme by inviting a user of sign language to demonstrate and answer questions in class.

The film *Mandy* may be hired for class showing. It cannot fail to appeal to pupils and will enrich the discussion of learning through the ears.

Braille

Braille is a code of 63 letters or characters composed of between one and six dots embossed on paper or card (see fig. 1). The dots are arranged in patterns based on six possible positions. The blind reader feels the raised dots with the tips of the fingers.

A	B	C	D	E	F	G	H	I	J

K	L	M	N	O	P	Q	R	S	T

U	V	X	Y	Z	and	for	of	the	with

W	Oblique stroke	Numeral sign	Poetry sign	Apostrophe sign	Hyphen	Dash

,	;	:	.	!	()	" ?	"

Figure 1

Braille is named after Louis Braille who was born on 4 January 1809 near Paris. The story of this gifted and courageous man will interest all children. (It is told on the cassette issued as part of the 'Awareness of Language' series. After hearing the story pupils are asked to answer questions, without benefit of visual prompts, as a blind pupil would have to do.)

When Braille was aged 3 he was cutting leather in his father's shop when the knife slipped and entered his eye. The eye became infected and the infection spread to the other eye, eventually rendering him totally blind. He then entered the National Institute for Blind Youth in Paris where he received his education. Having completed his studies in 1826 he stayed on as a tutor. When he began to teach at the

Institute he found only 14 books in the library with embossed type (the only kind of books the blind could read). This set Braille thinking. He was aware of an invention already used in the army, the work of a Captain Charles Barbier. This was a device for reading messages in battle at night. It used twelve raised dots arranged in a pattern. Braille simplified the system to six dots. For the first ten letters of the alphabet he used only four positions so as to keep the code as simple as possible.

Braille's last years were clouded by illness and he died on 6 January 1852 of tuberculosis. Despite the usefulness of Braille's invention it was accepted in his own Institute only two years after his death. Later, Braille was adapted for languages other than French. A universal Braille code for the English-speaking world was adopted in 1932. Special Braille codes exist for writing music, mathematics, shorthand, etc. Printing machines can now print whole books for blind readers. A recent invention (1982) has automated the process so that it can now be done twelve times more quickly than before.

In order to write in Braille a 'slate' is used. This consists of two metal plates hinged together. A sheet of paper is placed between the plates. The writer can then insert a pointer in one or more of six holes in the upper plate. Below each hole is a small pit in the lower plate which allows the pointer to emboss the dots on the reverse side of the paper. The writer writes from right to left, so that when turned over the message can be read in the normal way.

The Moon code

In 1845, before Braille's invention had been widely adopted, an Englishman, William Moon of Brighton, invented his own system of embossed writing for the blind. It uses many of the shapes of our Roman alphabet and so it can easily be learned by those who are blinded late in life and who find things harder to learn than when young. This is the Moon code for the blind (see fig. 2). It is still used, though it is much less widely known than Braille.

Stories of blind or deaf learners who have triumphed over their afflictions will always interest children, with their marked capacity for empathy with misfortune. The story of Helen Keller has many lessons for the language teacher. It is movingly told in her auto-biography (Keller, 1913). Especially interesting is the well-known passage where she describes the first time that she realised that things have names. It was the moment when, as the water from the fountain

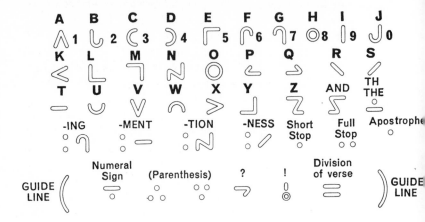

Figure 2: Grade 1 Moon

poured over one hand, her teacher traced out the signs for WATER on the palm of her other hand.

It may be possible to invite a blind reader of Braille into class to demonstrate reading aloud from a printed text and to answer pupils' questions. Copies of material printed in Braille and in Moon may be borrowed by schools from the Royal National Institute for the Blind, 224 Great Portland Street, London W1N 6AA (Moon Branch, Holmesdale Road, Reigate, Surrey).

FURTHER READING

1   The key text to refer to on the subject of spoken and written English and on English spelling is:
Michael Stubbs, *Language and Literacy* (Routledge and Kegan Paul, 1980)

2   Teachers who wish to read further in the history of the alphabet should consult:
I. J. Gelb, *A Study of Writing: A Discussion of the General Principles Governing the Use and Evolution of Writing* (Revised edn) (University of Chicago Press, 1963)

3   On the subject of the Initial Teaching Alphabet the recommended book for teachers is:
F. W. Warburton and V. Southgate, *ITA: An Independent Evaluation* (Murray and Chambers, 1969)

4   A most interesting collection of essays on learning via the ear and the eye is:
J. F. Kavanagh and I. G. Mattingley, *Language by Ear and Eye* (MIT Press, 1972)

5   An excellent source on the spelling of English, the effect of printing and of schoolmasters such as Mulcaster and dictionary makers such as Doctor Johnson is:
A. C. Baugh and T. Cable, *A History of the English Language* (3rd edn Routledge and Kegan Paul, 1978). This book is also an excellent guide to the history of English in America and to the differences between the American and British English in their attitude to 'authority' to which we have briefly alluded in the previous section.

6   On Chinese:
R. Newnham and Tan Lim-Tung, *About Chinese* (Penguin, 1971)

How Language
Works

The main themes introduced in this topic book are: why do we learn language(s)?; the sounds of our own and other languages; words as labels; joining words together; the nuts and bolts of language; doing things with words; gender and its effects; talking about the past and the future; word order and meaning; getting by in a foreign language.

This may be the most controversial part of the 'awareness of language' programme because it raises the difficult problem of grammar, which has become a bogey word. We have seen (p. 73) that Michael Halliday, introducing the Schools Council course *Language in Use*, deplored the fact that teachers of English had come to identify the study of language with teaching 'a rudimentary, inadequate . . . kind of grammatical knowledge'. He insisted that trying to heighten pupils' awareness of language was something quite different from an antiquated drilling in grammar. The approach adopted in *How Language Works* is to present grammar as an intriguing mystery to be explored rather than as a list of prescriptive rules and terminologies.

It is not a new approach. Eighty years ago, in his widely read book *How to Teach a Foreign Language* (1904), Otto Jespersen advocated what he called an 'Inventional Grammar', created by the student himself as he gained insight into the pattern of the grammar.

In this topic book pupils are invited to put themselves in the place of the baby learning how to 'do things with words', to echo the philosopher J. L. Austin. They are encouraged to use their ears, to observe, to trust to their own judgement and to draw their own conclusions from the evidence as they become more and more confident at seizing the 'pattern' in language.

It is known that insight into pattern underlies successful learning of a foreign language. It also underlies rapid and confident 'processing' of messages in the mother tongue. The significance of strengthening insight into pattern across the whole range of secondary school learning can scarcely be exaggerated.

The following notes concentrate on three aspects of the topic that teachers may wish to take further:

(i) how to arouse curiosity about 'grammar'
(ii) what to do about terminology
(iii) why bother about strengthening insight into pattern?

AROUSING CURIOSITY ABOUT PATTERNS ('STRUCTURE'? 'RULES'?) OF GRAMMAR

Teachers of language, both foreign languages and mother tongue, have allowed themselves to be manoeuvred into apologising for mentioning grammar, as a word to be ashamed of. It is not easy to reverse such an attitude. However language has its rules like the other social sciences. Our natural science colleagues do not apologise for teaching the structure of matter and the laws of physics, yet understanding the structure of language underlies much of the curriculum. We do not wish to oversimplify the problem but surely it is worthwhile taking some trouble to set up expectations in pupils' minds that grammar can be fun and interesting.

It may be helpful to describe a classroom activity that can initiate an exploratory approach to grammar. The teacher writes the following sentences on the board:

1 He put on his $\left\{ \begin{array}{l} \text{tweed} \\ \text{green} \end{array} \right\}$ jacket

2 She put on her $\left\{ \begin{array}{l} \text{red} \\ \text{nylon} \end{array} \right\}$ blouse

3 Boys wear a $\left\{ \begin{array}{l} \text{serge} \\ \text{grey} \end{array} \right\}$ blazer

4 Girls wear a $\left\{ \begin{array}{l} \text{blue} \\ \text{denim} \end{array} \right\}$ skirt

Pupils are asked to look at the words in the brackets and, since they are going to talk about them, to suggest what name they might call them, for convenience. In the discussion a number of names may be suggested, such as:

describing words/modifiers/adjectives/attributes/limiters

The merits of each word can be discussed. Why is 'adjective' less useful as a name than the other suggestions? Are the pupils sure what the word means? What does 'modifier' say about the category? Why might 'limiter' be a more exact description of the function than 'modifier'? Has each one been checked in a dictionary? Once pupils have agreed on a name the game can begin.

Pupils are asked to write out the four sentences, putting the two modifiers (as we may as well call them) in the order that feels the most natural when they say the sentences over silently to themselves. If pupils work in pairs, helping each other, the work is likely to be more successful. Pupils now report their results and discuss what they have observed. They will all agree that the words telling the *colour* come before the words telling the *kind of cloth* the garment is made of. So there is a pattern, or a 'rule' at work. Every pupil has followed the rule yet nobody had ever heard the rule before. Therefore we can follow rules of grammar without knowing that we know the rule. From this pupils can see that there are two ways of 'knowing' grammar – one conscious and the other subconscious.

But there is another problem about 'knowing' the rule. Pupils now know that words of colour come before words describing material but to observe this is not to *explain* it. Why should this happen? Why do we never say: her nylon red blouse? Perceptive pupils may at once point out that nylon is a noun acting as a modifier. This may suggest an explanation. Whereas 'red nylon' by itself makes sense (red nylon is a kind of nylon, like blue nylon or green nylon), 'nylon red' is not a kind of red. Yet 'rose red' is a kind of red though 'rose' like 'nylon', is a noun. Is the analogy exact? No, because the redness of roses is part of everyday experience. Then can the order of the modifiers in our sentences be explained by looking at the logical relationship that the ideas have with each other? In speaking the sentences we may (without knowing it) sense these logical relationships. But is it the *meaning* of the words that determines their order in the sentence?

To put this to the test, another, more complex game can be played. This time the following sentences are written on the board and the pupils are invited to take longer to work out, with their partners, their preferred order:

He put on his $\begin{Bmatrix} \text{tweed} \\ \text{green} \\ \text{trendy} \\ \text{new} \end{Bmatrix}$ jacket

She put on her $\begin{Bmatrix} \text{blue} \\ \text{cosy} \\ \text{nylon} \\ \text{old} \end{Bmatrix}$ blouse

Most pupils will produce the following results:

> He put on his trendy, new, green, tweed jacket
> She put on her cosy, old, blue, nylon blouse

There may be some debate in class about the order of 'trendy new' and 'cosy old', some pupils wishing to reverse the order of these two modifiers. But all will agree that the string cannot begin with either 'green', 'blue', 'tweed' or 'nylon'. Why should 'trendy', 'cosy', 'new' or 'old' be felt to be the logical first words in the string? Why not 'his green tweed, new, trendy jacket'?

An excellent plan, at this point, if pupils cannot agree on a specific preferred order, is to stage a little research project. Each pair of pupils will undertake to submit the sentences to three adult informants, including, say, one of their teachers of other subjects. The results can then be brought back and reports made in class.

Another way to play this is for the pupils to take to their adult informants the two sentences agreed in class and ask them to insert a further modifier in the place they feel is right:

> He put on his trendy, new, green, tweed jacket: insert: 'striped'
> She put on her cosy, old, blue, nylon blouse: insert: 'see-through'

The pairs of pupil researchers should ask their adult informers to say *why* they feel that the position they have chosen is the correct one. The reasons given should be reported accurately back to the class.

A further step in the game is for the teacher to write on the board:

> (a) He came in wearing his old smile
> (b) He came in wearing his old jacket

Pupils are asked to define the exact meaning of 'old' in each case.

> In (a) old means former (the smile he used to wear)
> In (b) old means old in time (not recently acquired)

So, does the 'company' old keeps determine its meaning? Or are there two different words having different meanings ('former' and 'more aged') which just happen to look and sound the same? But in that case how do we immediately recognise which one we are to understand? The same adult informants may be asked their answers to this. The report will probably be that they do not know why. They are operating a rule of which they were previously unaware and which they cannot formulate, and which linguists find equally baffling.

The lessons from this simple introductory game are:

(i) patterns in language are not hard to spot if two things are looked for:
   (a) meanings of words
   (b) the surface shape (order, spellings etc.)
(ii) Explanations of the patterns, however, are not at all easy and may baffle

linguists. There are two steps in grammatical explanation, or perhaps two levels or kinds of explanation:

(a) accurate description of the pattern (tells *what* is happening)
(b) finding a *reason* for the pattern (tells *why*)

Pupils will understand from their own experience that the explanation which simply describes the pattern is easier than the explanation which offers logical answers to the question: 'Why?' Another lesson to be learned from this is that we can all operate a great deal more grammar than we think we 'know' or than we can explain when asked.

The approach to grammar, then, in the 'Awareness of Language' series is exploratory, stressing that a great deal is not known by linguists and that finding out for ourselves is fun. It is this approach which determines our strategies regarding the thorny problem of grammatical terminology. It is also the approach, we believe, which will have the most directly helpful effect on the learning of the grammar of the foreign language.

Function words and content words

Having aroused pupils' curiosity about grammar it may be useful to explore the distinction between 'content' words (lexical items) and 'function' words (grammatical words and endings sometimes called 'formatives'). Some examples will make the difference plain:

> JOHN is OLDer than MARY
> MARY was as BRAINy as her SISTER
> the TEACHERS in our SCHOOL are the ones who TAKE the PUNISHMENT

It will be seen that the words in capitals carry meaning (content) while other words and endings serve to make a framework or structure into which the content words slot.

Bolinger divides the function items into two categories:

1 grammatical words:

	is (when purely linking)
prepositions	to, for, by
articles	the, my, our
quantifiers	many, few
conjunctions	and, also, yet
relatives	who, which
adverbial conjunction	because, when, while
intensifiers	too, quite
auxiliary verbs	can, may, do, be
pronouns	I, it, them

2 endings (inflexions):

plural	cat/cats
possessive	cat/cat's
verb present	earn/earns
verb past	earn/earned
participle present	earn/earning
participle past	fall/fallen
comparative	sweet/sweeter
superlative	sweet/sweetest

It will be seen that English has comparatively few inflexions. It is an 'analytic' language: that is, it shows changes of meaning by using separate words and word order. Latin, on the other hand, is 'synthetic': that is, meanings are shown by modifications to words, mainly changes of endings.

There are several observations to make about the 'function' and 'content' distinction:

(i) When English is spoken it is the content words that receive the tonic stress. This can be easily shown by saying aloud the well-known lines by Lewis Carroll:

> t'was BRILLIG and the SLYTHy toves
> did GYRe and GIMBle in the WABE
> or
> t'was SUMMER and the SILVER TROUT
> did DART and SLITHER all aBOUT

(ii) When we used to write telegrams it was the content words that we used and the function words that we omitted:

> (I shall) ARRIVE (at) KING'S CROSS
> (at) 3.15 (my) REGARDS (yours) DAVID

(iii) Babies acquiring English seem to learn the content words first, adding the function words later, by degrees and in a predictable order, though at varying speeds. (Do they respond partly to the fact that they hear the content words stressed?)

(iv) If we think of the speaker 'encoding' a message he seems to choose a succession of words to fit slots as the meaning to be expressed takes shape. Some of these slots are filled by words taken from a limited class which can be thought of as 'closed' or 'restricted'. These are the function words. Other slots have to be filled with 'open' class words. These are the content words. When the speaker comes to the slot to be filled by an open class word, with so many words to choose from, it naturally takes longer to review all the possibilities and select the exact one. Choosing the limited function words is more automatic. This is revealed by the slight pause often made just before the content word is spoken. (Note, too, the greater likelihood of the *reader* 'hearing' and imitating the *sound* of content words when he is 'silently' reading.)

(v) Statistically the function words are much more frequent in any text than the content words. The French scholar Pierre Guiraud (1954) has calculated that in the French language the 100 most frequently occurring words account for 60% of any text (mainly function words)

the 1,000 most frequently occurring words account for 85% of any text

the 4,000 most frequently occurring words account for 97.5% of any text

This might appear to mean that we only have to learn 100 words to understand two-thirds of any text. It is less easy than that, however. The fact is that the relatively infrequent content words carry most of the *meaning*. So merely recognising 60% of the words on a page does not mean that we can understand much of it if the few key content words are not known, though we can get some idea of the general sense as we saw with: t'was BRILLIG.

There is clearly a valid distinction between content words and function words. It is close to the difference between the dictionary and the grammar book, the two traditional tools of the linguist. However, caution is necessary. The distinction when pressed is seen to be rather arbitrary. Bolinger cites this example:

Did you see that man over there ('man': 'content' word)
What did he do?
He killed a man (de-accenting 'man'. The word 'man', Bolinger claims, is now merely filling an otherwise empty grammatical slot and is thus a function word)

In Bolinger's opinion statements about the distinction should be relative statements only.

'Duality' as a characteristic of human language

We referred (p. 104) to duality as one of Hockett's characteristics of human language and promised to come back to this idea.

Duality is the capacity of language to utilise a limited stock (some 44 in English) of low-level items, phonemes (the smallest discrete sounds that affect meaning), to make an almost infinite number of words and combinations of words. The phonemes 'b' and 'p' have no meaning by themselves but they affect the meaning of 'bat' and 'pat'. Phonemes combine to form 'morphemes' (the smallest items that carry discrete meaning). Morphemes can be 'bound' (that is, they only occur when tied to another morpheme, for example, '-ing' which never occurs by itself), or they can be 'free', for example, 'sing'. It is unnecessary to bother young pupils with the technical terms 'phoneme' and 'morpheme' but they should grasp the concept of duality as one of the key differences between human language and animal communication.

A simple beginning may be to play the game of making words (of more than three letters) out of a longer word. A word like SOUTH-AMPTON is written on the board and pupils have two minutes to write down as many words as possible from the letters of the word. The game can be made progressively harder by choosing a word with fewer vowels or consonants. The point can be made that duality makes for great economy and flexibility. A comparison might be made with the kits of construction items (such as 'Lego') that can be used and re-used to make a variety of models.

Cultural transmission

The concept of duality is linked with Hockett's other important characteristic: cultural transmission. Because the human language system is complex, with two levels of construction, it takes much longer to learn than animal systems. The human baby spends many months, perhaps eighteen, simply listening to language and respond-ing with all the senses, before beginning to put together morphemes to make sentences. The process would be complex enough without the additional complication that (in our society, not in all) the task of mastering the written form has to be faced as soon as the baby has achieved a limited grasp of the spoken form. Mastering the written form at increasingly complex levels makes language learning a necess-ary accompaniment to every other aspect of education. In some ways all the other fields of study can be thought of as 'linguistics' applied to particular kinds of questions.

GRAMMATICAL TERMINOLOGY

The simple principle to be followed throughout, we suggest, is to try to help pupils to conceptualise the *function* of each part of speech before seeking a *name* for it.

As far as possible pupils should be encouraged to invent their own preferred names, chosen because they best describe the function that has been clearly formulated. Pupils' suggestions for grammatical names are often surprisingly acute. It is in their attempts to invent suitable names that the real learning takes place. By discussing the *reasons* for the names proposed, the functions are clarified in pupils' minds.

Let us consider the key concepts 'subject' and 'object'. Teachers of Latin and of German have to teach the cases and establish the function of nominative and accusative. One of the objections to the old grammar grind was that inappropriate grammatical categories were imposed on the English language based on analogies drawn from Latin that were irrelevant to pupils' understanding of the grammar of English. An exploratory strategy might be as follows. Ask the pupils to consider the sentences:

> The master beats the servant
> The servant beats the master

Then ask the questions: What happens in each case? How do we know? After ascertaining that it is the order of the words which shows who did the beating and who was beaten, try and get pupils to suggest possible ways of referring to beater and beaten. Pupils might suggest:

> 1 the agent?
>   the doer?
>   the originator?
>   the one responsible?
> 2 the patient?
>   the done-to?
>   the victim?
>   the one affected?

When pupils have thoroughly explored the functions of the two slots in the sentence they may be told that some grammars use the terms 'subject' and 'object', terms which in themselves tell us little that is useful about the functions of the two parts of the sentence. Pupils may be asked to comment.

At this point it may be explained that in some languages, Latin and German being good examples, words which are in the 'doing' category are thought of as belonging to the set of 'doers' and that this is shown by a special ending on the word. This is also true of words that function in the 'done-to' slot. Explain that because the ending shows whether the word is a 'doer' or a 'done-to' word, the word order is less important. To show how this works the sentences above may be put into Latin:

> Dominus servum castigat
> Dominum servus castigat

Pupils can then be asked to identify the endings which show if the master is doing the beating and the servant being beaten or vice versa. It can be shown that in Latin the words can be put in almost any order. For example:

> Dominus servum castigat
> Servum dominus castigat
> Castigat dominus servum

On the model of the Latin, pupils may be asked to invent their own simple way of showing who or what is the 'doer' and who or what is the 'done-to'. They should try to be original in their ideas. When pupils are engaged in inventing their own markers or word endings to show which word is subject and which object the point may be made that English does have one way of showing whether a word is a 'doer' or a 'done-to' which is a bit like the Latin. Write the following sentences on the board and ask pupils to find out what is wrong with them:

> Him likes she
> Her likes he
> Me likes they
> Them like I

Pupils might discuss whether they usually say 'Whom did it?' or 'Who did it?' This may call for a longer discussion but at least we can see in 'who/whom' an echo of the way in which the change of ending and not the word order can decide the meaning. Compare in old-fashioned English: 'Who saw you?' and 'Whom saw you?'. Then try and decide on a name for words like 'he', 'him', 'she', 'her', 'who', 'whom'. Write a selection of words on the board and ask pupils to pick out those that are like 'he', 'him' etc. For example:

Paul	Mr Brown	they
she	football	that
him	us	often
Jane	whom?	you
who?	it	which?
we	yesterday	Sir

After agreeing on a word (such as pronoun) to describe these words, ask the pupils to try to write down a description of their function that would help a foreigner learning English. Pupils might then list all the pronouns they can think of and, working in pairs, arrange them in two sets: the 'doers' and the 'done-tos' or the subjects and the objects:

Subjects	Objects
I	me
(thou)	(thee)
you	you
he	him
she	her
we	us
who?	whom?

Note that some of these pronouns can be used to ask questions. You might ask pupils to find a word to describe these.

Point out that in Latin, and in German, these two sets of words are said to be in the 'nominative' and 'accusative' case respectively. Pupils might try and find out why. If they look in the dictionary they will find that 'nominative' 'names' the principal person or thing that the sentence talks about. As one old grammar book from the eighteenth century put it: 'The Nominative is that case without which there can be no regular and perfect sentence.' And the 'accusative'? This seems to mean nothing in English. The dictionary may help pupils discover that in Greek the word *aitiatike*, meaning 'the set or case into which words are put which are directly affected by the verb', was translated into Latin as *accusativus*. You might then discuss whether it is helpful or necessary to use 'nominative' or 'accusative' when talking about English grammar. Why not just say 'doer' and 'done-to' or 'subject' and 'object'?

The point may be made that in German there are not just two cases (nominative and accusative) but four (genitive and dative also) and that in Latin there are six cases:

1	Nominative	*dominus*	(the/a lord – subject)
2	Vocative	*domine*	(O lord!)
3	Accusative	*dominum*	(the/a lord – object)
4	Genitive	*domini*	(belonging to the/a lord)
5	Dative	*domino*	(to, for the/a lord)
6	Ablative	*domino*	(by, with, from the/a lord)

Point out that not all Latin nouns have endings like those of *dominus* and that it is traditional to group nouns into five sets or 'declensions' according to ending.

The four cases of German may be set out to be compared with the six Latin ones. It will be necessary to explain that, unlike Latin, but like English, German nouns take an *article*, which is marked by the case ending:

1	Nominative	*der Stuhl*
2	Accusative	*den Stuhl*
3	Genitive	*des Stuhls*
4	Dative	*dem Stuhl*

It will probably be agreed in class that though the resemblance of 'he'/'him', and 'who'/'whom' to the Latin and the German 'cases' is certainly interesting, English does not seem to have a 'case' grammar of the same kind and the use of nominative and accusative scarcely helps us to understand how English grammar works. For example, in

English, when someone knocks at the door and the person inside calls: 'Who's there?', the answer that most people would give is: 'It's me.' Now, it can be shown that in the Latin grammar the nominative case, not the accusative case, must follow the verb 'to be'. It will be seen that if Latin rules are applied to English peculiar answers will ensue. Another example of mistaken pedantry that might be pointed out is the use of the phrase 'For whom are you looking?' rather than 'Who are you looking for?' On the other hand German rightly uses the terms 'nominative' and 'accusative'.

Discussion of the problems of translation from English into another language may well be a useful kind of exercise, testing how firmly functions more complex than subject and object have been grasped. Many a student of foreign languages will attest the positive effect of such study on his grasp of the mother tongue.

As an interesting exercise, pupils might be asked into which cases they would put the following underlined words if they were translating them into Latin or German.

> *Paul* trapped *the ball*
> *He* kicked *it* into the net
> *The referee* signalled *a goal*
> *The linesman* raised *his flag*

This experience may be especially helpful when the grammatical going grows harder. The early mapping of subject and object to 'doer' and 'done-to' that we have been discussing is only a first step, and such a simple map soon has to be discarded. The underlying semantic structure does not always, in the adult grammar, match so simply the surface structure of the language. For example, in:

> John was bitten by the dog

John is clearly the grammatical subject but, far from being the 'doer', he is very much the 'done-to'!

The early grammar has to be reorganised and a much more complex matching of underlying meanings to surface structure has to be grasped. It is in this difficult part of the journey into awareness of the grammar that cross-language comparisons may be invaluable.

Languages of ethnic minorities

At a number of points *How Language Works* introduces pupils to the languages spoken by pupils from ethnic minorities. There are some 130 of these languages in British schools. Opportunities will be different for every teacher but they all should, of course, use every chance to widen the discussion by asking pupils to supply further examples of the grammar points from their own language; parents may also help here.

WHY BOTHER ABOUT INSIGHT INTO PATTERN IN GRAMMAR?

The reader may ask: why go to such lengths to try to help pupils to see the pattern in language and the function of the parts of the grammar before introducing them to terminology and before comparing the names of the parts of speech across different languages?

Our answer must be that there is a mass of research, too weighty to be disregarded, showing that insight into pattern lies at the root of successful foreign language learning and that it is also the key to efficient 'processing' of verbal messages in the mother tongue. Children's superficial use of vocabulary and syntax may mask wide differences in their understanding of language at a deeper level. These differences may be of two kinds: differences in the precision with which they have learned to match language to the concepts that they have categorised about the universe and differences in the degree of awareness they have acquired of their own use of language.

These differences are not easy to detect. We have no ready-made tests for the matching of language to concepts. Merely listening to children's talk and noting the surface features will tell us little about this matching. The differences between children are immediately revealed, however, when they face the two great language hurdles of the curriculum: learning to read in the infant school and learning a foreign language in the secondary school. The reader is referred to the earlier discussion (pp. 88 to 91) where evidence from three sources is reviewed:

(i) work on aptitude testing in foreign language classes
(ii) work on the effect of Short Term Memory constraints on language learning
(iii) work on cloze tests

The evidence seems to show beyond doubt that though it is by communicative use in real 'speech acts' that new language 'sticks' in the learner's mind, insight into pattern is an equal partner with communicative use in what language teachers now see as the dual process of language acquisition/learning. Grammar, approached as a voyage of discovery into the patterns of the language rather than the learning of prescriptive rules, is no longer a bogey word.

FURTHER READING

1 As general introduction:
S. P. Corder, *Introducing Applied Linguistics* (Penguin, 1973)
F. Palmer, *Grammar* (Penguin, 1971)

2 On the order of modifiers in the noun phrase:
See the chapter 'An Interlude' (p. 128) in *Linguistics* by David Crystal (Penguin, 1971). Professor Crystal discusses the order restrictions that seem to operate in phrases like: 'those large, new, red, English, wooden chairs' and examines possible explanations for exceptions to his rules.

3 For work on language courses in the curriculum in other countries see:
J. S. Falk, *Language and Linguistics: Bases for a Curriculum* (ERIC Clearing House. Center for Applied Linguistics, Arlington, Virginia. 1979)

4 On the role of insight into grammatical pattern in foreign language learning:
E. W. Hawkins, *Modern Languages in the Curriculum* (CUP, 1981)

5 For discussion of the grammar of West Indian Creole and ideas for teachers who wish to help West Indian pupils to cope with the standard English of the school curriculum:
V. K. Edwards, *The West Indian Language Issue in British Schools* (Routledge and Kegan Paul, 1979)
R. B. le Page, *Caribbean Connections* (Mary Glasgow Trust, 1982) available from CILT, London

6 Teachers who wish to read further on Short Term Memory are referred to the essay:
G. A. Miller, The Magical Number Seven – Plus or Minus Two: Some Limits on our Capacity for Processing Information. The Psychological Review 63, 2 1956

7 For a discussion of 'processing' messages and the role of the Short Term Memory:
J. W. Oller Jr, Cloze Tests of Second Language Proficiency and What they Measure (Proceedings of AILA Congress 1972, Copenhagen). In *Language Learning* 23, 1 (1973)
G. M. Olson, 'Developmental Changes in Memory and the Acquisition of Language', in T. E. Moore (ed.) *Cognitive Development and the Acquisition of Language* (Academic Press, 1973)

Using Language

This topic book is about the different ways in which we use language. The following themes are introduced: a day in the life of a language user; who are you speaking to?; who are you writing for?; what's it about?; 'good' and 'bad' language; playing with language and using the language tools.

The area covered by this topic book is probably one that will be familiar to many teachers of English. It is, at the same time, an aspect of language study whose importance will be readily accepted by teachers of many other subjects. Teachers of science, for example, have sometimes been most effective in showing their pupils how to write about their discipline succinctly and unambiguously. An example of such a teacher was the distinguished P. J. Hartog, a professor of chemistry whose book, *The Writing of English* (1906), was intended to help his undergraduate science students to write clearly and effectively and is still a model of its kind.

There are many possible approaches. One of the best-known sources is *Language in Use* (see p. 50). This offers a wealth of imaginative material which it is unnecessary to duplicate.

The classroom activities in *Using Language* are more selective in scope. They aim to help pupils, at the outset of the secondary course, to understand some basic aspects of language use as a preparation for the adventure into the use of language in the different secondary disciplines. The lessons to be grasped include:

the sheer variety of uses to which the 'articulate mammal' puts language
the need to be clear, if one is to 'do things with words' effectively, what meaning is intended and how the receiver of the message will take it
the importance of 'shared experience' between speaker and hearer, writer and reader as the base on which communication must build
the difference between 'good' and 'bad' in language
the verbal learning tools that have to be mastered and to be kept sharp, such as confidence in using the dictionary
the fact that although learning to 'do things with words' is a long job, it is well worth doing and can be fun on the way.

The topic book is self-explanatory. The following notes suggest possible supplementary areas that teachers may wish to explore *in addition to* the activities proposed in the topic book.

CHOICES TO MAKE WHEN USING LANGUAGE

We can distinguish two different kinds of choices that a speaker (writer) makes when using language. On the one hand there are choices in which the constraints are those of the grammar and the lexicon of the language. It is with these constraints that we were concerned in *How Language Works*.

It is not enough, however, that our language should be grammatically correct and that the words should mean what we intend. We also have to use language that is appropriate. Here a different set of constraints operates. We might say of the first kind of choices that the grammar has the last word. But what exactly determines our choice of what is *appropriate*? This is the theme of *Using Language*.

It may not be easy for pupils to grasp the difference between these two categories of language choice. A possible way to do this may be to take a realistic situation. Imagine that the school has booked a trip abroad; say the class is to pay a visit to its linked school in Spain. A week before the date agreed there is an outbreak of measles in the class and the trip has to be cancelled. The teacher in charge must quickly contact the linked school in Santander and warn them and try and rearrange the visit. He/she has a number of decisions or choices to make:

1 Should the teacher write (letter? telex?) or telephone?
2 Which language should be used? The teacher probably finds English easier but Spanish will be easier for the school secretary in Spain.
3 If English is chosen, and the decision made to telephone, should the teacher, who comes from Glasgow and has a strong accent, take care to speak very slowly and deliberately (i.e., to choose a particular way of speaking to suit the hearer)?
4 The teacher knows that the name of the Spanish teacher is Señorita Carmen Menéndez. Should she be addressed as 'Carmen'? (Under what circumstances would this be the right way to start?)
5 If Spanish is chosen, should the teacher use the '*tu*' form of address (as in English we use Christian names) or the formal '*Vd*'?
6 If the form '*Vd*' is chosen, the speaker is restricted to the verb forms that go with it, thus: '*Vd recuerda*', not '*Vd recuerdas*'. And since 'the visit' in Spanish is '*la visita*', the teacher must say '*nuestra visita*' not '*nuestro visita*'. (How much would it matter, however, if this slight error were made?)
7 The teacher must decide the date of the re-arranged visit. Here it is

essential that he uses the correct translation to avoid serious misunderstanding. (If the teacher thinks that the Spanish for eighteenth is '*diecisiete*' (which means seventeenth) it could be disastrous.)

8 At the end of the letter or conversation the teacher must choose the correct 'signing off' phrases: to end the letter or the phone call abruptly might give offence.

9 Since handwriting in a foreign language presents difficulties, the teacher may choose to use a typewriter.

10 When writing the letter the teacher must keep in mind what was said in previous correspondence and hence choose his words accordingly, as he must bear in mind previous conversations if telephoning.

If we look at the 10 choices made in the above situation we can see that they fall into two categories: choices *within* the syntax and meanings (semantics) of the language, and choices *outside* these. The speaker can scarcely alter the rules or the meanings of the language. Selection of the verb ending with '*Vd*', of the feminine adjective with '*visita*', of the correct word for 'eighteenth', of the acceptable pronunciation of these words are certainly all the result of decisions by the speaker but the *constraints on choice* come from within the language.

Typical of the choices of the second kind, however, would be: choice of the opening gambit ('Holá Carmen'), the choice of '*Vd*' not '*tu*', the decision to speak rather than write, the attempt to alter the Glaswegian accent, and when writing, use of a typewriter and attention to what the reader already knows.

A COMPARISON WITH CHOOSING OUR CLOTHES

It may further help pupils to see the difference between the two kinds of constraint on language use if we make a comparison with the way we choose our clothes.

When we choose what to wear on any given occasion we are constrained to a large extent by the limitations of our wardrobe. We can't use things we don't possess (words we don't know); nor can we very well wear, say, our shoes without obeying the 'rules' of shoe-wearing (the 'grammar') – if the laces aren't fastened the shoes will come off when we try to run! Our hat can't be worn as socks because of its shape and material. Our cotton shirt won't keep us dry in the rain. These limitations on our choice come from the nature, shape and material of the items of clothing themselves.

But we have other choices that are constrained by the conditions: Are we on holiday or on serious business? Are we going to climb a mountain or skate on the ice? Are spiked shoes allowed on the polished gymnasium floor?

Of course the analogy with language choices is not an exact one but it may help to make it clear that the 'intention' of the speaker plays an important part in determining exactly what is said, just as the wearer's 'intention' determines what is worn.

A lot of attention has recently been given by philosophers and linguists to the role of 'intention' in speech. The 'true speech act' is now seen as a combination of two elements: a 'proposition' (some meaning conveyed by the grammar) and the 'intention' of the speaker to achieve some result by his 'speech act'. It is now generally agreed that for linguists to leave out the 'intention', and merely to study the part of the speech act that can be analysed in grammatical terms, is not to study real language at all but to study an abstraction which only exists in the linguist's mind and not in the real world. This view connects with a long tradition in British linguistics of studying language in its context.

The teacher will not wish, of course, to trouble young pupils with this debate but he will wish them to grasp that in using language there is a constant interplay between two kinds of choices: those limited by the 'rules' of the grammar and the meaning of words, and those limited by the intentions of the speaker/writer and the situation or occasion when the words are used.

FUNCTION

Function in language has been approached in different ways by the linguist and the philosopher. Typical of the linguist's approach is that of M. A. K. Halliday. In *Learning How to Mean* (1975) he has described, from day-to-day observation of a child's acquisition of language, the functions that language serves in the child's life. He suggests that six functions are served by language for the very young child, all of which are 'extrinsic' to language. Each function has a small range of alternatives or 'meaning potential' associated with it:

1 Instrumental: enabling the child to satisfy basic needs ('I want')
2 Regulatory: controlling the behaviour of others ('Do as I tell you')
3 Interactional: enabling the child to interact with others ('Me and you')
4 Personal: expressing the child's uniqueness ('Here I come')
5 Heuristic: questioning about the environment ('Tell me')
6 Imaginative: creating an environment of his own ('Let's pretend')

To these functions the child later adds a seventh, highly sophisticated function, characteristic of adult language, the 'Informative'. It is intrinsic to language, that is, it can only be defined by reference to language itself. Moreover it can only develop after the child has grasped the principle of *dialogue*. Where this analysis links with that of the philosophers of language is that the motor that propels language acquisition, and moves the child to master these functions so early in its experience, is the drive to 'do things with words', as the philosopher Austin put it in the title of his seminal book (1962).

The theory of the 'speech act', propounded by Austin, was developed by his pupil, John Searle (1969). They argue that every time speakers utter a sentence they are trying to accomplish some intention. Examples might be:

(i) judge to prisoner: 'I hereby sentence you to six months in prison'
(ii) clergyman to couple: 'I pronounce you man and wife'
(iii) racegoer to bookie: 'I bet £2 on Moonraker for the 2.30'

The speech act can be thought of from two standpoints. Seen from the standpoint of the receiver it is a 'perlocutionary act' (for example, by arguing, the sender may convince someone of something – convincing him would be the perlocutionary effect of the speech act). Considered from the standpoint of the sender it is an 'illocutionary act'. Discussion has mostly centred on the latter. This, in Searle's terms, consists of two parts:

(i) the intention of the speaker (the 'force' of the illocutionary act)
(ii) the propositional content (the part that can be subjected to grammatical analysis).

Searle shows this as an equation:

$$F\ (p)\ =\ illocutionary\ act$$

where 'F' is the speaker's intention and 'p' the propositional content of what is said. To study sentences, as some linguists have done, without taking account of the 'intention' is, in Searle's view, to study non-language. The commonest kinds of illocutionary acts are assertions, questions and commands. There are, however, many more, expressed by verbs like 'sentence', 'pronounce', 'promise', 'appoint', 'bequeath', 'warn', 'announce', 'nominate', 'guarantee' and so on. Austin claimed that there were over 1,000 such 'performatives' in English.

An aspect of speech act theory that has attracted much attention, since Searle's work was published, is the 'indirect speech act'. To take an example, the 'force' of a command can most obviously be conveyed by a verb in the imperative. But there are indirect ways in which a command can be given without use of an imperative verb form. For instance:

Command	'Open the window.'
Indirect command	'Why is the window closed?'
	'That window should be open.'
	'I would like that window opened, please.'

The topic book includes some exploration of the 'indirect speech act' in ways which lend themselves to classroom discussion. For an invaluable introduction to this subject see G. M. Green (1975) and A. Davison (1975).

LEVEL OF FORMALITY

An important constraint on use of language and especially on the speaker/writer's choice of a possible indirect form of the intended speech act is the level of formality felt to be required by the occasion and by the relationship of the sender and the receiver of the message.

The range from intimate dialogue to most solemn, even frozen, exchanges is very wide but the steps from one to the other are not easy to plot. Linguists have suggested that it is possible to distinguish as many as five different levels or degrees of formality/informality. It is, however, by no means easy to decide exactly where the line between the different levels should be drawn.

The linguist's five levels of formality are, after Joos (1967) and Bolinger and Sears (1981)):

1 oratorical (frozen)	the professional speaker (something of an art form)	both usually monologue	both aimed at an audience
2 deliberative (formal)	less polished than 1		
3 consultative	words chosen with care the register of business discussions	typically dialogue	
4 casual	absence of social barriers	typically between fellow students	
5 intimate	not only absence of barriers but some special closeness	typically between family or close friends	

In practice teachers may prefer to suggest that pupils distinguish three levels only:

1 formal or oratorical
2 deliberative or consultative
3 intimate or casual

The clearest way in which the different levels appear may be in forms of address. A useful classroom activity may be to ask pupils to collect forms of address which they have actually met. These can be pooled and, in class discussion, allotted to one or other of the three levels, for example:

1 Mr Chairman
  My Lords
2 Dear Sir
  Good morning
3 Morning, dear!
  Hey Andy!

Levels of formality are not only marked by the words used. They are also shown by the tone of voice, by gesture, by elisions and by the way in which particular words are pronounced. For example, some speakers from the north of England who normally pronounce the 'a' in 'bath' as [a] seem to lengthen the sound slightly to approximate to southern pronunciation when they feel that they are in a more formal situation. Similarly initial 'h' sounds are omitted in intimate contexts but sounded at more formal levels. For example: 'is 'e?' for 'is he?'

It will be obvious that the discussion of function and levels of formality in connection with this topic book overlaps with some aspects of language which are treated in the topic book *Language Varieties and Change*. A somewhat arbitrary distinction had to be made. We discuss such features as 'register', 'dialect' and 'slang' in the next section, as part of our discussion of language varieties.

WHAT DOES THE HEARER/READER ALREADY KNOW?

All of these aspects of languages are linked. The speaker/writer's expectation of what the hearer/reader already knows and expects underlies much else in language use.

In the topic book we approach this by asking pupils to try to imagine how they would explain to a blind listener the effect that the different colours make on a sighted person, and to describe the effect of hearing different melodies to someone who has been deaf since birth.

Of all the constraints on effective use of language possibly the most important one for pupils (and still more for teachers!) to grasp, is: how (sometimes incorrect) notions of the hearer/reader's expectations shape what people say or write.

FURTHER READING

1   The pioneering contribution in this area is undoubtedly:
P. Doughty, G. Thornton and J. Pearce under the chairmanship of M. A. K. Halliday, *Language in Use*, Schools Council Programme in Linguistics and English Teaching. (Edward Arnold, 1971)
The teachers' book explaining the new approach of *Language in Use* is:
P. Doughty, J. Pearce and G. Thornton, *Exploring Language* (Edward Arnold, 1972). The bibliography is practical and helpful.

2   On language in society:
M. A. K. Halliday, Language in Social Perspective. *Education Review* 23, 3, 1971
M. A. K. Halliday, The Functional Basis of Language in B. Bernstein (ed.) *Class, Codes and Control*, Vol. 2 (Routledge and Kegan Paul, 1973)

3   A most useful book for pupils produced by Mike Raleigh and based on work by a working party at the English Centre of the Inner London Education Authority is:
The Languages Book (ILEA English Centre, 1981)
Also recommended is: T. Penman and A. Wolff, *Web of Language*. (OUP, 1981)

Language Varieties and Change

This topic book seeks to set pupils thinking about the following themes: how English, as a member of the vast Indo-European language 'family', fits into the world language map, which contains over 4,000 languages; the other mother tongues that go to make up the rich language map within the UK; the relationship of British English, with its comparatively few speakers, to the other varieties of English spoken as first or second language by hundreds of millions in countries such as America, Australia and Africa; how the forms of English spoken in a particular district (or by a particular social group) fit into the dialect map of the UK; the effect of borrowings between languages on the language that we use; the ways in which languages change over a period of time.

A principal aim of the topic book is to promote awareness and understanding of the way others use language and thus to combat prejudice which is often based on misunderstanding and suspicion of the unknown. Though the topic book will obviously be useful in multi-lingual schools and in schools where the pupils speak a 'non-standard' dialect, the materials and activities are also designed for use in schools where there is less linguistic diversity. Here the examples of language and dialect variety provided on the cassette accompanying the series should prove useful. At the same time it is hoped that the topic book will help to prepare pupils who are beginning to learn a foreign language in school to accept more open-mindedly the changes (in speech habits and in cultural expectations) that are involved when one 'goes to meet' a foreign speech community.

The notes which follow offer some background information and further teaching ideas to help teachers to exploit the materials in the topic book.

CLASSROOM PROJECTS

The subject lends itself to practical activities and projects, many of which, as so often in language work, are best tackled by pairs of pupils helping each other. The following suggestions may be found useful (some of them are worked out in greater detail in the topic book):

(a) Pupils are given an outline map of the world on which they show the main language families and approximate numbers of speakers, using a colour code (the relevant data are supplied later in this section).

(b) As (a) but the exercise is limited to a map of the British Isles.

(c) Both (a) and (b) can be followed up by inviting a small team of pupils to make a colourful wall display of the information, after discussing alternative ways of setting it out.

(d) Pupils choose a concept shared across all languages, for example:
the numbers 1 to 20
school
mother
water
food

Groups of pupils are asked to make inquiries and report back with the written symbols representing these cross-cultural concepts. A multilingual chart is then prepared for display in class.

(e) A colour-coded chart is prepared showing the origin of a selected number of words which English has borrowed from other languages (see suggested list in *Language Varieties and Change* and fuller list later in this section).

(f) A language census is carried out by teams of pupils to discover how many different mother tongues are represented in the school population. A chart is drawn to show location of countries of origin. A 'cross-cultural' chart is prepared of shared concepts and written names as in (d) above.

(g) Following the language census, notices are prepared for school corridors, dining room, library etc. in the different mother tongues giving useful information or instructions ('Keep to the left'). In this project the parents of pupils from ethnic minorities can be brought in as linguistic informants.

(h) Members of ethnic minorities are asked to bring to school examples, written in their mother tongue, of:
proverbs
short sayings from wise men
short poems
nursery rhymes
jokes
riddles

These are transcribed attractively for wall display with translations into English (parents should be involved as closely as possible).

(i) Pupils from ethnic minorities are encouraged to bring from home examples of the picture books with captions that young children are given when they begin to read. Pupils from ethnic minorities and English-speaking pupils pair up to translate the captions in the picture books into English for use as classroom wall displays.

(j) Pupils from ethnic minorities bring into class examples of:
local community newspapers
cinema advertisements and programmes

advertisements for goods

Again in pairs, pupils work out appropriate translations.

(k) Pupils working in teams try to list the commonest boys' and girls' names in all the languages represented in the school or studied in the foreign language lessons.

(l) Writing systems are compared; for instance, examples of languages in which the writing goes from left to right are displayed for comparison with writing systems that go from right to left or vertically; diacritics used in the different languages are illustrated.

(m) An illustrated project on writing through the ages is done by a group of pupils. Examples of early writing materials are drawn. The following data may be useful.

Early writing materials:

clay and wax tablets; papyrus; scrolls; parchment; the stylus; the brush; the quill pen

sixth century BC –

the earliest known instance of a quill pen being used (early ink was made from carbon black, soot, lamp oil and gelatine)

a bronze pen was found in the ruins of Pompeii

Modern writing instruments:

1564 the world's first commercial graphite mine near Borrowdale, Cumbria, opened: the purest deposit of graphite for pencils ever discovered

1780 first steel points (nibs) made in Birmingham

1884 Waterman, New York, made the first fountain pen

1888 John H. Loud, an American, patented the first ball-point pen

1944 Lazlo Biro, a Hungarian living in Argentina, patented a ball-point and gave his name to this writing instrument

More recently – fibre-tip pens.

(n) It may be possible to attempt a study (using recordings made by pupils themselves) of the main phonological features of the dialect of their own region. Some comparison may be attempted with the 'standard' dialect used, for example in radio and television news broadcasts. Members of the teaching staff or visitors to the school from various dialect backgrounds may decide to record an agreed passage in their home dialect for detailed study by the class. A form 'library' on cassette may be assembled of the regional dialects of English. (A selection of dialects can be heard on the cassette which accompanies this series.)

LANGUAGES OF THE WORLD

The 22 most widely spoken languages, with approximate numbers of mother tongue speakers, are:

1 (Chinese) Peking Dialect (Mandarin): 515 million

2 English: 300 million (plus hundreds of millions of non-native speakers)

3 Spanish (Spain and America): 225 million (including the Ladino spoken in Turkey and Israel)

4 Hindi: 180 million
5 Russian: 150 million (plus some 42 million who speak it fluently as second language)
6 Bengali: 125 million
7 Arabic: 120 million (plus many millions who have some knowledge of it)
8 Portuguese: 103 million (including 3 million Galicians)
9 Japanese: 100 million
10 German: 100 million
11 Bantu: 100 million (more than one hundred Bantu languages)
12 French: 75 million (including Creoles; plus many more familiar with it)
13 Italian: 60 million
14 (Chinese) Cantonese: 55 million
15 Korean: 51 million
16 (Chinese) Min dialect: 50 million
17 (Chinese) Wu dialect: 50 million
18 Javanese (Indonesia): 45 million
19 Telegu: 45 million
20 Tamil (India and Sri Lanka): 45 million
21 Urdu: 35 million (plus some 45 million who speak it as second language)
22 Ukrainian: 35 million

(after Kenneth Katzner, *The Languages of the World*. Routledge and Kegan Paul, 1977).

The first 10 languages listed above account for two-thirds of the population of the world.

LANGUAGE 'FAMILIES'

There are estimated to be over 4,000 languages in the world. Fewer than half of them possess a written form. They can be classified into several hundred language 'families', that is, languages whose origins can be traced to a common ancestor. The most important 'families' or related groups are:

(a) **The Indo-European languages**
Branches
Indo-Iranian or Aryan (classical Sanskrit, Bengali, Hindi etc., also Persian, Kurdish)
Greek and the ancient Hellenic dialects
Italic (Latin and its Romance descendants: Italian, Spanish, French, Catalan, Portuguese, Romanian, Provençal etc.)
Celtic (Gaulish, Cornish, Breton, Gaelic, Welsh)
Baltic (Lithuanian, Lettish)
Slavonic (Serbo-Croatian, Bulgarian, Czech, Polish, Russian)
North Germanic (Icelandic, Norwegian, Danish, Swedish, Faroese)
East Germanic (Gothic, Vandal, Burgundian)
West Germanic (German, Dutch, Frisian, English)
Minor Branches
Albanian, Armenian, Anatolian

Over one thousand million people speak an Indo-European language as mother tongue. These include: over 300 million who speak a Germanic language; over 250 million who speak an Indian language; and over 200 million who speak a Slavonic language.

All the languages of this enormous family, it is thought, are descended from a common, prehistoric language which linguists call Proto-Indo-European, spoken by peoples living on the plains of central or eastern Europe. About 2500 BC, after a number of different dialects had begun to form, the speakers began to expand and disperse to the south-east, the south, the north and the west.

(b) **Semitic** (named from Noah's son Shem) includes Arabic, Ethopian, Hebrew

(c) **Hamitic** (named from Noah's son Ham–related to Semitic) includes ancient Egyptian, Coptic, Somali, Berber

(d) **Ural–Altaic** Finnish, Hungarian, Estonian, Lappish, Turkish, Mongol, Manchu

(e) **Sino-'Tibetan**
includes Thai, Burmese, Tibetan, Chinese

(f) **Japanese, Korean**

(g) **Dravidian**
includes Tamil, Telegu

(h) **Malayan–Polynesian**

(i) **Bantu**
includes Swahili, Zulu

(j) **Sudanese–Guinean**
includes Nubian, Hausa

LANGUAGES IN THE UK

Where English came from

The Roman legions withdrew from Britain in AD 410. When the Saxons, Angles and Jutes invaded England in 449 the long process of establishing English as the main language of the British Isles began. Anglo-Saxon domination of England was not complete until about 700. Wales remained a stronghold of the 'British' who spoke a Celtic language established before the Romans came. The Celtic language persisted in its three forms (Cornish, Welsh and Gaelic) where the mountains sheltered the inhabitants from invasion. The language that became established in England, now referred to as Old English, was originally one of a number of Low German dialects of northern Germany. Its nearest cousin is Frisian, then spoken along the North Sea from northern Holland to central Denmark but now confined to a few coastal regions of Holland. At first England was divided into a number of kingdoms in which men spoke different dialects. The language that became standard was West Saxon: the language of King Alfred, the West Saxon king who led the unification of the country in the ninth century. It was also the language in which *Beowulf* was written.

Old English possessed many features found in modern German, such as the three grammatical genders, (masculine, feminine and neuter) and a system of four cases (nominative, accusative, genitive and dative). Nouns belonged to four declensions. Old English also had the German liking for making compounds: literature was 'book-skill'; arithmetic was 'numberskill' and astronomy was 'starskill'.

The substratum language, Celtic, had little influence on Old English. Only the occasional names were taken over: London, Leeds, Kent, Devon, the Avon (Celtic for 'water'), the Ouse (stream), the Thames (dark river), the Trent (a river liable to flood), down (upland). Celtic had little prestige with the invaders. The Old English word 'wealh', originally 'foreigner', came to mean both 'Welshman' and 'slave'! Most place names that have come to us from Old English were not Celtic but Anglo-Saxon in origin, for example, the endings -ton (enclosure), -ham (homestead), -hamm (meadow), -ley (glade or wood), -worth (enclosure), -field (open country), -ing (the people of). Thus Buckingham means the meadow of Bucca's people; Chorley means the wood of the churls; Brighton means the homestead of Beorhthelm.

Two further invasions were to change Old English into the language we now speak. These were the Viking (Norwegian and Danish) incursions which began in 800 and the Norman conquest dating from 1066. (The 'Normands' were of course themselves the descendants of Norsemen who had earlier established themselves in Normandy.) The language of the Viking invaders, Old Norse, was very similar to Old English: Englishmen and Danes probably understood one another much of the time. Many words of Scandinavian origin came into English. Common Scandinavian endings for place names are: -by (village), -thorp (outlying farmstead), -toft (plot of land), -thwaite (woodland clearing). The many borrowings from Scandinavian include: 'egg', 'kirk' – a Scandinavian pronunciation of an originally Greek word, 'husband' (from 'husbondi', literally 'house-dweller'), 'to take', 'law', 'by-law', 'window', 'bag', 'cake', 'wrong', 'low', 'fellow', 'sky', 'skull', 'skin', 'skiff', 'anger', 'ill', and pronouns: 'they', 'them', 'their'. A feature of such borrowings is that they are mostly commonly used words: the 'popular language'.

The effect of the Norman conquest was still more profound. It meant that for some two hundred years English ceased to be the language of the governing class. Perhaps more important, it ceased to be *written* and it was not taught in schools.

The Norman conquest completed the disruption started by the Vikings of the Anglo-Saxon tradition in literature, scholarship and art. Latin and French became the prestige languages for two hundred years, during which time English survived by oral tradition outside the Court, the schools and the manor houses. Latin was almost exclusively the language of the Church and an international lingua franca. French was used for administration in Britain. This was the situation until the late 14th century. The reign of Henry V (1413–22) marks the turning point in the recovery of English as a written language.

Why did English (though much altered) win the struggle and replace French? One reason was that the variety of French spoken by the invaders, the Norman dialect, steadily lost prestige in France itself as Paris gained political ascendancy over the rest of the country. Under the influence of English the Norman dialect developed into a form of French that aroused ridicule on the continent. French speakers in England began to apologise for their dialect. Another reason was the rise of a powerful middle class and the increasing importance of craftsmen and merchants. At the same time the catastrophe of the Black Death, beginning in 1348, wiped out 30% of the poorest of the population who could not take evasive measures. The result was to increase the economic importance of the labouring class. Merchants, craftsmen and labourers spoke English, not French. Already by the end of the twelfth century the children of the aristocracy were being taught French as a foreign language. Special measures were being taken to 'revive' French. Textbooks for the teaching of French began to appear. In the fourteenth century English was generally adopted. In 1362 the Statute of Pleading enacted that all lawsuits should be conducted in English. By 1385 the practice of using English for teaching in schools had become general.

The 'Middle English' that emerged was much altered from the Old English of *Beowulf*. Two hundred years of oral transmission had enabled rapid grammatical changes to develop, which schooling and written transmission might possibly have delayed. The three grammatical genders disappeared. (In Old English these were chiefly indicated by concord of adjectives and of the demonstrative, especially in the singular.) Nearly all trace of the four cases disappeared with the gender. Of the declension endings only the two plurals -es and -en remained.

By making English the language mainly of uneducated people, the Norman conquest made it easier for grammatical changes to go forward unchecked. (Baugh and Cable, 1978, p.167)

The effect of these changes in making English more accessible to foreign learners and so becoming the world vehicle language was to be incalculable.

The vocabulary of Middle English was also immensely enriched by borrowings from Norman French and from Latin. It is usual to distinguish two kinds of borrowing from Norman French: those that entered English before 1250 (some nine hundred) and those (many more) borrowed later.

In the first category were words learned by the English-speaking lower classes from contact with their masters, such as: baron, noble, dame, servant. A great number of ecclesiastical words were also borrowed in this period. After 1250 the borrowings were mainly of words carried over into English by the upper classes, accustomed to speaking French, and now, perforce, speaking English and using the French words to eke out their English vocabulary. The borrowings can be grouped under headings such as: government words (govern, crown, parliament, tax, treasury); ecclesiastical words (sermon, religion, sacrament, miracle); legal terms (justice, assize, advocate, jury, trespass); army and navy words (army, battle, soldier); fashion, meals etc. (apparel, chemise, garter, 'kerchief, jewel); words from art and learning (sculpture, poetry, study, logic, apothecary, plague). In addition many French words were given English endings and then made into compounds with English suffixes: for example, *gentille* became 'gentle' (gentlewoman, gentleman, gentleness, gently); or *foi* became 'faith' (faithless, faithful, faithfulness). Sometimes a French word was borrowed more than once: for example, *gentille* became 'genteel' in the sixteenth century and 'jaunty' in the seventeenth century. Often the English word and a French borrowing continued to exist side by side:

English	*French*
to deem	to judge
love	affection
hearty	cordial
smell, stink, stench	aroma, perfume, fragrance

and there were the well-known examples of 'master's language' and 'servants' language' (see p. 80).

English thus became a compound of two broad lexical traditions, the Anglo-Saxon words being on the whole shorter and simpler than the Latinate words and being associated with everyday, homely experience. They are the 'bread and butter' words, learned earliest by children, and, for that reason if for no other, carrying strong emotive connotations (mother, father, brother, sister, house, milk, water). Also, of course, the demotic vocabulary (swear words, words of sexual connotation) tends to be Anglo-Saxon except in 'formal' contexts (for example in the doctor's surgery) where Latinate words are substituted.

Modern English

Modern English is a rich mongrel language, yet, despite its rich lexical mix, it remains structurally a Germanic language. Britain is, like the USA in Kennedy's phrase, 'a nation of immigrants'. Seafaring and a world-wide trading empire have brought foreign borrowings into English from over 50 languages. It would be a useful class exercise to ask pupils, working in pairs, to track down the countries of origin of the following words:

1 garage; chauffeur; fuselage; rouge; suede; promenade; boutique; cafe; moustache; menu (France)
2 balcony; design; granite; violin; pizza; spaghetti; volcano; stanza; studio; fiasco; influenza (Italy)
3 alligator; cannibal; canoe (via West Indies); siesta; corral; cedilla; cocoa; embargo; hammock; sombrero; canyon; hurricane; mosquito; potato; tobacco (Spain and Portugal)
4 pyjama; bungalow; dungarees; shampoo; thug; rajah; juggernaut; cot; loot; tom-tom (India)
5 budgerigar; boomerang; kangaroo; wallaby, koala (Australia)
6 schooner; deck; dock; freighter; dollar; gin; easel; landscape; yacht; skipper (Holland)
7 paraffin; quartz; blitz; dachshund; kindergarten; yodel; poodle (Germany)
8 tomato (Mexico)
9 bamboo (Malaya)
10 coffee (Turkey)
11 sauna (Finland)
12 vodka; sputnik (Russia)
13 goulash (Hungary)
14 geyser (Iceland)
15 maize (West Indies)
16 ski (Norway)
17 judo; kimono (Japan)
18 apartheid (South Africa)
19 tea (China)

20 sidewalk; elevator; cookie; movie; fall (USA)
21 algebra (via Italian); giraffe (Arabic)
22 rabbi (Hebrew)
23 anorak (Eskimo)
24 bog; brogue; bard; glen; whiskey; slogan (Gaelic)
25 blarney; shamrock; colleen (specifically from Irish Gaelic)
26 clan; sporran; loch (specifically from Scottish Gaelic)

Another useful 'dictionary investigation' is to discover the origins of scientific words

- from Latin roots: bacillus, focus, genus, saliva, vitamin
- from Greek roots: mono, graph, hydro; and prefixes such as micro-, phono-, thermo-
- of mixed Latin and Greek origin: haemoglobin, television

or technical words based on names of individuals:

ohm, to pasteurise, a 'bobby', mackintosh, cardigan, derrick (name of a seventeenth century hangman!), a diesel, sandwich (the fourteenth Earl unwilling to leave the gambling table – even to eat!), to boycott, raglan, wellingtons

or proprietary names:

thermos, primus

Similarly pupils may be challenged to put a date on the invention of words that were not in use when their parents were born, such as: microchip, hovercraft, word-processor, blue jeans, miniskirt, wedge-heels, sweatshirt, flyover, babysitter.

Modern English can be said to have begun to emerge in the fifteenth century as the East Midlands dialect (one of the many local dialects of Middle English) won general recognition. London was the chief centre of the 'East Midlands', the most populous and prosperous region of England. The speech of London was a compromise between the extremes of the dialects of the north and south of the country. East Midlands dialect was also the language of official documents emanating from the capital. The two great universities gave the dialect further prestige. Finally, it gained ground because it was the dialect in which Chaucer wrote. So 'London standard' gradually became accepted in most parts of the country. From 1476 printing introduced by Caxton made London the centre of book publishing and Caxton used the current London speech.

By 1640 over 20,000 printed titles had appeared. Books, previously an expensive luxury, suddenly became accessible. This was a powerful force for producing a standardised dialect (and a standardised spelling, see pp. 121 to 127). In Shakespeare's London probably one-third of the population could read. In the seventeenth and eighteenth centuries education spread considerably and there was a growing reading public to encourage the expansion of journalism (consider the great output of Defoe) and the growth of the novel. Printing, while slowing down structural changes and serving to 'standardise' the language, greatly speeded up the acceptance of new lexical importations and new creations.

Minority languages in the UK

It is a modern-day paradox that while Britain is becoming, year by year, a more multi-lingual community, the English language itself spreads ever wider across the globe as the world vehicle language, especially in the fields of higher education and technology and in specialist areas such as air traffic control, satellite communications and computer technology.

The minority languages spoken in the UK and in Ireland can be divided into two categories:

(i) the mother tongues older than English which are still spoken in Wales, Scotland and the Republic of Ireland
(ii) the newer mother tongues introduced by the incomers from Europe and from the former British colonial territories in Africa and the East

The numbers of speakers of the older mother tongues are estimated (Katzner, 1977) to be:

> Welsh: 600,000 (approximately 25% of the population of Wales)
> Scottish Gaelic: 75,000 (approximately 1.5% of the population of Scotland)
> Irish Gaelic: 500,000 (approximately 16.5% of the population of the Republic)

The newer minority languages have been introduced as a result of various factors:

> political upheaval: for example, the Polish speakers who settled in the UK after the Second World War, or the Vietnamese 'boat people'.
> the immigration of citizens of the former British Empire: for example, those from India and Pakistan, or those who were victims of persecution in a former British colony such as the Ugandan Asians who held British passports.
> immigration by groups with enterprise and special skills: for example, Chinese restaurant workers or hotel staffs from Europe.
> a deliberate policy of recruiting workers needed in a particular industry: for example, the Italian brick workers brought into the Bedfordshire area.

Speakers of these minority languages are mainly concentrated in the big urban areas. The best-documented city is London. Here the Inner London Education Authority's surveys have shown that the 12 commonest minority languages are:

Bengali
Turkish
Greek
Spanish
Punjabi
Italian
Urdu
Chinese (mainly Cantonese)
French
Arabic
Portuguese

These languages represent some 80% of the bilingual pupils in the ILEA area. Each is spoken by more than 1,000 pupils.

The proportions of pupils in the different language groups have recently altered. A few years ago Greek was the most widely spoken language. It has now been overtaken by Bengali. A recent census shows that more than 5,000 pupils in ILEA schools speak Bengali, an increase of perhaps 50% in a few years. Just two years ago Bengali pupils formed the majority in some 9 schools. Now there are 18 schools with a Bengali majority. From 1978 to 1981 bilingualism increased significantly in London: in primary schools from 12.6% to 16.1%; in secondary schools from 6.2% to 11.5%. The total number of languages spoken by pupils in all London schools is now estimated to be 131.

This picture of growing bilingualism is repeated in many cities. Leicester, for example, has a range of languages including Latvian, Ukrainian, Polish, Chinese, Punjabi, Gujerati, Bengali and Italian. Nor is the phenomenon confined to metropolitan areas. In Bexley, Kent, there are no fewer than 17 languages and dialects.

An increasing number of studies have taken place in recent years from which two points have emerged on which there is a growing consensus:

(i) the reservoir of bilingualism in our population is a potential resource of great richness, *if it can be developed*

(ii) a bilingual child's mother tongue is a most important channel for learning which should be exploited wherever possible

The DES document, 'The School Curriculum' (1981) commented:

> Far more pupils than in the past have a first language that is not English or Welsh. This constitutes a valuable resource, for them

and for the nation. How should mother-tongue teaching for them be accommodated within modern language provision so that this resource does not wither away and the pupils may retain contacts with their own communities?

The EEC Directive on the Education of Migrant Workers (1977), which the Secretary of State declares it his intention of applying in the UK, regardless of the country of origin of the children, states:

> Member states shall, in accordance with their natural circumstances and legal systems, and in co-operation with States of origin, take appropriate measures to promote, in co-ordination with normal education, teaching of the mother tongue and the culture of the country of origin (Article 3).

The immense difficulties of doing this, in the face of such a variety of languages, some represented by quite small numbers, will be obvious. The shortages of trained teachers and of suitable teaching materials, the conflicting demands for time on overcrowded time-tables, the overriding need to acquire competence in English (the vehicle of higher education) – all are daunting challenges as much to the pupils concerned and their parents as to the hard-pressed administrators and teachers in the schools.

There are no easy solutions. But it can be claimed at least that a first step, within the capacity of every school with ethnic minority children on roll, is to build into the curriculum a language element which brings together the diverse language experience of the pupils while offering to the different kinds of language teacher (English mother tongue, ESL, foreign language) a shared responsibility.

It is here that the 'awareness of language' programme can make a small contribution to the language education both of the ethnic minorities and of their classmates with English as a mother tongue.

VARIETIES WITHIN A LANGUAGE

Discussion of varieties of language must raise questions of definition. What exactly is a 'dialect'? What is meant by 'register'? How does 'slang' differ from 'jargon'? What is a speaker's 'repertoire'?

Teachers will be the best judges of how far it is helpful to tackle such definitions with their pupils. Whether or not they think their classes are ready for such discussion, they may themselves welcome some clarification of the issues.

Dialect

A dialect is a variety of speech used in a particular geographical area and/or by a particular social group. But could that not also be a definition of a language? A distinction commonly made in the attempt to clear this up, is that different languages are mutually *unintelligible*, whereas different dialects (of one language) are mutually intelligible, to a large degree, across the dialect boundaries.

This may work as a rule of thumb distinction but it is not satisfactory because no way has been found of drawing a sharp line between closely similar 'languages', which must have some degree of mutual intelligibility, and 'dialects' whose mutual intelligibility is greater but still limited. In China the different 'dialects', such as Peking or Cantonese, are as mutually unintelligible as, say, Dutch and Swedish but, unlike Dutch and Swedish, they share a common written form which can be read all over China. In Europe there might be no agreement about the exact status of, say, Dutch and Frisian, or French and Provençal. Are they dialects of one language or separate languages?

Linguists confess that there is no clear answer to give. When linguists wish to discuss what they clearly accept as varieties of a common language they prefer to use the term 'standard' to describe the variety used in schools and the media, or taught to foreigners in language schools, and 'non-standard' to describe forms which differ from the standard form to some degree in vocabulary, grammar or pronunciation.

Slang

Slang is defined as language of a highly colloquial kind, considered to be below the level of standard educated speech and consisting either of new words or of current words used in some special sense. It is a special vocabulary coined within a particular group or set, for example, soldiers' slang, schoolboys' slang or prison slang, which feels itself to be free of the restraints that limit use of the 'standard' form. If we relate slang to the levels of formality discussed earlier (p. 157) slang will only be used at the 'casual/intimate' level.

At the level of slang innovation in language is most rapid. Slang is correspondingly ephemeral, however, and dates more quickly than the 'standard' forms. (It may be less ephemeral in an enclosed, static world such as prison.) The ephemeral aspect of slang makes its acquisition a minefield for the foreigner coming into the language, who may find that, say within the short time that a language course at university lasts, the student slang expressions acquired in the year of study abroad may have dropped out of use as an entirely new generation of students replaces its predecessors.

Jargon or code

A jargon or code is the special vocabulary (and very occasionally syntax forms) used within a profession, for example, the language used by actors or lawyers. It is not, unlike slang, felt to be 'low' or free from the restraints of the 'standard' or the schoolmaster in some way. Jargon will be used at quite formal levels. It expresses technical meanings that are part of the experience of the profession concerned and can only be understood by those who share that experience.

Register

A register is a variety of language that is not typically identified with any speech community but is tied to a communicative occasion or context. The speaker/writer is affected by the situation but is also attentive to the audience and adopts a register to suit both.

What kinds of factors affect choice of register? The following may be the most important:

> the speaker/writer's knowledge of the hearer/reader's intentions, state of mind, age, education, nationality, knowledge of the language
> the speaker's constraints (in a hurry? on the telephone?)
> the context (urgency: is someone ill? is there a fire?)
> the number of people listening/reading

There is clearly a close connection between choice of register and the levels of 'formality' discussed earlier (pp. 157 to 159).

Repertoire (or repertory)

A speaker's repertoire (or repertory) is the set of linguistic varieties he has at his command, each of which enables him to play a defined role within the speech community and in different contexts.

All speakers must master a repertoire of varieties of their language, and the human language learner seems to be innately programmed to do this effortlessly. It has been observed that some pupils (for example, those of West Indian origin in city schools) have to master varieties of English (of the home, of the peer group, of the class-room) which differ very widely indeed. Some observers have claimed that the differences between the home variety (Creole) and the school variety (standard) are differences not between varieties (dialects) of one language but rather differences between discrete languages. (See earlier discussion, p. 173.)

Whether we accept this or not, the repertoire of such pupils covers a very wide spectrum and the resulting misunderstandings, on the part of both pupils and teachers, and the uncertainties and loss of confidence that follow, deserve the closest and most sensitive study. Teachers know that to discuss someone's language is as sensitive a matter as to discuss his or her appearance. On the other hand teachers will be able to help such pupils best if they are aware of what is involved in 'switching' between parts of the repertoire. There is nothing unusual about it. All speakers are adept at it to some degree, though not all pupils have to make such abrupt and marked switches as, say, the West Indian pupil or any other pupil who learns at home a variety of English that is markedly different from the 'standard'.

The point that teachers will wish to stress, and the point made in the 'Awareness of Language' topic books, is that the switch is between varieties of language which have their rightful and proper place in the repertoire, because they each serve good purposes, not between a 'good' and a 'bad' variety of the language.

FURTHER READING

1   Strongly recommended for the staff room library as a source of reference both on British and American English:
A. C. Baugh and T. Cable, *A History of the English Language* (3rd revised edn) (Routledge and Kegan Paul, 1978)

2   On dialects:
M. F. Wakelin, *English Dialects: An Introduction* (University of London Press, 1972)

3   On word formation in English:
V. Adams, *An Introduction to Modern English Word-Formation* (Longman, 1973)
L. Bauer, *English Word-Formation* (CUP, 1983)

4   On place names:
K. Cameron, *English Place Names* (Batsford, 1978)

5   On names:
E. H. Partridge, *Name into Word: Proper Names that have Become Common Property. A Discursive Dictionary* (Secker and Warburg, 1949)
N. Addison, *Understanding English Surnames* (Batsford, 1978)

6   On words that have changed their meaning:
S. I. Tucker, *English Examined: Two Centuries of Comment on the Mother Tongue* (CUP, 1961)
S. I. Tucker, *Protean Shape: A Study in Eighteenth Century Vocabulary and Usage* (Athlone Press, 1967)

7   On where our language came from:
K. Cripwell, *Man and Language* (Harrap, 1979)
S. Potter, *Our Language* (Revised edn) (Penguin, 1966)
C. L. Barber, *The Story of Language* (Pan Books, 1964)

8   On the world map of languages:
K. Katzner, *The Languages of the World* (Routledge and Kegan Paul, 1977)
Mario Pei, *The World's Chief Languages* (3rd edn) (George Allen and Unwin, 1954)

9   On the European languages:
B. Brown, *Outlook Europe: People and Languages* (Macdonald, 1979)
T. Jordan, *The European Culture Area* (Harper and Row, 1973)
P. Freeman, *Europe Today and Tomorrow* (Longman, 1977) (on the role of languages in European politics)
C. Jenkins, *Language Links: The European Family of Languages* (Harrap, 1980)

10   On multi-lingual Britain:
H. Rosen and T. Burgess, *Languages and Dialects in London School Children: An Investigation* (Ward Lock Educational, 1980)
A. Little and R. Willey, *Multi-ethnic Education, The Way Forward* (Schools Council, 1981)

11   On the older mother tongues of Britain:
C. V. James (ed.), *The Older Mother-Tongues of the United Kingdom* (CILT, 1978)
A comprehensive account of language in the United Kingdom will be the forthcoming *Language in the British Isles* to be published in 1984 by CUP and edited by Peter Trudgill.
On the language of West Indian pupils see the references to works by V. K. Edwards and R. B. le Page on p. 151. See also: M. Raleigh, *Making Use of Language Diversity* (ILEA English Centre, 1981)

How do we Learn Languages?

This topic book explores two main aspects of language learning: the acquisition of language by the baby and the very different process by which second or foreign languages are learnt in the classroom. One aim, in arousing curiosity about language acquisition by the baby, is to provide a basis on which later discussion can build in 'preparation for parenthood' courses for school leavers.

It is also hoped that the study of the 'universals' of language acquisition across different language families will be something to which all pupils in multi-racial classes can contribute. In such discussion all can start level and contribute their experience, or that brought in from home. In this way diversity of language background becomes a positive enrichment, not a problem.

The topic book is particularly intended to help pupils who are just starting or about to start learning a foreign or second language in school. They may be English speakers learning, say, French, or instead, as in some schools, choosing to learn the language of one of the ethnic minority groups. Some of the members of the class may be speakers of minority languages who are learning English as a second language.

One of the problems that these groups will share is the need to unlearn ingrained speech habits in their mother tongue and to master new ones. This will call for a 're-education of the ear' in which they can help each other. The work in the topic book links directly with the programme of 'learning to listen' set out in Appendix A to this book (pp. 186 to 210). The topic book activities require no explanation. In the following notes some background matters are discussed which may help teachers to develop particular aspects of the topic. These are:

> How does mother tongue acquisition differ from learning L2 in school?
> What is the role of the LAD (Language Acquisition Device) hypothesised by Chomsky and how does it relate to the Language Acquisition System (LAS) suggested by Bruner as being possibly more important?

What do learning to *read* the mother tongue and learning L2 have in common?
What does recent research suggest regarding:
 (i) the role of insight into pattern in L2 learning?
(ii) the effect of 'real speech acts' in economising L2 learning?
How important is 'awareness of language' in the preparation of young parents?

MOTHER TONGUE AND FOREIGN LANGUAGE LEARNING

The differences between acquiring the mother tongue and learning a foreign language under school conditions are broadly of two kinds: circumstantial and psychological.

The circumstantial differences are huge. Just consider the time available. By the time they embark on their foreign language, secondary school pupils will have spent 11 years in full-time practice in order to achieve their modest command of the mother tongue, and still may have far to go. They cannot expect to be granted another 11 years of full-time immersion in French, Spanish or German to repeat the experience.

In fact they will be given four or five lessons per week, each effectively of some 30 minutes' actual learning time at most. Each pupil will share the teacher's attention with 30 other pupils, instead of being, like the baby, one learner surrounded by many language informants in the home and family circle. If the teacher's voice is heard only for half of each lesson, each individual pupil can hope that his or her voice will be heard for, at most, 30 seconds each lesson or two and a half minutes each week. Compare this with the estimate of Nelson Brooks (1960) that the average 5-year-old speaks some 10,000 to 15,000 words per day in the mother tongue. Consider further the fact that in between the foreign language lessons the 'gale of English' blows relentlessly.

The psychological differences are equally striking. Learning the mother tongue in infancy is largely learning to 'categorise' the universe: not simply learning the names for things, but learning how to manipulate the conceptual universe via the grammar. The 3- or 4-year-old learning how to talk about parts of the body or items of clothing is learning at the same time that these items exist and what they are like. Learning to interpret the clock face is also learning that time is divided in the way our culture has chosen (arbitrarily) to divide it. The discovery is exciting and intrinsically rewarding; it is also extrinsically rewarded by smiles and response from the environment. Contrast this with the pupil answering the routine question in the French lesson, as the teacher holds up the wooden clock face: 'Quelle heure est-il?' Here there is no discovery. Telling the time is 'old hat'. The pupil merely substitutes a new number code for the well-practised mother tongue numbers. Where is the motivation?

THE LAD OBJECTION

Discussion of the processes of L1 acquisition and L2 learning may sometimes not have been helped by uncritical application of the notion of an innate Language Acquisition Device. This is a hypothesis proposed by some linguists to account for the way in which babies acquire their mother tongue.

The theory assumes that babies are born with an inherited 'grammar searching device', that is, a ready-programmed expectation regarding the (limited) range of language 'universals' (regularities common to all languages) that they are going to meet, regardless of the particular language community in which they happen to find themselves. It supposes that the environment provides samples of a particular language (sometimes more than one), and that, from this evidence, however degenerate the samples may be, the LAD effortlessly infers the 'rules' to be internalised. Observation of babies acquiring language certainly seems to support much of this hypothesis.

Some commentators, however, have gone further, and argued that *because* the LAD is innate, the role of the linguistic informants met by the child is not important. Since all children bring to the task their LAD (except for children with physical or mental handicap) it is supposed that all can learn language with equal success, given only minimal data from the environment.

Psychologists who have observed children do not accept this. Jerome Bruner, formerly professor of psychology at Oxford and Harvard Universities, has stressed that more than the LAD is needed. Children also need what he has called an 'LAS', a 'Language Assistance System': 'It matters terribly to the child that somebody is attending to what he is attending to' (Bruner, 1979).

This view is supported by a great deal of evidence. Nobody who has read, for example, the sensitive account by Gina Armstrong (1975) of the home-visiting project in the South Yorkshire colliery village of Denaby, near Conisbrough, could fail to share the project team's conviction that

the socialisation and learning processes of a child begin as soon as he is born, and begin in the home. If the home environment is not conducive to certain forms of early learning then some ground will have been lost before the child is three, and the pre-school programme which begins at this point will already be on a remedial or 'compensatory' basis. (p. 136)

Specifically regarding language development, Armstrong found, from her weekly visits to the families in the Denaby study, that

the deciding factor seemed to be whether or not the child received undivided attention from an interested adult every day ... Children who were looked after by grandparents, who were regularly talked to and played with, were as verbal as children who were looked after by their mothers all day. (p. 152)

The report on Armstrong's home-visiting project adds the comment:

Most parents are aware of the importance of their children's early physical development, the need for care of teeth, hair and skin, adequate diet and injections against sickness and disease. The importance of feeding the child's imagination, helping him to move gradually towards independence in learning, to an increasing interest in thoughts and ideas, and a sense of achievement, is less well understood. (p. 164)

There need not be any conflict between accepting an LAD hypothesis and giving proper weight to the linguistic environment. The process of language acquisition does indeed show some similarities with 'maturational' processes such as beginning to walk on two legs. This process can be seen developing, like an alarm-clock timed to go off, from the baby's early flexing of the leg muscles in the womb, through exercise of the thighs in crawling and pulling upright in the play-pen, to walking, without need of teaching. So it is possible to observe similar 'programmed' sequences in language acquisition. Nevertheless the evidence also shows how vital is dialogue with a sympathetic adult.

The uncritical acceptance of the LAD hypothesis may have confused discussion of language learning by tending to distract attention from the vital role of the parent as language model, informant and often teacher.

LEARNING TO READ AND LEARNING A FOREIGN LANGUAGE

However much linguists and psychologists may disagree among themselves about the degree to which acquisition of speech is innately programmed and how far it is dependent on the environment, there is no evidence that children are equipped from birth with any innate expectation of meeting the *written* language or of having to learn a foreign language under school conditions. It is when these two linguistic hurdles in the 'vertical curriculum' are met that the need for *teaching* becomes clear, and that the *role of the parent determines success or failure, whatever the school may do*. Neither learning to read nor learning a foreign language in class are primary language activities, in the way that hearing and speaking are primary. Children do not differ greatly in their performance of the primary activities but this superficial similarity can mask more subtle differences in the way that children 'map' the language they use on to their conceptual universe. There are no easy tests of such mapping. It is not apparent, without very sensitive listening over a long period, how precisely children are conceptualising or with what discrimination they are distinguishing, through the language they have acquired, concepts that are related but subtly different.

This hidden dimension in language acquisition, which has been largely ignored in all the debates about children's learning in school, only begins to be apparent when they attempt the secondary activities of reading and writing. Learning to read is thus 'parasitic' upon 'awareness', that is, insight into the structure of the primary activity. In its turn, learning the foreign language under school conditions is also parasitic upon the learned skills of reading and writing and of matching sounds to symbols, with the added complication that long-practised speech habits, and well-worn listening expectations, must be unlearned.

LEARNING A FOREIGN LANGUAGE IN SCHOOL – APPLYING THE LESSONS OF RESEARCH

We have already discussed in some detail (pp. 88 to 97) the process of learning a foreign language in school. Effective learning, we saw, calls for a dual strategy:

(i) development of the pupil's insight into pattern in language
(ii) getting the pupil to transact real 'speech acts' in the foreign language

It is time to review briefly some of the implications for the classroom of this dual strategy (see Hawkins, 1981 for a further development of these ideas).

Development of insight into pattern

This has been a thread running through much of the argument of this book and it is a theme that is developed in the topic book *Using*

Language. The following are some ways in which the foreign language teacher can help pupils to develop confidence in spotting pattern:

(a) Frequently present pairs of phrases in the foreign language asking pupils to say whether they are of exactly the same pattern or not, and if not where they differ.

(b) Include in all language tests from the earliest stage such pattern-spotting challenges, using, as far as possible, familiar language items in new combinations.

(c) Regularly ask pupils to write the grammatical pattern or regularity or 'rule' that the class has recently discovered and discussed in their own words. This forms a good homework task. The aim is to encourage pupils to express the pattern clearly and succinctly or in an original formulation. The class may well be asked to decide, after discussion, which formulation of the 'rule' is preferable, and give reasons.

(d) Encourage every pupil to keep a personal 'inventional grammar' of the rules discovered, expressed in the wording invented by the class.

(e) Propose a limited number of short phrases in the foreign language to be learned by heart, at the rate of perhaps one each fortnight, and recorded in pupils' 'inventional grammar'. The phrases should be regularly revised and quoted whenever fresh instances of the pattern they exemplify are met. Each of these phrases should exemplify a particular pattern. The sum of the patterns (perhaps some 18 to 20 in a school year) represents a syllabus of insights into structure that is solidly understood and on which the next year's work can build. It is a great advantage that the stock of 'master patterns' is known to all the class and can be referred to by the teacher (and by subsequent teachers of the class) as old friends.

(f) In school examinations at the end of the year, ask pupils to examine phrases that they have never met before and to comment on their pattern, in the light of the insights achieved during the year.

Promoting real 'speech acts' in the foreign language

This theme is also developed in the topic book *Using Language*. The following are some ways in which the teacher can promote the use of 'speech acts' in the foreign language:

(a) Constantly use the foreign language in class as the language of instruction, especially whenever individual or class movement is involved. As far as possible try to combine this use of the foreign language with some physical response by the pupils. Experience in the USA in using the foreign language to evoke a 'total physical response' from learners encourages us to believe that reacting physically to the foreign language greatly facilitates mastery. For discussion of pattern in the language, of course, English must be used in the early years, but such use of English should be closely monitored and not allowed to squeeze out active use of the language for classroom control.

(b) Experiment with 'intensive sessions' (mornings, days or weekends when no English at all is allowed).

(c) Bring into class 'posses' of students from training establishments to promote dialogue in the foreign language in these intensive sessions.

(d) Utilise older pupils (fifth and sixth formers) to stimulate group work (such group leaders can be briefed for their role in lunch times or at short after-school meetings). The point can be made that schools which have experimented with this kind of tutoring have found that the gain for the older pupils was at least as great as for the younger ones. Having to answer questions one has not thought about, or check facts one is unsure of, is one of the best ways of learning, as many a young teacher fresh from university studies has found.

(e) Seize every chance to bring native speakers into class, especially children.

(f) Exploit the resources of the linked school for exchange of taped letters on cassette, giving messages from class to class but also, if possible, messages which have reference to individuals in the class. These greatly motivate careful listening by the individuals concerned and by their friends.

(g) Arrange an annual 'reciprocal' course for matched teams of pupils from linked schools (for details see Hawkins and Perren, 1978).

(h) Make it a fortnightly task for pupils in fourth, fifth and sixth forms to write a short personal message (of, say, no more than 10 lines) to the school's native-speaking assistant, asking a purely personal question about the foreign country or the language. The assistant can respond to these messages either face to face, in class, during the next week or in a written note or, if all pupils are issued with their personal cassette, by recording the reply on each pupil's cassette for study at leisure.

(i) When planning the whole syllabus keep in mind that foreign language learning is a dual process. Classroom work has its rightful place but ultimately the language is acquired in dialogue with native speakers and in the foreign country. The obstacles in the way of providing this opportunity for *all* pupils are formidable but the language teacher's professionalism must be judged partly on his ability to overcome these obstacles.

AWARENESS OF LANGUAGE IN CHILD-CARE COURSES

In our first chapter we recalled the Bullock Committee's insistence that future parents should have help in understanding the heavy responsibility they will bear for their children's language development. In a later section (p. 46) we described the pioneering efforts of a distinguished modern linguist headmaster in devising and teaching a language element in his school's 'child-care course' for 15/16-year-olds. Everything we have learned from recent work, both on L1 acquisition and on foreign language learning, strengthens the case for much greater understanding among parents of their role as language models and informants: as, in fact, the key members of Professor Bruner's Language Assistance System. This understanding is critical at three particular stages in the child's 'vertical curriculum':

in the pre-school years
when the breakthrough to literacy has to be made
when the child faces the challenge of learning a foreign language

The present curriculum offers no help to the future parent. There must come a time when it is realised how many of our difficulties have their roots in the pre-school years. We may then get what we have long needed: a minister with sole responsibility for the under fives, the 'language learners'. Only with such a minister are we likely to see effective support for young parents at the ante-natal clinics along the lines that the Bullock Committee recommended, with seminars and demonstrations, films and literature. Only with such a minister will the media, and especially the radio and television, provide the on-going education and support that young parents deserve. And finally only with such a minister can we hope to win the battle for adequate financial support for families and the provision of the precious 'adult time' of which so many children are cheated at the critical age.

In the meantime we can at least make a beginning in our 'awareness of language' course, by asking questions and arousing expectations. The interest that our introduction will generate among the 11/12-year-olds and, it may be hoped, among many of their parents – for this is not the least of the benefits of the new element in the language curriculum – may be the best preparation for the later exploration in more depth with fourth and fifth formers of the role of the family unit as the community's 'language laboratory'.

FURTHER READING

1   On the development of the child's language an excellent introduction is:
V. J. Cook, *Young Children and Language* (Edward Arnold, 1979). This is based on thorough research and close observation of children. It is written in a most readable and attractive style, accessible to parents and to teachers with no previous knowledge of the literature.
A more difficult account, by a psychologist, is:
A. Elliot, *Child Language* (CUP, 1981)
A widely read linguist's account is:
M. A. K. Halliday, *Learning How to Mean* (Edward Arnold, 1975) based on his observation of his own child's language development.

2 On children beginning to put sentences together:
L. Bloom, *One Word at a Time* (Mouton, 1973)
For those who wish to read further the following are now classic works:
On the psychology of language:
H. H. Clark and E. V. Clark, *Psychology and Language* (Harcourt Brace Jovanovich, 1977)
On language acquisition:
R. W. Brown *A First Language* (George Allen and Unwin, 1974)

3 On children's thinking and learning to read:
M. Donaldson, *Children's Minds* (Fontana, 1978)

4 On recent advances in second language learning:
E. W. Hawkins, *Modern Languages in the Curriculum* (CUP, 1981). This includes a detailed discussion of the roles of 'awareness' and of 'force' in second language learning.
Stephen D. Krashen, *Second Language Acquisition and Second Language Learning* (Pergamon Institute of English, 1981). In these collected papers Krashen's 'monitor theory' of language learning is described.

5 Earl W. Stevick, *Teaching and Learning Languages* (CUP, 1982). Gives a non-technical account of how the mind deals with foreign language data and describes a wide range of techniques with discussion of their advantages and disadvantages.

Appendix A:
Learning to listen

Some teachers may find it hard to accept the idea of a specific programme of activities aimed at helping pupils to learn to listen to language. The Bullock Committee, as we saw (p. 34), was divided on the need for 'education of the ear', though the Committee's final word was: 'deliberate strategies may be required, for it cannot be assumed that improvement [in listening] will take place automatically'.

An eminent exponent of such deliberate strategies to educate, or re-educate, children's listening, was the late Peter MacCarthy, former head of the phonetics department of the University of Leeds. He carried out a research programme in primary and secondary schools in Yorkshire looking specifically at the problems children meet when beginning their study of French. In his book *The Teaching of Pronunciation* (1978) he wrote:

To leave pronunciation [in the foreign language] to take care of itself is virtually to ensure that a really acceptable standard is never reached – save possibly by the quite exceptional individual. [There is] a crucial distinction between learning the mother tongue initially and learning another language at a later date: any other language must be 'superimposed' on the mother tongue, which is already there in the mind and cannot be obliterated... Each individual is conditioned by his mother-tongue experience to react in terms of its specific phonological structure. This creates problems as soon as he is required to react differently when confronted with the different phonological structure of the foreign language...

Systematic de-conditioning – which in the nature of things can only be partial, never complete – must be embarked upon for its own sake before any new system(s) can be effectively mastered... The education of the ear, then, is a prerequisite for efficient foreign language study. (p. 14)

It is not only the learner just beginning a foreign language who needs education of the ear, however. Hans Furth, whose work on the thought and language of the deaf has given him an international reputation, described in *Thinking Goes to School* (1974), written with his teacher colleague Harry Wachs, the 'auditory thinking games' developed in their 'School for Thinking' project in Charleston, West Virginia. Working with children of primary school age the authors devised a series of games, which they call 'thinking games', to promote 'intellectual health' and especially to help pupils who might otherwise not succeed at school.

The listening activities and games described in this Appendix owe a debt to the work of Peter MacCarthy, Hans Furth and Harry Wachs. Their usefulness has been proved over many years of experiment by the author with two categories of pupil:

(i) pupils aged 11 beginning the study of French in a comprehensive school in York, where the listening games were among the most popular of the week's activities with the pupils and contributed clearly to the confidence with which quite ordinary learners, some with limited aptitude for French, attacked the work.

(ii) groups of pupils aged between 9 and 13 at the annual intensive summer schools for pupils from ethnic minorities and slower learners organised by the Language Teaching Centre of the University of York. Here the games were much enjoyed and, though they could only be tested over the period of the summer school, there was clear evidence that they increased the confidence, both of the (mainly Asian) children learning English as a second language and of pupils with English as mother tongue who were having difficulties with their reading.

SYLLABLE-TIMED V. STRESS-TIMED LANGUAGES

The need for 're-education of the ear', when pupils begin to study a foreign language or when they begin to learn English, becomes clearer when we consider the peculiar status of English as a 'stress-timed language'. The languages of the world are broadly of two kinds: 'syllable-timed' and 'stress-timed'. English belongs to the second category; most of our European neighbours speak syllable-timed languages.

What this means, simply, is that the speakers of, say, French (syllable-timed) utter all the syllables in a phrase at an approximately uniform rate. The more syllables there are in a phrase, the longer it takes to say it. In English, however, it is the strongly stressed syllables that mark approximately equal beats. If there are few syllables between the stresses, they are uttered more slowly. If a larger number of syllables comes between two stresses, they are uttered more quickly. The native speaker of English learns to make this subtle adjustment of speed subconsciously, constantly speeding up and slowing down. By contrast the French native speaker learns subconsciously to utter all syllables at a steady, if not staccato, rate.

Thus speakers of either language trying to learn the other have a deeply ingrained set of habits, *of which they are quite unaware*, to *unlearn* and a new set of habits to learn.

Pupils can be shown the difference between stress-time and syllable-time quite simply if they are asked to count aloud in English and French.

In English. Beat (on stressed syllable only)

FOURteen	FIFteen	SIXteen	SEV'Nteen	EIGHteen
1	2	3	4	5

In French. Beat (on each syllable)

QUA	TORZE	QUINZE	SEIZE	DIX-SEPT		DIX-HUIT	
1	2	3	4	5	6	7	8

The consequences of this fundamental difference between the two languages are far reaching. The music of the verse and much of the prose of English is stress-timed music. In French the typical rhythm of poetry is the strict syllable beat of the Alexandrine.

Using a simple metronome in class the teacher can demonstrate how stress-time works in short dialogues. The metronome is set beating at a steady rate and against the beat the class recites such a sequence as:

Beats	1	2
Are you GO ing		HOME?
I'm GO ing		via CREWE
And THEN		to LONdon?
And BACK		to MANchester

As pupils grow confident they can be set to compose their own dialogues and record them against a metronome for the class to listen to. A splendidly witty collection of such dialogues, recorded against the metronome beat, can be found in C. Mortimer, *Stress Time* (1976).

It is, of course, this difference between stress-time and syllable-time that makes the translation of songs and opera into English so hard. The great merit of the translations made by Edward Dent of the Mozart operas was that this problem was faced and overcome. Music written to fit a libretto in a syllable-timed language was for the first time heard in perfect match with a language whose natural rhythms are based on equal timing between stresses. The stressed syllables of Dent's translation had to fall exactly on the stresses required by Mozart's music. In our programme of activities below we suggest some simple class projects in this area to be tackled when pupils have gained confidence in their listening (p. 208).

Teachers of pupils who are learning English as well as teachers of the European languages will find that the translation of simple songs with close attention to the rhythm of the words in both the languages involved greatly helps 'awareness' of this important aspect of spoken language.

'CROSS-MODAL' ACTIVITIES

A particularly useful listening activity is the one requiring 'cross-modal' co-ordination: that is, involving a dialogue between the ear and one of the other senses. Cross-modal activity of this kind is something for which the human cerebral cortex is uniquely well equipped (compared with the brain of animals) because of the 'association areas' of the human cortex which act as telephone exchanges for the messages received through different sensory channels.

It has been argued that it is this cross-modal facility that makes language learning possible. Certainly the advanced skill of reading makes constant demands on the ability to interpret simultaneously messages received by two different sensory paths. Our listening games will therefore include ploys to develop confidence in doing this by asking pupils to 'listen and look'.

HOW TO PLAN THE LISTENING SESSIONS

What follows does not aim to offer a complete course of listening activities, to be followed by all classes in the order set out.

Pupils will differ greatly in the experience they bring to listening and in their special needs, just as teachers will not all have the same time to devote to 'education of the ear'. It is important for each teacher to be free to tailor the listening activities to suit the pupils' needs. The games described are therefore to be taken as *examples* to be copied or developed, rather than as a syllabus.

Experience seems to show that variety is most important and that pupils must always be challenged to the limit of what they can do. When the games are too easy (or when they are impossibly hard) boredom sets in. The aim should be to offer in every session some activities that all pupils can succeed at but also to include some which really stretch them all.

A useful guiding principle is 'little and often'. Ten minutes at the start of a lesson, two or three times a week, spread over the first year or two of secondary school, or the last year of primary and first year of secondary school, to accompany the attack on the foreign language has been found best. (Such listening activity will, of course, in some LEAs, rightly be part of the Middle School course.)

Each game should be kept short. At first no more than five items should be given, with the answers, and praise for keen listening, coming at once. Later the game can be extended to ten items, the first five being repeated, to help the slower learners, and the next five being said only once, to stretch all pupils and to build good habits of 'listening first time'.

SILENCE IS GOLDEN

It is important to ensure that, from the start, great self-discipline is shown during the playing of the games: no shuffling of feet or creaking of chairs; even breathing has to be controlled while the test is on.

The stillness and disciplined listening that are called for make a good start to a language lesson, to which pupils may arrive from a number of sometimes very energetic, breathless exertions. Perhaps we may have underrated the value of silence in language work. Teachers in the USA who have worked with C. Gattegno's book (1972), subtitled *The Silent Way*, have been struck by the gain in learning that ensues when aural input is followed by a short silence. This seems to give the mind the best chance to extract the information from the message and process it. When there is no silence:

the barrage of utterances from teacher and fellow students is like a handful of stones thrown onto the surface of a quiet pond; we are unable to follow the ripples from any one of them because of interference produced by the others ... the silence that surrounds the new words both allows and compels maximum attention ... this use of silence means that the student derives much more benefit per audible model from the teacher. (E. W. Stevick, 1976, p. 139)

There need be no conflict between this regular training in silent listening and the proper wish of the language teacher to encourage maximum active use of language by pupils in the lesson, especially if the listening sessions are at once followed by 'lesson starters' which bring all pupils into the action. Such a lesson starter, which the author thought that he had invented until he saw it in use with English classes in China recently, is the game of 'try to beat the record' in the number of different questions that the class can correctly ask in two minutes. The game is played against the clock – a kitchen egg-timer which rings a bell at the end of two minutes. A running tally of correct questions accepted by the teacher is kept on the board for all to see, with the previous best score recorded by the class shown plainly as the goal to beat. As the tally approaches the previous best score the excitement mounts and pupils strive mightily to think of questions in the foreign language that they have not already used. The excitement is even greater if they know that beating their record will be rewarded by remission of homework!

In the English lesson a similar 'starter' which has been found to complement the silent listening session is to ask pupils to take turns at opening the lesson by giving a short account of exactly what was said and done in the previous lesson. The account is then briefly discussed by the class and assessed for accuracy and delivery.

LISTENING FOR MEANING

The final point to make is that all the listening activities are aimed to lead up to 'listening for meaning'. It is recommended that, from the start, the less 'contextualised' games should be mixed with 'listening for meaning' activities so that the two kinds of listening reinforce each other. Suggestions are given for 'listening for meaning'.

CASSETTE

There is a cassette issued with the series 'Awareness of Language' which contains some model listening games that teachers may wish to exploit in class, as an alternative to their own versions. Listening activities included in the cassette are marked ★ in the list which follows.

LISTENING GAMES

The games are set out under headings showing the particular features for which pupils are to listen as the game is played.

★ 1 Learning a notation for playing the games
Many pupils will not previously have used a written notation to show elements such as rhythm or syllable division in speech. It is worthwhile spending some time making sure that all can do this confidently.

Begin very simply: beat simple rhythms (on a drum, tambourine, or empty milk bottle) and show pupils how to represent the number of beats and then the rhythm of the beats by a simple musical notation of dots along a line. The spaces between the dots show, very approximately, the rhythm of the beats.

Then the following game can be played. Write a rhythmic sequence on the board. Pupils study the notation on the board while they listen to the beat (or, if using the cassette, to the beat in the recorded games). If the notation *seen* is exactly what is *heard*, pupils mark their example with a tick (✓). If the two are different, pupils mark a cross (✗). Example:

Written on board	Heard (teacher or tape)	Pupil writes
1 ●● ●● ● ●	●● ●● ● ●	✓
2 ● ●● ● ●●	● ●● ● ●	✗
3 ● ● ●● ●●	● ● ● ●●	✗
4 ●● ●● ●● ●	●● ●● ●● ●	✓
5 ● ●●● ● ●●●	● ●●● ● ●●	✗

Pupils can later be asked to invent their own 'tunes' and tap them out for the rest of the class to note down.

When the accurate matching of rhythms heard with written notation has been mastered by all pupils the task can be made more complicated. Now introduce two beats, one at a higher pitch than the other (for example, with an empty milk bottle and a half-full bottle, or a drum and a glass bottle). Pupils now draw a horizontal line on their paper and show the beats above or below the line, according to pitch:

As pupils become proficient and confident at this listening and writing they should be challenged to do it in a harder way. Tap out a rhythm and, *only after it has been heard*, write the notation on the board. Pupils mark their paper with a tick or cross but now they are relying on their memory of what they have heard.

The above games can be kept going as 'warm-up' activities to start listening sessions long after the class has progressed to more demanding listening.

★ 2 Discrimination of syllables

Some pupils may be unsure of how words divide into syllables, those learning English and slow readers often having special difficulty.

The best way to begin may be by counting with the class the syllables in the names of well-known towns:

Manchester/Aberdeen/Bristol/Bombay/Karachi
● ● ●/ ●● ● / ● ●/ ● ● / ●● ●

Then proceed to count syllables in simple phrases such as:

'Have a cup of tea'

Pupils can then be asked to tap out the rhythm with rulers saying how many syllables they hear. Write the rhythm on the board thus:

●● ●● ●

This exercise can then be repeated with a phrase such as:

'Have a cup of coffee'

Pupils can now count the syllables in the phrase and write down the rhythm in the way they have learned:

'Have a cup of coffee' ●● ●● ●●

The game can then be played with the following phrases:

1 Have a cup of tea. ●● ●● ●
2 Have you got a spoon? ●● ●● ●
3 Put it in the saucer. ●● ●● ●●
4 The milk is in the cupboard. ●● ●● ●● ●
5 Thank you very much. ●● ●● ●

The next step (when all pupils are confident that they can hear the number of syllables and the rhythm) is to write five simple rhythms on the board in the agreed notation and then to ask pupils to listen as each one is spoken. If the spoken rhythm agrees with the written notation, pupils write a tick ✓; if not they write a cross ✗. For example, write on the board:

●● ●● ●

Then say:

'Have a cup of coffee'. Pupils answer with a cross ✗ .

A (more difficult) development is to speak two phrases and ask pupils to mark ✓ if they are exactly the same in rhythm and ✗ if not. Example:

1 What a pretty colour
  Can I have a cutting? } ✓

2 I planted them last autumn
  You must have done it well } ✗

3 Put them in your basket
  Put some paper round them } ✓

4 Will you take some roses?
  Only if you wish me to } ✗

5 What a lovely smell
  Put them straight in water } ✗

★ 3 Tonic stress on syllables

Rhythm and stress combine in a subtle way as illustrated in the following game. Ask pupils to listen once again to the phrase 'Have a cup of coffee' and write the rhythm on the board. Tell pupils to listen carefully and say whether some of the syllables have more stress or strength than others. Demonstrate that a refinement of notation is needed to show this by writing on the board:

Have a cup of coffee   ● • ● • ● •

Ask pupils to write the stress pattern for a simple phrase such as 'Have a cup of tea':

● • ● • ●

and repeat the exercise with the following phrases:

Have you had your supper?   ● • ● • ● •
I *could* make some   ○ ● • •
No yòu couldn't!   ● • ● •

After this introductory practice pupils will be ready to tackle the following (note that it is always helpful to repeat one of the phrases that have already been used to ensure that all pupils begin with complete confidence):

1 Have a cup of tea   ● • ● • ●
2 Can you see the point?   ● • ● • ●
3 No, I can't   ● • ●
4 Wait a bit!   ● • ●
5 Now I get it.   ● • ● •
6 Don't you know any more?   ● • ● • • ●
7 What a sense of humour!   ● • ● • ● •
8 What about me then?   ● • ○ ● •
9 Waste of time!   ● • ●
10 Don't be so rude!   ● • • ●

(As explained in the introduction, the first five items can be repeated to help slower pupils: the remaining five are said only once, to teach listening first time.)

As with many of the games, the way to follow the initial practice of the notation is to develop a 'listen and look' game by writing several patterns on the board and then asking pupils to indicate whether the spoken pattern is exactly the same as the written version.

As always in this work, only the teacher who knows the class will be able to judge how easy or difficult to make the game. It may be advisable at the start to speak the phrases with slightly exaggerated stress on the accented syllables. Later the game can be made harder by marking the stressed syllables only lightly. It is even better if, sometimes, pupil volunteers can take over the teacher's role. The game can be made very hard by asking pupils to show by the spaces between their dots the approximate time intervals between syllables.

★ 4 Intonation combined with syllable division and tonic stress

The first step is to accustom pupils to distinguish rising from falling intonation. They may be taught a simple notation to distinguish the two and given practice at writing phrases and showing the movement of the voice:

You said six? ➚ (question)
You said six! ➘ (statement)

Write these five phrases on the board and show the movement on each one:

1 You said six! ➘
2 You said six? ➚
3 Only one? ➚
4 Only one! ➘
5 Ready? ➚

A variation is to ask pupils to listen to the following phrases and mark (Q) or (S) after each:

1 Ticket for London!   (S)
2 Return?   (Q)
3 Back to the engine?   (Q)
4 Near the buffet!   (S)
5 Platform?   (Q)

Now ask pupils to listen to the following five pairs of phrases. If pupils think the tune is exactly the same for the pair they should mark ✓. If they are different they should mark ✗.

1 You said six! ⎫ ✓
  You said six! ⎭

2 Return? ⎫ ✗
  Return! ⎭

3 Two lumps? ⎫ ✗
  Two lumps! ⎭

4 You're watching Arsenal? ⎫ ✓
  You're watching Arsenal? ⎭

5 You prefer Liverpool? ⎫ ✗
  You prefer Liverpool! ⎭

As soon as pupils begin to learn a foreign language this game should be played with phrases in that language, preferably recorded on tape by a native speaker. He or she may need careful coaching before being entrusted with the recording as some experience is needed to secure good quality of sound and to make the distinctions clear.

The second step is to introduce pupils to the way in which intonation and tonic stress work together. In a phrase like:

He said he was going to Mary's party on Friday

the meaning will depend on the intonation and stress. Two possible readings are:

He said he was going to MARY's (not Jane's) party on Friday
He said he was going to Mary's party on FRIDAY (not on Saturday)

The voice will *rise* on the accented word and, more precisely, on the accented syllable in that word:

• • • • •• • ● • •• • ••
He said he was going to MARy's party on Friday

• • • • •• • •• • •• • ● •
He said he was going to Mary's party on FRIday

The mastery of even this simplified notation, assuming only two possible levels of the voice, and showing the tonic stress in the way practised·in earlier games, may take some time. It is worthwhile giving plenty of time and making the games easy at first, in order to ensure that all pupils gain confidence at hearing and transcribing the tunes and stresses.

When confidence is attained pupils may be asked to take a phrase and transcribe it showing several possible meanings by the different intonation contours. For example: ask pupils to transcribe the following, giving it five possible meanings:

JOHN said that MARY's PARTY was on FRIDAY EVENING

(John not David said/Mary's not Jane's/party not disco/Friday not Saturday/evening not afternoon).

A further development of this listening game, which may stretch the more able listeners, is to distinguish, from the intonation, the difference between an ironical (untrue) statement (I) and a truthful and sincere one (S):

ironic: That's a big help! (intonation implies: I must say!)
sincere: That's a big help! (intonation implies: I am really grateful!)

Ask pupils to mark each of the five phrases (S) or (I)

1	That's a big help!	(I)
2	That helps a lot!	(S)
3	Thanks a lot!	(I)
4	Very kind, I must say!	(I)
5	Great!	(S)

Or ask pupils to listen to the following pairs of phrases (either ironic of sincere) and if they think they are identical, mark ✓ ; if they are different in meaning, mark ✕ :

1 That's a big help! (I)
  That's a big help! (S) — ✕
2 That explains a lot! (I)
  That explains a lot! (I) — ✓
3 Very interesting, I must say! (S)
  Very interesting, I must say! (I) — ✕
4 Thanks a lot! (I)
  Thanks a lot! (S) — ✕
5 Don't let me interrupt you! (I)
  Don't let me interrupt you! (I) — ✓

★ 5 Pure vowels and glides

Write the following sounds on the board and ask pupils to listen to them:

[u] (as in 'mood')
[ɔu] (as in 'Oh!')

Point out that the second one was really two sounds (o-u) called a glide and that the first was a pure vowel.

Get pupils to listen to the following sounds and mark P (for pure) or G (for glide):

1	Oh!	(G)		6	sow	(G)
2	mood	(P)		7	saw	(P)
3	food	(P)		8	low	(G)
4	grow	(G)		9	mow	(G)
5	I know	(G)		10	law	(P)

A variation of this for pupils who have begun French is to ask them to listen to the following pairs of sounds. If they think they are identical, pupils mark ✓ . If they think one is pure and the other a glide, pupils mark ✕ :

1 know
  know — ✓
2 know
  l'eau — ✕
3 rude
  mood — ✓
4 *le thé*
  tray — ✕
5 sew
  mow — ✓

(In speaking these examples the teacher may at first exaggerate the glide on vowels in 'know', 'tray' etc.)

The same games can be played with the following pairs:

> French [e] (as in *école*) and [ei] (as in eight)
> French [y] (as in *du*) and [u] (as in you)

6 Pairs of sounds in the foreign language

The next step may be to introduce pairs of sounds within the foreign language which pupils must learn to differentiate confidently. For example:

> In French: [y] as in *du* from [u] as in *vous*
> [e] as in *j'ai* from [ɛ] as in *est*
> The four nasal vowels:
> [œ̃] as in *un*
> [õ] as in *bon*
> [ɛ̃] as in *vin*
> [ɑ̃] as in *blanc*
> In German: [y:] as in *Güte* from [u:] as in *gut*
> [ɔy] as in *Fräulein* from [au] as in *Frau*
> [Iç] as in *ich* from [Iʃ] as in *Tisch*
> In Spanish: [r] as in *pero* from [rr] as in *perro*
> [b] as in *vamos* or *Badajoz* from [v] as in *leve* or *recibía*

The same 'tick'/'cross' procedure is used as in 5 above.

★ 7 Voiced and unvoiced consonants

Say to the class: 'Say these "th" sounds after me while lightly placing a finger on your "Adam's apple" which guards your voice box. Try to tell me on which of the "th" sounds your voice box vibrates.' Use the following words as examples:

> ha*th*, *th*eatre, *th*umb, *th*ing, ma*th*s: no vibration (unvoiced)
> *th*is, *th*en, *th*ough, wi*th*out, o*th*er: vibration (voiced)

Then ask pupils to listen to the following five pairs. If they think that the 'th' sounds are exactly the same, they should mark ✓ , if they think they are different, they should mark ✗

> 1 thin ⎫
>   this ⎬   ✗
> 2 thumb ⎫
>   thistle ⎬   ✓
> 3 though ⎫
>   then ⎬   ✓
> 4 other ⎫
>   without ⎬   ✓
> 5 theatre ⎫
>   then ⎬   ✗

(Pupils should be warned to listen *only* to the 'th' sounds and not to be distracted by the rest of the word.)

When pupils have learned the technical names 'voiced' and 'unvoiced' the game can be played asking them to listen and mark each sound (v) or (u). Other voiced and unvoiced distinctions to practise are:

[z] as in $\begin{cases} \text{razor} \\ \text{zeal} \end{cases}$ v. [s] as in $\begin{cases} \text{racer} \\ \text{seal} \end{cases}$

[b] as in $\begin{cases} \text{nab} \\ \text{bad} \end{cases}$ v. [p] as in $\begin{cases} \text{nap} \\ \text{pad} \end{cases}$

[d] as in $\begin{cases} \text{had} \\ \text{dip} \end{cases}$ v. [t] as in $\begin{cases} \text{hat} \\ \text{tip} \end{cases}$

[g] as in $\begin{cases} \text{sag} \\ \text{got} \end{cases}$ v. [k] as in $\begin{cases} \text{sack} \\ \text{cot} \end{cases}$

[v] as in $\begin{cases} \text{veil} \\ \text{live} \end{cases}$ v. [f] as in $\begin{cases} \text{fail} \\ \text{life} \end{cases}$

★ 8 Order in which sounds are heard

This series of games may be especially useful for pupils who have reading difficulties but it should also help to prepare the way for spelling unfamiliar sound clusters in the foreign language. Ask pupils to listen to these two sounds:

[ʃ] sh (as in ship)
[tʃ] ch (as in chip)

Ask pupils to say which one they hear first:

which ship? (ch first)
Ashchurch (sh first)

The following game can then be played. Pupils draw a diagram like this:

	ch	sh
1		
2		
3		
4		
5		

They then listen to the phrases and mark 1 or 2 in the appropriate column to show which sound they hear first and which second:

	ch	sh
1 fish and chips	2	1
2 which do you wish?	1	2
3 Cheshunt	1	2
4 He shouldn't charge you	2	1
5 Chester is sheltered by a wall	1	2

As pupils become confident they should be challenged to do harder games with phrases such as:

> Which fish is cheaper?
> He washes the dishes cheerfully.
> I wish Ashchurch would change his shoes.

★ *9 Presence or absence of a particular sound*

Tell pupils that they are going to listen for a rather hard sound: [ŋ] (as in sing). Can they hear it in:

> song? wing? ping-pong? hungry? going?
> singe? hinge? plunger? the pin goes here?

Only when all pupils can confidently hear the difference between 'ping' and 'the pin goes here' should the game start. the game proceeds in the following way. If pupils hear the sound [ŋ] they should mark ✓ , if not, they mark ✗ .

1	hinge	✗
2	single	✓
3	ring	✓
4	kingly	✓
5	singe	✗
6	in goes the pin	✗
7	hunch	✗
8	plunger	✗
9	going	✓
10	angle	✓

The game might be continued with the following, more difficult phrases:

1	anger	✓
2	Anne got it	✗
3	ping	✓
4	the pin got stuck	✗
5	the run gets longer	✗
6	ring Gordon	✓
7	that thing gets heavier	✓
8	the pan got heated	✗
9	she sang out of tune	✓
10	she ran Gladys home	✗

Similar games can be played with sounds:

> French: [e] [ɛ] [y] [u] and the nasal vowels: [œ̃] [õ] [ɛ̃] [ã]
> Spanish: [lj] [ɲj] [rr] [b]
> German: [ç] [y:] [u:]

10 Finding words containing particular sounds

This is merely a variant of the above game. Give pupils a sound and ask them to find, say, three words that contain the same sound. For example: given the word 'plough', pupils find: cow; now; out. The game can be made into a useful revision of the early vocabulary in the foreign language if pupils are asked to draw simple pictures illustrating the words they find. Example:

> sound: [y] (as in *la plume*)
> pupil writes and draws: *la lune, les lunettes, le mur* etc.

If the rule is made that all the drawings of feminine objects are done in *red* the game will also serve to establish genders in the early stages. It is useful to keep a supply of red ball-point pens for this purpose, to be given out and collected up again by team captains elected for the purpose. 'Grammatical' words (*sur, du* etc.) should be written in blue or black, like the masculine objects. The colour code helps to give to the slower learner an additional clue to associate the correct gender with the word. If a further clue is needed it has been found useful to suggest to pupils that they consistently write the feminine objects and their drawings on the right hand side of the page, with masculines on the left. Spatial code and colour code, used consistently throughout the first year or two, greatly strengthen pupils' grasp of the gender of the *vocabulaire de base*.

★11 Sounds that are not phonemic in the mother tongue

This game is particularly useful for pupils learning English as a second language.

Ask pupils to listen for the sound of the vowel [ʌ] in: cut; but; hut. Can they hear the same vowel in:

> cat?   ✗
> nut?   ✓
> cot?   ✗
> rut?   ✓
> foot? ✗

Now ask pupils to listen to the following pairs and if the sounds are exactly the same they mark ✓ , if not, they mark ✗ :

> 1 I have a cut on my knee ⎫
>   I have a cat on my knee ⎭   ✗
> 2 Can you see his hat? ⎫
>   Can you see his hat? ⎭   ✓
> 3 Where is her hat? ⎫
>   Where is her hut? ⎭   ✗

4 That's a dangerous cat }
  That's a dangerous cut }   X
5 I don't eat butter }
  I don't eat batter }   X

Depending on the composition of the class, you may find it useful to select pairs of sounds that cause difficulty to particular pupils. The following pairs may give most trouble:

vowels:	[ʌ] [a]	cut/cat
	[a] [ɑː]	cat/cart
	[iː] [i]	sheep/ship
	[ɔ] [ou]	cot/coat
	[u] [uː]	pull/pool
	[ɛ] [ei]	met/mate
consonants:	[b] [v]	ban/van
	[k] [h]	carry/harry
	[d] [ð]	den/then
	[f] [v]	fine/vine
	[g] [k]	goat/coat
	[æz] [hæz]	as/has
	[liːk] [liːg]	leak/league
	['beri] ['beli]	berry/belly
	[p] [b]	pike/bike
	['reizər] ['reisər]	razor/racer
	[æks] [æʃ]	axe/ash

As pupils make progress you may limit the listening games to the dwindling number of distinctions that still give trouble to particular pupils, while all the time inventing more searching tests of discrimination.

★ 12 Short Term Memory

(a) The simplest way to begin the discussion of the STM with pupils is to practise the retention of strings of random digits. Read the digits out at about two per second without 'bunching' or imposing an intonation pattern on the string. The average adult STM capacity is seven bits of information (seven random digits) plus or minus two. It is best therefore to begin with no more than four digits in a string, to make sure that all pupils get the first ones right. You might conduct the game in the following way. Ask pupils to listen to the following numbers (it might help to point out that the string resembles a telephone number) and to write down the string when, and only when, you have finished reading it out:

8 2 7 4

5 4 9 6 1

8 1 3 9 4 5 2

9 3 4 7 2 6 1

7 5 9 6 4 1 2 3

8 3 1 5 4 9 2 7 6

(b) One variant that stretches pupils' listening, as they become more confident and able to concentrate for longer periods, is to tell them that in some of the strings they hear, one number (and only one) may be repeated. They are to listen and write down the number that is heard twice. If no number is repeated, they write 0. Example:

5 2 3 4 7 2 8	2
4 8 1 6 9 4 5	4
2 5 1 9 3 1 8	1
1 6 2 7 4 3 9	0
2 5 4 6 9 5 7	5

(c) Another variant is to nominate a number to listen for. If pupils hear the number in the string, they mark ✓ , if not, they mark ✗ . Example:

Pupils listen for 9:

    1 3 5 4 9 2 7 :   ✓
    3 6 8 1 7 2 4 :   ✗

(d) A harder variant is to read out the string and, *only after reading it*, name the number to be identified. Example:

    3 6 8 1 7 2 4

Did pupils hear 5? Answer: ✗

(e) As pupils become increasingly confident at holding the strings of digits in the STM it will be useful to introduce:

    (i) perception of pause in the string

Ask pupils to listen to the following numbers and write them out as before but this time showing with a stroke where the pause comes:

6 9 3 4 2 7	6 9 3 / 4 2 7
2 4 7 9 5 2	2 4 7 9 / 5 2
2 7 4 9 5 2	2 7 / 4 9 5 2

(ii) perception of a signal between two digits in a string

Ask pupils to listen to the following numbers. During the reading they will hear a tap. Pupils write the string down and show by a stroke where the tap comes:

6 8 3 (tap) 4 2 7   6 8 3 / 4 2 7

Another way to play this is to ask for the number that comes *before* the tap (or *after* it) to be written down. Example:

6 8 3 (tap) 4 2 7   Number before the tap: 3

From an early stage the STM games can be played in the foreign language. This is especially useful for fixing numbers in the first year.

13 STM and phrases in the foreign language

The best-known version of this game is that beginning 'I packed my bag and in it I put' followed by items suggested one by one by the pupils. Each successive player has to recapitulate the list and to add one item. Care must be taken to give genders correctly each time (always using article to show gender). As the list grows long it is helpful if the teacher writes the initial letter of the objects on the board. Here a colour code (red for feminine objects) can be used to help to fix correct gender.

As pupils grow more confident they can graduate from simple lists of items to dialogue played by pairs of pupils as follows:

> first pupil: Holà David, ça va?
> second pupil: Oh, oui, pas mal, et toi?

The next pair repeat these phrases and add:

> first pupil: Où vas-tu?
> second pupil: Je vais à la piscine.

The third pair repeat the dialogue and add:

> first pupil: Et après ça?
> second pupil: Oh, je ne sais pas ... chez moi probablement.

★ 14 Oral cloze games

This and the following game (15) should be practised well in the mother tongue until pupils have a firm grasp of the function of the different parts of the grammar. Then the games can be played in the foreign language.

This game can be played in several ways. The simplest is probably to ask pupils to listen to a story read out with selected words omitted (replaced by a buzzer). At first, read the story straight through. Then give a second reading with a short pause after each buzz to allow pupils to write down the word they think is missing. A most useful follow-up is to discuss in groups the suggested 'fillers' for the buzz slots. The various suggested fillers should be arranged in order of probability and suitability. A variant of this is to read out the story, inserting nonsense words for certain key words in the passage. Pupils spot the nonsense words and write down the words they think should replace them.

★ 15 Identifying components of a spoken sentence

Read out five phrases and ask pupils to spot various components in the sentence. They might first listen for verbs, then subjects, and later, direct objects, adjectives, prepositions etc.

The usefulness of this listening game is that it draws pupils' attention to the *function* of each part of the phrase, rather than simply concentrating on terminology. It helps to develop the insight into pattern that is vital for rapid learning of a foreign language, and for confident 'processing' of messages in any language.

★ 16 Listening for meaning

The games listed in this section are intended for both mother tongue and foreign language classrooms. It was stressed in the introduction to this Appendix that 'listening for meaning' games should be introduced from the start and constantly combined with the more formal listening activities.

(a) *Comparing two versions of a spoken story*
Read a story (perhaps twice) and then announce that you are going to repeat it in a slightly different version, perhaps changing some of the key words at first; later, as the class grows more confident, make more subtle changes. You may ask pupils to make notes, during the last reading, of the words or phrases altered and to use their own shorthand to recall the changes made. Alternatively, for younger pupils, you may suggest that they interrupt (perhaps with a signal) whenever they notice a change in the story.

(b) *Comparing a spoken story with a text*
A variant of the above is for the class to read a story, after which, with the text in front of them, the pupils listen to a spoken version which differs in some ways from the text. You may ask pupils to mark on the text the words or phrases that have been changed.

(c) *Comparing a written story with a spoken commentary*
Pupils read a story and become thoroughly familiar with the details.

They then listen to a dialogue between two people who exchange information, some of which corresponds to the text and some of which does not. Ask pupils to note discrepancies between the written story and the commentary.

(d) *Comparing a visual with an oral message*
Show pupils a picture (a street scene, perhaps, or a landscape). Then give a commentary and ask pupils to note discrepancies between the commentary and the information contained in the picture. The discrepancies can at first be obvious; for example, a bus in the street might be the wrong colour, or a cyclist might be on the wrong side of the road. Later the discrepancies can be more subtle.

(e) *Correcting a visual display after spoken commentary*
Give pupils a railway timetable, some parts of which have been torn away. They then listen to a spoken commentary over the station loud-speaker giving information about train departures, platform changes etc. From the spoken information pupils complete and correct the timetable.

(f) *Identifying 'force' of an utterance from the intonation*
One form of this game has been described earlier (p. 196). Another way of playing it is to give pupils a phrase which might carry various kinds of 'force' and ask them to add words to the phrase to show clearly whether it is a question, a threat, a statement etc. Example: Give pupils the phrase:

> I'll be waiting for you

Then ask pupils to add words, making it clear that the statement is a threat:

> I'll be waiting for you *with a gun*

or a promise:

> I'll be waiting for you *with the theatre tickets*

After they have practised the game with your help in deciding the 'force' of the statement, ask pupils to infer the 'force' from your intonation only.

(g) *Exploitation of language given (particularly useful in foreign language classrooms)*
Propose a phrase which has already been met and practised in class and challenge pupils to see how many variants (different ways of expressing the same meaning) they can propose in two minutes (using the egg-timer device described on p. 190). Example:

teacher: What's the time? (or the appropriate phrase in the foreign language)
pupils: Have you the time? How's the time? Got the time? etc.

Keep a list of useful everyday phrases met in the foreign language which lend themselves to this activity in the early stages of the course (date, weather, age, address).

(h) *Exploiting a spoken commentary on slide sequence*
Show pupils a short sequence of slides of a common activity (cashing a cheque in a bank, buying apples in the market). Pupils listen to a simple commentary as the slides are shown. Repeat until the pupils are familiar with the commentary. Then invite volunteers to make a commentary as the slides are shown again. The class assesses each effort for accuracy, omissions etc.

(i) *The game of 'Simon says'*
This is too well known to need explanation. In the foreign language classroom, use the appropriate equivalent phrase. For example, the phrase in French is 'Jacques a dit'.

An alternative way of playing the game, encouraging pupils to listen and look and to respond physically, is to give an instruction:

'Touch your right ear'

At the same time touch your right ear: the class obeys. BUT if at the same time you touch your *left* ear: the class does not move.

There are many variants.

Note: when these games are played by both mother tongue and foreign language teachers it will help if the teachers can keep in step with one another, by following similar procedures and instructions. It can be disconcerting if pupils are expected to play the same game according to different rules in adjacent classrooms. It is also helpful if teachers know what stage colleagues have reached in the 'listening' programme. This all points to the need for joint language boards of studies to plan this and other parts of the 'awareness of language' programme.

★ 17 Listening comprehension
The 'listening for meaning' activities suggested above lead naturally into the kind of listening comprehension work that is already widely practised both in mother tongue and in foreign language classrooms. There is no shortage of published comprehension material for classroom use at different age levels. Some recommended texts are listed at

the end of this Appendix. The cassette issued with the series 'Awareness of Language' contains a listening comprehension exercise of a slightly different kind to be used in connection with the topic book *Spoken and Written Language*. It accompanies the section which discusses the problems of blind learners and the role of Braille in enabling them to read.

Pupils are asked to close their eyes and imagine that they cannot see. They then listen to the tape-recorded story telling of the invention of Braille and the remarkable courage of its inventor. They are then asked to answer some questions on what they have heard.

One object of the exercise is to bring home to pupils some of the problems faced by the blind child in learning and remembering without written notes. It may also serve to show pupils something of the kind of concentration on listening that blind learners can achieve: the intense 're-education of the ear' that blindness necessarily brings. The discipline of listening with eyes closed may be a valuable part of regular comprehension practice.

18 Language and music

This is a rich and neglected area. The language teacher and the music teacher have much to contribute to each other's work. We have space here to suggest only a few elementary activities.

(a) *Matching words to music*

Play a catchy song to pupils in a foreign language until pupils become thoroughly familiar with the words and the rhythm. The language should preferably be one that the pupils are studying in class but it need not be. Short extracts of songs in other European languages ('*Che sarà sarà*'), or in languages spoken by pupils from ethnic minorities, would be excellent for the purpose. The essential thing is that the words in the foreign language must be thoroughly explained and understood and their pronunciation exactly copied. Pupils then work in pairs to find English words that snugly fit the rhythm. To take an elementary example:

> Au   clair   de   la   lu – ne
> ●   •   ●   •   ●   •
> Stan-ding in the moon light

fits the rhythm of the French better than

> ●   •   ●   •   •   ●
> In the light of the moon

(though this may seem to be a word for word translation).

(b) *Matching words to well-marked drum rhythms*

Beat a rhythm on a drum and ask pupils to think of phrases to fit the rhythm exactly. Example:

The Morse code signals are traditionally given names by instructors to help learners remember them:

      C = — • — • Charlie Charlie
      Q = — — • — God Save the Queen
      K = — • — And the King

You may ask pupils to invent their own phrases which fit the rhythm of some of the other Morse code signals and help the learner to remember them.

(c) *Matching words to well-known musical passages*

Ask pupils to invent words to match well-known musical passages. For example, the opening bars of Beethoven's Fifth Symphony or the entry of the cellos with the second theme in Schubert's Unfinished Symphony:

'I hear a knock. What can it be?'

'This is the second tune, the second tune played on a cello.'

Note: music teachers may wish to follow up these activities by discussing in class the difficulty of translating songs and operas into English from the (syllable-timed) European languages: for example from French (Bizet's *Carmen* with an illustration from such a well-known tune as the Toreador's Song) or from Italian (Mozart's *Figaro*, with an illustration from: 'If you go out for a little amusement').

If you go out for a lit-tle a-muse-ment.

Modern pop songs clearly offer a rich source for such exploration of the pitfalls of translation.

The problem is commonly said to arise from the comparative lack of 'pure' vowels in English compared with, say, Italian and this is obviously part of the difficulty. Much more significant, however, may be the fact that English is not a syllable-timed language, as are French, Spanish, Italian. (See discussion pp. 187 to 189.) It is this that makes singing in the foreign language such a useful activity. When words are well set to music the stresses required by the music match the spoken stresses exactly and thus reinforce good habits of pronunciation.

But this is only a small part of the value of co-operation between teachers of music and teachers of language (both English and foreign languages). So much of the way of life of a speech community is expressed in its music, especially its folk music.

Folk song, by its rhythm and melody, helps the learner effortlessly to retain many of the basic patterns of the grammar, thus sub-consciously furnishing the mind with a stock of models. For example, a simple song such as 'Au clair de la lune' exemplifies much of the basic grammar of French:

> *prête-moi!*
> *ouvre-moi!*
> *je n'ai plus de . . .*
> *je n'ai pas de . . . va chez . . .*
> *je crois que . . .*
> *elle y est*
> *on bat*
> *P. répondit . . .*
> *je suis dans . . .*
> *car . . .*

Language teachers and music teachers should be partners and it is hoped that the 'Awareness of Language' programme may contribute to bringing them fruitfully together.

FURTHER READING

1   On 'thinking with the ears':
H. G. Furth and H. Wachs, *Thinking Goes to School* (OUP, 1975)

2   On the need for 'education of the ear':
S. W. Lundsteen, *Listening. Its Impact on Reading and the Other Language Arts* (Revised edn 1979) (ERIC Clearing House on Reading and Communication Skills, National Inst. of Education, 1971)
P. MacCarthy, *The Teaching of Pronunciation* (CUP, 1978)

3   On 'syllable-time' v. 'stress time':
P. MacCarthy, *The Pronunciation of French* (OUP, 1975)
P. MacCarthy, *The Pronunciation of German* (OUP, 1975)
C. Mortimer, *Stress Time* (CUP, 1976)

4   On listening comprehension:
P. Ur, *Teaching Listening Comprehension* (CUP, 1983)

Appendix B: Language in education

TWO EXAMPLES OF A BASIC LANGUAGE COURSE FOR TEACHERS

The Bullock Committee recommended (see p. 28) that all teachers, whatever their special subject, should have a course in Language as a part of their initial training. It was suggested that at least 100 hours should be given to the course. In order to promote further discussion the committee offered two model syllabuses for the proposed course:

TWO EXAMPLES OF A BASIC LANGUAGE COURSE

Example 1

(1) THE NATURE AND FUNCTION OF LANGUAGE
(based on (a) the students' own language and (b) the language of school children).
Language as rule-governed behaviour: reference to phonology, grammar, lexis.
Accents, dialect, standards.
Spoken and written media.
The functions of language – some theoretical models.

(2) LANGUAGE ACQUISITION
Pre-speech behaviour in the family.
'Speech for oneself' and the regulative role of language.
Speech and the development of higher mental processes (Piaget, Vygotsky).
Creativity and language (Chomsky).
The development of syntax; transitional grammars.

(3) SPEAKING AND WRITING AS SOCIAL PROCESSES
The context of situation.
Language and role relations.

Language and social control.
Language and the presentation of self.
Conversation and the validation of social reality.

(4) THE PROCESSING OF CODED INFORMATION
Stages in data-processing (a) perceptual, (b) encoded in speech, (c) encoded in writing.
'Ear language' and 'eye language'.
'Linguistic awareness' and reading.
Storage and retrieval of information.

(5) LEARNING TO READ
The initial stages: sight, vocabulary, phonics, reading for meaning, context cues, the role of expectations.
Reading and the internalisation of written language forms.
Reading and the purposes of the curriculum.
Developmental reading: suiting the skill to the purpose.
Diagnosis, testing, observational techniques.
The rôle of fiction in developing reading.
Children's literature and patterns of individual reading.

(6) LANGUAGE IN SCHOOL
The language behaviour of the teacher (the language of instruction, of questioning, of control; the teacher as listener).
The language of text books.
The heuristic function of language – talking and writing as ways of learning.
The development of expressive, transactional, and poetic writing.
Literature as language.
Language across the curriculum – a language policy for a school.
Organisation: class organisation for talk, for writing, for
　　　　　　　　reading.
　　　　　　　　organisation of resources.
　　　　　　　　diagnosis and recording.
Evaluation: educational aims and the uses of language in school.

Example 2
(1) INTRODUCTION
　　(a) An historical introduction to language change and stability.
　　(b) A sketch of linguistic theory, with psychological and sociological links.

(2) COMMUNICATION IN THE CONTEXT OF COGNITIVE AND AFFECTIVE DEVELOPMENT

(a) Goals of communication in speech and writing: information needs; negotiation processes; control processes; thinking; forms of self expression.

(b) Sociological and psychological factors affecting communication

    (i) accents and dialects; styles of print and writing; conventions of presentation; linguistic constraints in a multicultural society; attitudes and preconceptions; knowledge structures; motivations.

    (ii) social context and style; comparative study of a range of texts; the kinds of writing required of children at school; and kinds of writing relevant to a teacher's professional role.

(3) THE COMMUNICATIVE EVENT

    (i) Strategies and tactics used in accomplishing communication goals.

    (ii) Receptive organisation – information access and selection procedures.

(4) SKILLS AND STRUCTURES

(a) Primary skills – Language substance.

    (i) the sound system of English, with an emphasis on intonation, auditory perception and discrimination.

    (ii) the graphic system of English, including punctuation, visual perception of letter shapes and groupings.

    (iii) correspondences and anomalies in the sound and graphic systems. Auditory and visual association.

(b) Intermediate skills – Language form.

    (i) Syntactic structures in speech and writing.

    (ii) semantic structure: words and collocations semantic relationships.

    (iii) inter-sentential structures in speech and writing; the paragraph and beyond.

    (iv) redundancy as a feature of natural language: context cues in reading and listening, writing and speaking, arising from redundancy; stochastic processes.

(c) Comprehension skills – Language function.

    (i) kinds of comprehension – literal, interpretative, reor-

ganisation, inferential, evaluative, appreciative, applicative.
  (ii) factors affecting comprehension.
     (*a*) reader/listener preconceptions; reader/listener goals.
     (*b*) behaviour of speaker/writer: language variation (e.g. restricted codes); sensitivity to situations (e.g. registers, language for special purposes); awareness of audience – aiming at target groups of listeners/readers.
  (iii) Aids to comprehension: questions; note-taking techniques, models and diagrams.

(5) SELF-DEVELOPMENT, SKILLS AND STRATEGIES
  (a) Developmental analysis and evaluation.
  (b) Learning to use verbal skills in communication; self-evaluation, recording techniques and personal resource management.
  (c) Interdependence of resources and skills: the limiting effect of deficiencies in either: techniques for overcoming transitory and developmental deficiencies.

(6) ORGANISATION OF LANGUAGE AND READING IN THE CURRICULUM
  (a) Varieties of media for learning.
     A Reading: reading schemes and workshops
                 subject-area textbooks and materials
                 other types of printed media
     B Speech: the language of the teacher
                 verbal styles and strategies
                 recorded and broadcast speech
                 other varieties of spoken language
                 language interaction in group learning situations.
  (b) Evaluation of media for learning.
     A intelligibility, legibility, readability of media.
     B analysis of content: logical and ideological
  (c) Language across the curriculum.
     (i) activities for developing the full range of language/reading behaviour in each curriculum area.
     (ii) organisation of learning situations within the normal curriculum.

(7) TEACHING THE INDIVIDUAL CHILD
- (i) Assessment of individual language and reading perform-ance; record keeping.
  Creative analysis of the child's idiolect, using the skills acquired earlier in the course.
- (ii) Devising of individual learning activities based on the assess-ment of analysis.
  Assessment and selection of appropriate materials to match individual needs.
- (iii) Special individual problems in language and reading; an awareness of the various influencing factors.

(8) DEVELOPMENT OF THE LANGUAGE CURRICULUM
- (a) Evaluation of teaching materials and procedures in use.
- (b) Resource development.
  - (i) storage and retrieval systems for the teacher.
  - (ii) management of audio-visual resources.

Bibliography

This bibliography lists books and papers cited or referred to in the text. In addition there are further reading suggestions for teachers using the topic books of the 'Awareness of Language' series at the end of each section of Part 2 (pp.: 111, 136, 151, 159, 175, 184 and 210). (Place of publication is London unless stated otherwise.)

Armstrong G. (1975) The Home Visiting Project. In G. Smith (ed.) *Educational Priority*, Vol. 4. HMSO

Aplin T. R. W. et al. (1981) *Introduction to Language*. Hodder and Stoughton

Austin J. L. (1962) *How To Do Things with Words*. (2nd edn 1975) Oxford: OUP

Ball B. N. (1967) *Basic Linguistics for Secondary Schools*. 3 vols. Methuen

Barnes D. et al. (1969) *Language, the Learner and the School*. (Revised edn 1971) Harmondsworth: Penguin Education

Baugh A.C. and Cable T. (1951) *A History of the English Language*. (3rd edn 1978) Routledge and Kegan Paul

Bernstein B. (1965) A Socio-Linguistic Approach to Social Learning. In B. Bernstein *Class, Codes and Control*, Vol. 1: *Theoretical Studies towards a Sociology of Language*. (1971) Routledge and Kegan Paul

Beveridge M. and Jerrams A. (1981) Parental Involvement in Language Development: an Evaluation of a School-Based Parental Assistance Plan. *British Journal of Educational Psychology* 51, 3, 259–69

Bolinger D. and Sears D.A. (1981) *Aspects of Language*. (3rd edn, revised) New York: Harcourt Brace Jovanovich Inc.

Brooks N. (1960) *Language and Language Learning*. (2nd edn 1964) New York: Harcourt Brace and World

Bruner J.S. et al. (1966) *Studies in Cognitive Growth*. New York: Wiley

Bruner J.S. (1975) Language as an Instrument of Thought. In A. Davies (ed.) *Problems of Language and Learning*. Heinemann

Bruner, J.S. (1979) mimeograph. *Lecture to the Assoc. for the Study of the Curriculum Annual Conference*. Univ. of Edinburgh

Bullock A. (Lord Bullock) (Chairman) (1975) *A Language for Life*: Report of the Committee of Inquiry appointed by the Secretary of State for Education and Science. HMSO

Burstall C., Jamieson M., Cohen S. and Hargreaves M. (1974) *Primary French in the Balance*. NFER

Carroll J.B. (1971) Implications of Aptitude Test Research and Psycholinguistic Theory for Foreign Language Teaching. In Research Memorandum RM71. 14 Princeton, New Jersey: Educational Testing Service

Chomsky C. (1969) *The Acquisition of Syntax in Children from 5 to 10.* Cambridge, Mass. MIT Press

Chomsky N. (1959) Review of B.F. Skinner: *Verbal Behavior* (1957). *Language* 35, 1, 26–58

Clark H.H. and Clark E.V. (1977) *Psychology and Language: An Introduction to Psycholinguistics.* New York: Harcourt Brace Jovanovich Inc.

Cockroft W. (1981) *Mathematics Counts*: Report of the Committee of Inquiry into the Teaching of Mathematics in Schools. HMSO

Cook V.J. (1979) *Young Children and Language.* Edward Arnold

Corson D.J. (1981) Social Class, the Semantic Barrier and Access to Curricular Knowledge. Ph. D. thesis, University of London

Corson D.J. (1982) The Graeco-Latin (G-L) Instrument: A New Measure of Semantic Complexity in Oral and Written English. *Language and Speech* 25, 1, 1–10

Coulthard M. (1977) *An Introduction to Discourse Analysis.* Longman

Crowther G. (1959) *15 to 18*: Report of the Central Advisory Council for Education, England. HMSO

Davie R. et al. (1972) *National Child Development Study.* (1958 Cohort) Longman

Davison A. (1975) Indirect Speech Acts and What to Do with Them. In P. Cole and J.L. Morgan (eds.) *Syntax and Semantics*, Vol. 3: *Speech Acts.* New York: Academic Press

DES (1981) *The School Curriculum.* HMSO

Donaldson M. (1978) *Children's Minds.* Fontana

Edwards V.K. (1979) *The West Indian Language Issue in British Schools.* Routledge and Kegan Paul

EEC (1977) *Directive of the Council of the European Community on the Education of Migrant Workers.* Brussels

Englemann S. and Osborn J. (1969) *Distar Language.* Henley-on-Thames: Science Research Associates

Franklin B. (1768) A Scheme for a New Alphabet and a Reformed Spelling. In A.H. Smyth (ed.) *Writings of Benjamin Franklin*, V, New York: Macmillan, 169–78 1907)

Furth H. and Wachs H. (1975) *Thinking Goes to School.* New York: OUP

Gardner K. (1968) The State of Reading. In Smart N. (ed.) *Crisis in the Classroom: An Enquiry into State Education Policy.* Hamlyn (out of print)

Gattegno C. (1972) *Teaching Foreign Languages in Schools : The Silent Way.* New York: Educational Solutions Inc.

Goodlad S. (1979) *Learning by Teaching.* Community Service Volunteers. 237 Pentonville Rd, London N1 9NJ

Gordon J.C.B. (1981) *Verbal Deficit : A Critique.* Croom Helm

Green G.M. (1975) How to Get People to Do Things with Words. In P. Cole and J. L. Morgan (eds.) *Syntax and Semantics*, Vol. 3: *Speech Acts.* New York: Academic Press

Green P.S. (ed.) (1975) *The Language Laboratory in School: Performance and Prediction. The York Study.* Edinburgh: Oliver and Boyd

Guiraud P. (1954) *Les caractères statistiques du vocabulaire.* Paris: Presses Universitaires de France

Halliday M.A.K. (1971). In P. Doughty, J. Pearce and G. Thornton

Language in Use. Schools Council Programme in Linguistics and English Teaching. Edward Arnold.

Halliday M.A.K. (1975) *Learning How to Mean: Explorations in the Development of Language*. Edward Arnold

Hartog P.J. (1906) *The Writing of English*. Oxford: The Clarendon Press

Hawkins E.W. (1974) Modern Languages in the Curriculum. In G.E. Perren (ed.) *The Space Between: English and Foreign Languages at School*. CILT Reports and Papers 10. CILT

Hawkins E.W. (1979) Language as a Curriculum Study. In G.E. Perren (ed.) (1979) CILT

Hawkins E.W. (1981) *Modern Languages in the Curriculum*. Cambridge: CUP

Her Majesty's Inspectorate (1977) *Matters for Discussion 3: Modern Languages in Comprehensive Schools*. HMSO

Her Majesty's Inspectorate (1978) *Curriculum 11–16: Modern Languages*. A Working Paper of the Modern Languages Committee of the Inspectorate. HMSO

Her Majesty's Inspectorate (1980) *Matters for Discussion: A View of the Curriculum*. HMSO

Hewes G.W. (1973) An Explicit Formulation of the Relationship between Tool-Using, Tool-Making and the Emergence of Language. *Visible Language* 7, 101–27

Hewison J. and Tizard J. (1980) Parental Involvement and Reading Attainment. *British Journal of Educational Psychology* 50, 209–15

Hockett C.F. (1977) *The View from Language*. Athens, Ga: University of Georgia Press

Holberton R. (1977) The First Generation of a New Experience. *ILEA Contact* 6, 23

Hunter I.M.L. (1964) *Memory*. (Revised edn) Harmondsworth: Penguin Books

Inner London Education Authority (1980) *Literacy Survey*. ILEA Research and Statistics Group

Jespersen J.O.H. (1904) *How to Teach a Foreign Language*. George Allen and Unwin

Joos M. (1967) *The Five Clocks*. New York: Harcourt Brace Jovanovich Inc.

Katzner K. (1977) *The Languages of the World*. Routledge and Kegan Paul

Kavanagh J.F. and Mattingley I.G. (1972) *Language by Ear and Eye*. Cambridge, Mass.: MIT Press

Keller H.A. (1913) *The Story of my Life*. Hodder and Stoughton

Krashen S.D. (1981) *Second Language Acquisition and Second Language Learning*. Oxford: Pergamon

Labov W. (1982) The Black English Trial at Ann Arbor: Objectivity and Commitment in Linguistic Science. *Language in Society* 11, 2

Langer S. (1942) *Language*. In S. Langer *Philosophy in a New Key*. (Reissued 1957) Cambridge, Mass: Harvard University Press

Laye, Camara (1959) *The African Child (L'Enfant noir* trans. J. Kirkup). Collins

MacCarthy P. (1978) *The Teaching of Pronunciation*. Cambridge: CUP

Miller G.A. (1956) The Magical Number Seven – Plus or Minus Two: Some Limits on our Capacity for Processing Information. *The Psychological Review* 63, 2

Miller G.A. (1951) *Language and Communication*. New York: McGraw-Hill

Mulcaster R. (1582) *Elementarie*. E.T. Campagnac (ed.) (1925) Oxford: The Clarendon Press

National Congress on Languages in Education *see* Perren G.E. (ed.) (1979) and Trim J. (ed.) (1980)

Oller J.W.Jr (1972) Cloze Tests of Second Language Proficiency and What They Measure. (Proceedings of AILA Congress, Copenhagen.) *Language Learning* 23, 1 (1973)

Olson G.M. (1973) Developmental Changes in Memory and the Acquisition of Language. In T.E. Moore (ed.) *Cognitive Development and the Acquisition of Language*. New York: Academic Press

Palmer H.E. (1917) *The Scientific Study and Teaching of Languages*. Harrap. Reissued Harper D. (ed.) (1968) Oxford: OUP

Parliamentary Select Committee for Education, Science and Arts (1981) *The Secondary School Curriculum and Examinations*: Second Report 16 December, 1981. HMSO

Perren, G.E. (ed.) (1974) *The Space Between: English and Foreign Languages at School*. CILT Reports and Papers 10. CILT

Perren G.E. (ed.) (1979) *The Mother Tongue and Other Languages in Education*: NCLE Papers and Reports 2. CILT

Pimsleur P. (1966) Testing Foreign Language Learning. In A. Valdman *Trends in Language Teaching*. New York: McGraw-Hill

Plowden B. (Lady Plowden) (Chairman) (1967) *Children and Their Primary Schools*: Report of the Central Advisory Council for Education, England. 2 vols. HMSO

Rampton A. (Chairman) (1981) *West Indian Children in our Schools*: Interim Report of the Committee of Inquiry into the Education of Children from Ethnic Minority Groups. HMSO

Rosen H. (1972) Review of J.C.B. Gordon *Verbal Deficit: A Critique*. *Times Educational Supplement* (9 April)

Sachs J. S. and Johnson M. (1976) Language Development in a Hearing Child of Deaf Parents. In Engel. W. von Raffler and Y. Le Brun (eds) *Baby Talk and Infant Speech* (Neurolinguistics 5) Amsterdam: Swets and Zeitlinger

Sapir E. (1921) *Language: An Introduction to the Study of Speech*. New York: Harcourt Brace and World.

Searle J. (1969) *Speech Acts*. Cambridge: CUP

Scarr S. et al. (1983) Developmental Status and School Achievements of Minority and Non-Minority Children from Birth to 18 years in a British Midlands Town. *British Journal of Developmental Psychology* 1, 31, 48

Schools Council (1976) *Writing Across the Curriculum: 11–16 Project*. Ward Lock Educational

Skinner B.F. (1957) *Verbal Behavior*. New York: Appleton-Century-Crofts

Snow et al. (1976) Mother's Speech in Three Social Classes. *Journal of Psycholinguistic Research* 5, 1–20

Start K.B. and Wells B.K. (1972) *The Trend of Reading Standards*. NFER

Stevick E.W. (1976) *Memory, Meaning and Method*. Rowley Mass.: Newbury House

Stubbs M. (1980) *Language and Literacy: Sociolinguistics of Reading and Writing*. Routledge and Kegan Paul.

Sweet H. (1899) *The Practical Study of Languages.* (Reissued 1964) Oxford: OUP

Tacke O. (1923) *Der Sprachunterricht muss umkehren.* Leipzig: Oldenburg

Taylor M.J. (1981) *Caught Between: A Review of Research into the Education of Pupils of West Indian Origin.* NFER, Nelson

Tizard J. et al. (1981) Collaboration between Teachers and Parents in Assisting Children's Reading. *British Journal of Educational Psychology* 52, 1–15

Trim J. (ed.) (1980) *Issues in Language Education:* NCLE Papers and Reports 1, 2 and 3. CILT

Trudgill P. (1974) *Sociolinguistics: An Introduction.* Harmondsworth: Penguin Books

Vygotsky L.S. (1962) *Thought and Language.* Cambridge, Mass.: MIT Press (First issued, posthumously, 1934; suppressed 1936)

Webster N. (1828) *An American Dictionary of the English Language.* 2 vols. Springfield. Mass.: G. and C. Merriam

Wijk A. (1959) *Regularised English.* Stockholm: Almqvist and Wiksell

Young M.F.D. (ed.) (1971) *Knowledge and Control.* Collier Macmillan

Yuen Ren Chao (1968) *Language and Symbolic Systems.* Cambridge: CUP

Zachrisson R.E. (1932) *Anglic: An International Language.* (2nd edn) Uppsala: Almqvist and Wiksell

Index